Landscape Lessons

Book 1

Ning 17

Ning Yeh

Also in this series by Ning Yeh:

Landscape Lessons
Book 2

Tree • Pine and Moon • Pavilion • Alley Flowers •
Courtyard Willow • Hua Mountain • Aerial Guilin •
Yangtze Gorge • Wuyi Mountain • Tibet Palace

First Edition

Huntington Beach, California
ISBN: 9780961830564

Printed in Taiwan

Contents

www.orientalartsupply.com

Preface

I have taught brush painting for over 40 years. I love it. To me, a teacher is a student who shares the joy of his own learning experience.

When I first started teaching in the early 70s, I was earning my Ph.D. I taught with an academic zeal, using big words like "homogeneity" and "proximity." After a lesson, an elderly lady pinched my cheek, "You are sooo cute." It brought me down to earth. Decades later, a young student came to class with her toddler, "Say hi to Grandpa Ning." These days, I use words like "getting along" and "being close." I think I am a better teacher now.

Generations have come through my classroom door—folks just like me who love to paint. The young lady's toddler is now a teen. She has been my student for even longer. Mayee Futterman is a devoted Chinese brush artist who helped me produce these landscape volumes. I am grateful to her and to generations of students—the most inspiring happy dots in my landscape—for their encouragement and support.

Since 1978, I have taken many friends as the American Artists on our Dream Journey tours throughout China. Each trip is a new beginning with so much inspiration and surging energy.

In 1995, Congressman Kuan, an elder Chinese statesman, offered a reception for our tour group at the old Palace in Chengde, China. When I presented him with my art album, Mr. Kuan studied each page. "I regret to say," he began, "in order to find the true spirit of Chinese art, we Chinese have to look abroad." There was some heartfelt truth in his humble remark.

In 1949, General Chiang Kai-shek took the entire Palace Museum collection to Taiwan. I was only three but I might as well have been 5003. I feel I am among the luckiest Chinese whose generation grew up enjoying cultural continuity and valuing one of mankind's greatest heritages.

I love to take pictures, make movies, write, and paint. I collect the seeds of culture. The search is fun, and the discovery is more fun. I organize and internalize my findings by blending them with my thoughts and experiences.

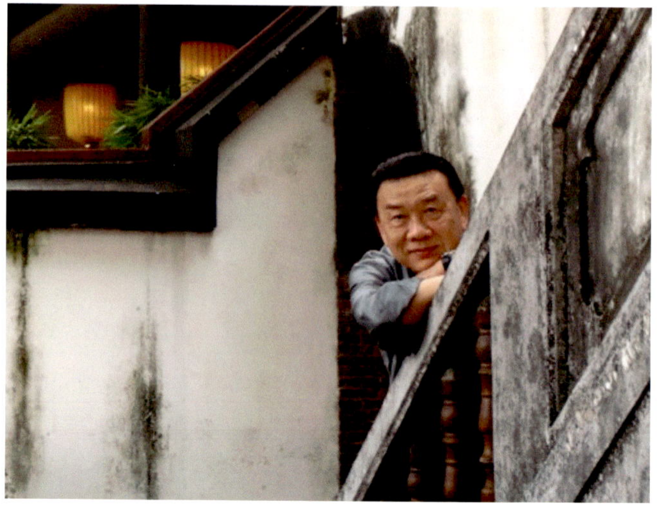

When spontaneous, creative inspiration comes along, something magical takes place. The ultimate reward is sharing this process with people who have the same interests.

Landscape is "shan shui" in Chinese. Shan is mountain, and shui is water. Landscape is the harmonious union of land and water. Chinese landscape painting is a journey. It allows one's mind to reach tranquility. As a young artist, painting landscapes was my first love. It was my dream world. With music playing, I danced with my brush. Allowing the mist to unveil herself. There, I was the great explorer, discovering mountains beyond mountains.

Now, let our dream journey begin.

Landscape Basics

1) Set Up

Felt

Use a piece of white felt under the paper.

Water Bowl (porcelain with 3 divisions)

Leave 1" between the water and the rim.

Stackable Porcelain Dish Set

A set comes with 5 dishes for storing Chinese chips and frequently used colors (like green).

Flower Plate

Keep most colors in pasty condition. Arrange colors from light to dark according to the brush loading sequence.

Mixing Plate

Choose a white saucer for blending purposes.

Paper Towel

Fold a couple of sheets under the mixing plate.

Spray Bottle

Use a small pump-spray bottle that produces a fine mist to moisten the colors.

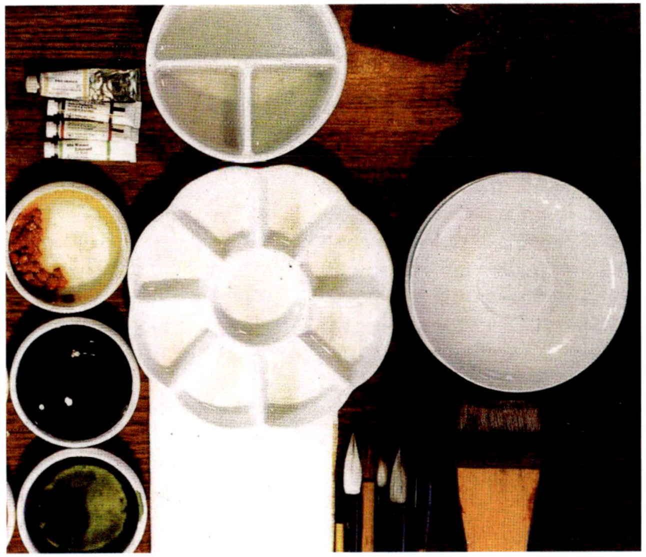

2) Materials

Pi Paper

All the lessons in this volume are horizontal. The vertical to horizontal ratio is 2:3. For example, use a 16"x24" sheet for larger paintings or a 12"x18" sheet for smaller paintings.

Brushes

OAS Flow: main brush for line work, dots, and coloring

OAS Large Flow: useful for larger subjects (like mountains)

Mountain Horse (Small or Medium): sharp lines (like pine needles), irregular lines (like rocks), and texture

OAS Happy Dot: fine lines and dots

Wash Brush: Wash and mist

Mixing Brush: use a small, tough-bristle brush to prepare colors

Colors

Chinese Chips

Yellow, Vermillion, Sky Blue

Sakura or DaVinci Goache

White

OAS

Best Bottle Ink

Schmincke Horadam Aquarell Tubes

Cadmium Red Deep

Winsor & Newton Artist's Water Colour Tubes

Indigo, Manganese Blue, Perylene Violet, Winsor Violet, Winsor Green, Lamp Black, and other colors as specified in each lesson

3) Preparing Colors

Ink

The stackable porcelain dishes are the ideal size and depth for preparing three shades of ink. Pour a couple of teaspoons of water into a dish plus a dab of ink to produce Light Ink. Prepare another dish with water and slightly more ink to produce Medium Ink. Pour fresh, undiluted ink in a dish for Dark Ink.

White

In a separate dish, dilute some White with water into a semi-transparent, milk-like condition.

Yellow

Melt Yellow chunks with 2 tablespoons of water in a small jar (for 1 hour or more). Use a mixing brush to smash the softened Yellow into a thick liquid.

Chinese Chips (Vermillion and Sky Blue)

Store Chinese chips in stackable dishes. Pour the whole package of chips into the dish. Gather the chips to one side. Spray wet the chips. Allow time for the chips to stick together and onto the dish. When painting, wet the chips with a light spray. Use a mixing brush to work colors into a thick paste.

Vermillion:

Sky Blue:

Mixed Colors

Squeeze the tube watercolors into each section of the flower plate. Use a dry mixing brush to flatten the colors. Keep dark colors pasty. Add a touch of water to the lighter colors. If colors dry up, lightly spray them with water. Depending on each lesson, the ink, white, and/or colors may need to be diluted with water or kept in a pure or thick/pasty condition.

Greens

Light Green:
  Yellow + Indigo (strong)

Dark Green:
  Light Green + Indigo (thick)

White Green:
  Light Green + White (diluted)

Shade:
  Winsor Green + Lamp Black + Dark Brown (pasty)

Earth/Warm Colors

Brown or Dark Brown:
  Vermillion + Ink (thick)

Light Brown or Beige:
  Dark Brown + White + Vermillion (diluted; may add a touch of Yellow or Light Green)

Ochre:
  Yellow + Vermillion + Green (diluted)

Purples/Blue

Purple or Dark Purple:
  Winsor Violet + Perylene Violet + Green (strong)

Light Purple:
  Purple + White (diluted)

Manganese Blue:
  diluted with water

Reds

Red:
  Cadmium Red Deep (pasty)

Pink:
  Red + White (thick)

Dark Red:
  Perylene Violet (pasty)

4) Preparing a Draft

Draft

Sometimes it is a good idea to prepare a draft of the composition on Pi paper. Place it under the painting paper as a guide. Attach it with removable tape.

Color Chart

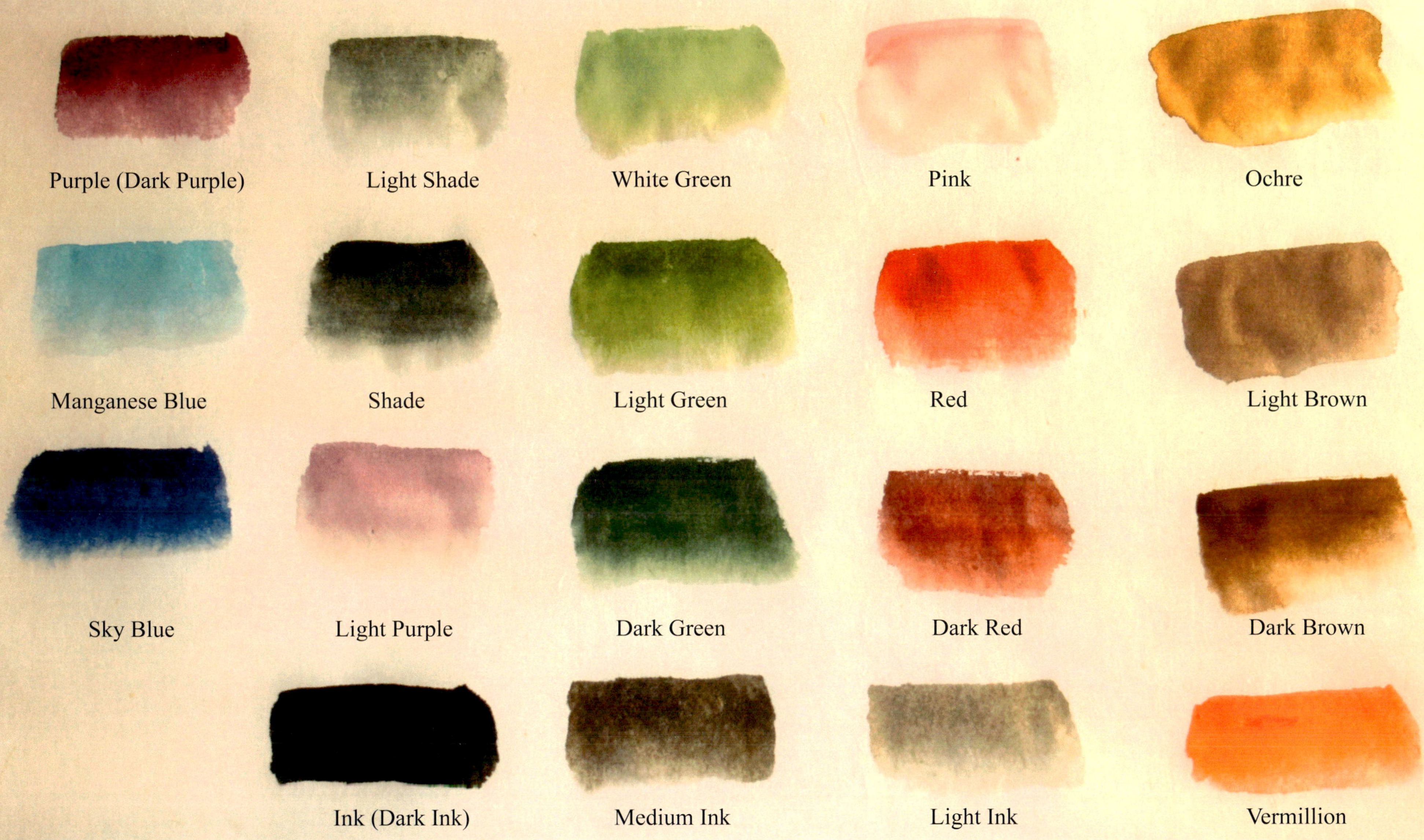
Purple (Dark Purple)
Light Shade
White Green
Pink
Ochre
Manganese Blue
Shade
Light Green
Red
Light Brown
Sky Blue
Light Purple
Dark Green
Dark Red
Dark Brown
Ink (Dark Ink)
Medium Ink
Light Ink
Vermillion

Run a centerline both vertically and horizontally to help the placement of scenery. Additional grid lines are helpful to keep vertical elements straight and horizontal elements leveled.

Sketch the draft with a No. 2 pencil. Optionally, use multiple colored pencils or waterproof pens as a reminder of which color goes where. You may darken the pencil sketch with ink in order to see things better when the painting paper is laid over it. Wait until the draft dries before painting.

Testing Paper

Use an extra piece of Pi paper for testing colors and moisture.

5) Brush Selection

OAS Flow Brush

When in doubt, go with the Flow brush. The Flow does lines and coloring equally well. I have students who own a half-dozen Flow brushes. When the tip wears out, it becomes an excellent brush for dots.

Mountain Horse Brush

The Mountain Horse brush is one of the most amazing brushes for creating textured line work. It is also a brush designed to outline shapes. Shape outlines require a fine point. Texture is done with a dry brush and sometimes with a tip that is not as well behaved. If we have more than one size of Mountain Horse, use the Small for sharp lines, and the Medium for texture work.

Happy Dot Brush

The Happy Dot brush is used to do fine lines (hair-like), fine dots (smidges), and the artist's signature. We rarely use this brush in a tilted position. Keep it vertical.

Wash Brush

The Wash Brush is used to shade the sky and water, and to define the mist.

6) Brush Fundamentals

Most brushes are treated as described in this section. The Wash Brush is an exception because of its shape and function. It is described separately.

Holding the Brush

Use the first section of the thumb and index finger to hold the middle section of the brush handle. Slide the middle finger down the front and press the nail of the ring finger from the back. Keep the small finger attached to the ring finger.

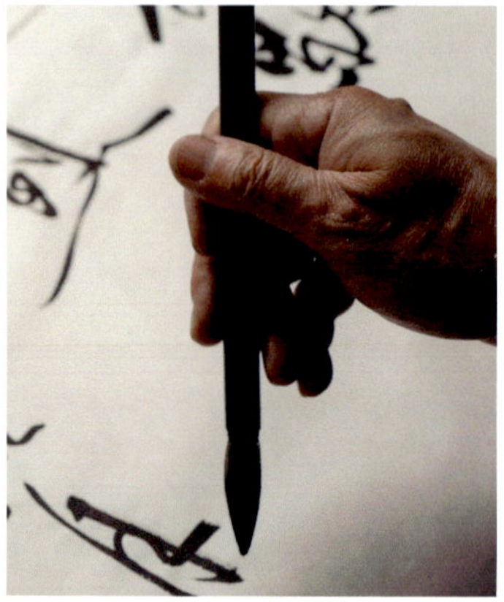

Preparing the Tip

Wet the brush bristles in water. Stroke the bristles with pressure on the rim of the water bowl. Wipe all sides dry on the paper towel and form a tip.

Loading Water

After forming the tip, we begin by loading water. Dip only 1/4" of the tip a couple of times into water. Stroke off the excess along the rim of the water bowl. That is all the water we need on the brush. The secret is wet tip, dry body. Do not roll the brush on the paper towel. Keep all the hair straight. We need to realize how little water and color is needed to work on rice paper. A little dry texture adds strength to our lines. This is referred to as "dry brush" in these lessons.

Loading One Color

Whether using ink or color, follow these instructions for loading the brush. Load one color 1/8" into the tip. Blend until the color fades about 1/4" into the tip. Dip the tip 1/8" into the color again. If the color is thick, blend the tip a little.

To test the color, tilt the tip and press the brush with half-length of the bristles making contact with the paper. Lift the brush. If the brush is loaded correctly, we should see a shape with the point showing more intense color, and then the color fading naturally into nothing (A). If we see a solid shape with no fading, we have loaded the color too deep. There will be no transparency and no variation. Flat colors produce no joy.

Loading Multiple Colors

The exciting moment is when multiple colors blend spontaneously in one brush stroke. Load the lightest color first then progressively load stronger and darker colors. Each successive color covers a shorter length of the bristles. For instance, we load Light Green 1/4", add Dark Green 1/6", then add Ink 1/8". Blend.

Positioning the Brush

After spending the effort to load colors on different parts of the brush, painting with just the tip becomes self-defeating. Color variations will not show. We need to use the brush body with the tip. With the brush tilted, pressure is exerted to allow the body of the brush to make contact with the paper.

By design, only half the length of the brush body is intended for painting. We never paint with the full length of the bristles. For example, the Flow brush is 1" long (B). So the effective part of the bristles is only 1/2" (C).

We do watercolor. It is obvious that color needs to work with water. We save half of that 1/2" for water. Therefore, the most we load color will be 1/4" (D) deep.

Where to Begin a Stroke

From the diagrams in this book, we can study the intensity of colors in a stroke to learn the direction and path of the brush tip. The color is more intense at the beginning of the stroke and then it fades. The brush tip may travel in the middle of a stroke or along the edge (E). Work a shape from the corners and edges inward. Allow colors to blend in the middle. If a shape is not enclosed, we allow the colors to fade in the open edges.

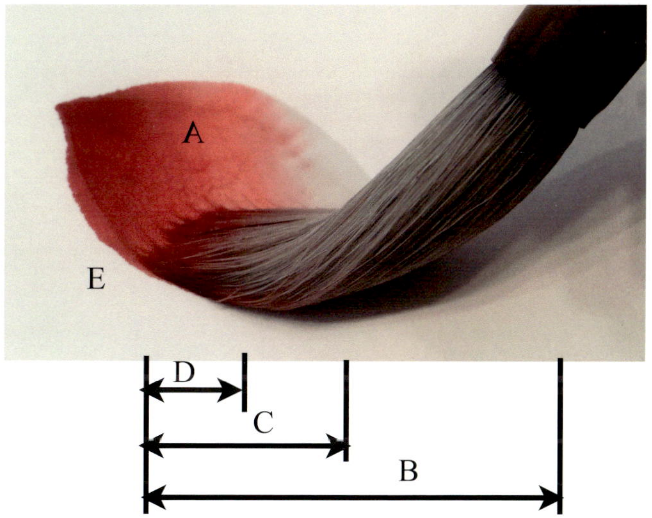

When to Show the Brush Tip

The tip color is the strongest. The brush tip is the dragon head and like the popular phrase, "crouching tiger, hidden dragon," we try to conceal it. Hide it near the border of a shape, do not let it show up in the middle of a painted area. Study each shape to be colored, place the brush tip at the edge and fan strokes out to fade. The trick is tilting the brush and moving it with the body in front of the tip.

7) Wash Brush Fundamentals

Preparing the Wash Brush

Wet and dry the bristles, wipe both sides and allow the bristles to form a line.

Loading Water on the Wash Brush

Dip 1/3 the length of the bristles (A) into water and stroke off the excess along the rim of the water bowl. Do this a couple of times. The brush should never be too wet. Most of the time, wash is applied onto a paper that is already wet.

Ways to Load Colors on the Wash Brush

Prepare colors in flat saucers so the full width of the brush (B) can land into the colors.

ONE COLOR ON ONE CORNER

We load thick and dark color on one corner of the brush (C) while fading gradually toward the other corner (D).

The width of the color on the brush varies according to coverage needs, but rarely does the color go beyond half the width of the bristles. We do load color generously into the length of the bristles so we do not need to reload it frequently.

To blend, hold the brush vertically, and press the entire body of bristles in a grinding motion to fade the color. Reload and blend several times to ensure enough color is on the brush.

MULTIPLE COLORS ON ONE CORNER

After loading one color, load the second color on the same corner, but cover less width of the brush. Blend and reload.

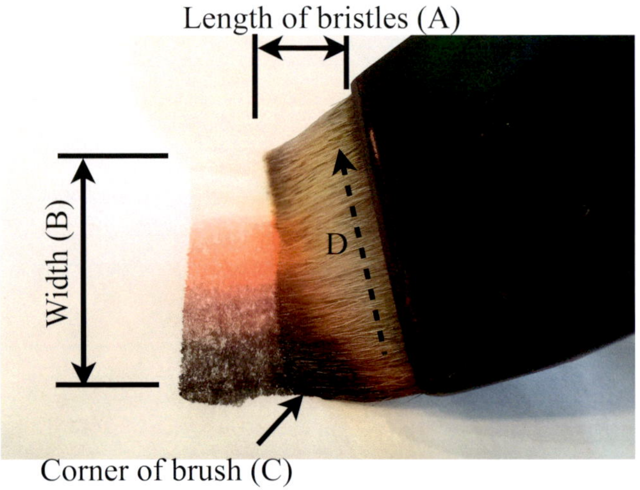

Typically, the colored corner of the brush is down to do mist and water. The colored corner is up to do the sky. The entire width makes contact with the paper.

COLOR ON THE ENTIRE BRUSH

Dip the whole width into color, dip the two corners in water to minimize hard edges.

8) Landscape Techniques

There are four essential elements of Chinese landscape painting: 1) line work; 2) shading and coloring; 3) dots; and 4) wash.

Chinese painting was originally an extension of calligraphy or writing skills. As such, traditional Chinese landscape painting begins with lines; followed by ink shading and color rendering; then accented with dots. The sky and water elements are left unpainted including rivers, mist, waterfalls, etc.

While I respect this sequence as exemplified by some lessons in this book, I also like change and experimentation. I modify the sequence in some lessons. For example, we do tree dots in color, then add ink shading to show depth.

My students have inspired many of these modifications. To overcome moisture control problems, we start with shading and coloring the mountain before adding outlines. Occasionally, I omit a step or two. For instance, if a mountain is misty, lines and ink shading are not necessary. Sky, water, and mist are rendered last. Sized rice paper like Pi allows us to rewet the entire paper.

I also apply Western principles of perspective. Even imaginary scenes are based on my photo records of the many wonderful places I visited in China. There is a humanistic spirit that remains the theme in all paintings. For instance, mountains embrace each other or trees gesture politely to one another.

Line Work

BONE STROKE

The bone stroke is used to do branches, tree trunks, architectural features, and other strong linear elements. Hold the brush vertically and land on the paper with a little pressure. Apply pressure while keeping the brush vertical throughout the stroke. The tip travels in the middle of the stroke. End the stroke with pressure and withdraw backward.

Some strokes may not have pressure on both ends but the tip still travels in the middle of the stroke and the brush handle stays erect throughout.

IRREGULAR LINES

There are no lines in nature. Lines are used to express the contours of objects like rocks or the texture of tree trunks. It is best to do lines not like lines. Therefore, we want most of our lines to begin and end with fading; to show various widths; to discontinue and reappear; and to overlap with different tones, textures, and spirit.

Most of the irregular lines are done with the brush tip tilted; using the brush like a chisel to scratch, tease, and chip. Splitting the tip can also create natural textures.

LINE TONES

We do light lines to define a shape. Strengthen lines by adding medium and dark. Keep their ends dry and light to ease lines into space or mist. A fading effect is created when lines go from dark to light; from wet to dry; and from solid to broken. On occasion, we use light line work, and frame it with the dark lines to add shadow and depth.

Shading and Coloring

MOVING THE BRUSH

After loading the brush with ink or color (see "Brush Fundamentals"), tilt the handle and press the body halfway onto the paper. Move the brush like a mop, with the body in front and tip trailing behind. Stop abruptly while the body is still in contact with then paper. Lift the brush up, rather than allowing the tip to travel on the paper. The tip, therefore, is always hidden and the stroke ends without color.

BLENDING

Larger shapes such as mountains are covered with multiple colors and shade to create depth and variation. If the brush runs out, reload the color but dip the tip in water to tone it down then continue. To blend areas with different colors, start from one edge with one color then work another color from opposite end by reversing the tip. Push strokes together to join and blend.

FADING

Fading is the most important task in landscape painting. Fading takes place in every stroke. We fade when we approach the mist area or when we lead one color to meet another color.

The key to fading is properly loading, positioning, and moving the brush as described in "Brush Fundamentals."

If the body of the brush stays in front of the tip, fading should occur naturally. If fading does not occur, the following may be the reasons: we loaded the colors too deep; we did not press the body; or we let the tip continue its movement on the paper while lifting. The most common problem is that we went back to an already colored area to repeat strokes so the brush body picked up colors and got dirty.

Going back to repeat a stroke is one of the worst crimes in brush painting. With the exception of applying colors to ink work or strengthening lighter ink/color with darker ones, we never go back. We do apply overlapping strokes often. We may alter a stroke by adding strokes next to it, overlapping into it, but not repeating on top of it. If a hard edge happens, clean the brush. Reload matching colors then continue the shape a little longer to fade. Wet and dry the brush. Rubbing the hard-edged area with dry brush will soften the hard edge if the painted shape is still wet.

BUILDING A WALL

Sometimes we want to keep two shapes separate and prevent strokes from blending or bleeding into each other. So just like doing a paint job, we line the edge where we want to avoid bleeding, then fill in the rest. "Building a wall" means doing a stroke along the edge of a shape and using it as a platform to launch other strokes. Chinese are well-known for building walls.

LEAVE A HAIRLINE SPACE

Leave a hairline space between strokes that we do not wish to blend. The hairline space prevents adjacent strokes from bleeding into each other. It also adds a sense of light to our shape. When "building a wall," leave a hairline space between the "wall" and the adjacent stroke to prevent bleeding.

SHOWING CONTRAST

The purpose of Chinese landscape painting is tranquility. It is based on the harmonious union of contrasting elements. Land elements are painted, but water elements as left as space. The land needs to fade into water to achieve harmony.

To express harmonious contrast, think of host (dominating) and guest (supportive): line and shape, light and dark, wet and dry, thin and thick, warm and cool, mass and detail, shape and space. Allow them to coexist in harmony.

SHOWING SPACE

Whenever we feel misty, whenever the brush wants us to, we leave space. In a spiritual sense, the blank paper is the mist where everything emerges from and returns to. Any opening between strokes can be an indication of light. Since we do not totally paint from real scenery, we can "stage" the lighting to feature certain areas. Leaving them unpainted is most effective.

We need to fix our eye on the space around our stroke. If the space is boring, we modify it with our strokes. Space is the essence.

SHOWING SHADOW

In general, each shape has a shadow near its base area and to its sides. This is how we create the dimension of a shape. We naturally want to darken the dominant features to lead viewer there too. We color a shape from the light side and stop half way. To do shadows, we mix a "Shade" color (see Preparing Colors). Work the Shade, Ink, or other dark colors from the shadow side to blend with the existing colors.

If we want to apply Shade onto a colored area, do it when the color area is still wet. Do the Shade diluted first, with a dry brush. Then add stronger Shade to the center area of the diluted Shade.

Dots

Happy dots are lively strokes of various shapes and sizes used for trees, rocks, and foliage. Do foliage with overlapping dots. Add shadow dots. Apply shadows in the lower areas of the foliage clusters and near the trunks. Show foliage dots in the back and outreaching points. Make the overall contour of the foliage go in and out. Show host and guest, continents, and islands.

Wash

WETTING THE PAPER

Wash is used to shade the sky and water, and to define the mist. Traditional Chinese landscape painting is done on raw paper and does not use wash for the sky and water. I wanted to add wash to my landscapes. I found that raw paper like Double Shuen (Xuan) bleeds and streaks. Instead, I resolved use to sized paper like Pi. The sizing allows the wash to blend.

Wetting the paper allows the wash to blend evenly and integrate with other elements. It also softens the mist lines. It is an awesome feeling to see everything come together in harmony.

To do a wash, remove the draft from underneath before wetting the painting. Load the Wash Brush with water. Apply strokes horizontally. Make sure the whole painting is wet. Carry the strokes off the paper. If we lift near the edge, the corner may fold into the painting. Check the surface, if there are puddles, blot them with a paper towel.

If any painted part starts to bleed, blot it off with a paper towel. Alternatively, wet and dry the Flow brush and use it to blend and fade the bleeding parts. This happens when colors are still wet, the colors are too thick, or the colors want to run no matter what. If the latter occurs, do not use these colors next time.

APPLYING WASH

Load the Wash Brush as described in "Brush Selection." Hold the brush vertically. Work strokes horizontally with the whole width of the brush making contact with the paper. Do not tilt the handle. Overlap the strokes to have smooth coverage of the area. Try not to jump all over the place.

Wash the top of the painting (sky) with the colored corner of the brush up. Do the lower base of the painting (water, mist) with the colored corner of the brush down. Let the wash fade into the painted scenery.

SHOWING MIST

With the Wash Brush, darken selected areas with Shade color in the lower parts of our mountain to show mist and to highlight the space below.

We fade the mountains in order not to show a hard edge. Applying Shade color by wetting the paper is also a way to avoid hard edges. We want to define the mist line. Apply strong Shade with a dry brush. Align the base of the Wash Brush with the base of the mountain. Work one side of the base area then the other side. Hold the brush vertically. Allow the whole width of the brush to make contact with paper. Stroke horizontally to create a soft curving mist line. Our eye is looking at the space (mist) below.

With proper loading and execution, the stroke should define a bottom edge while the top of the Shade fades to nothing. Mist comes and goes. Sometimes it gathers, other times it disperses. We should not form too long or too solid a definition all along. Wet and dry the Flow brush and use it to soften and blend the shade into the rest of the areas, if we wish.

Do not tilt the edge of Wash Brush. Make full contact with the paper. Otherwise, the Shade will not fade upward into the mountain.

Do mist decisively. Do not go over or fuss with detail. The more we do, the worse it gets. Wet paper does unpredictable things.

Mist is one body. It breaks and embraces a mountain from the base with two arms. After developing the mist line, taper the ends to make it disappear. We do this by turning the handle clockwise on the right side of the mist line, and counter clockwise on the left end. The color will narrow as a result. I call this "fanning."

TO WET OR NOT TO WET

For snow scenes or scenery where contrasting colors or shapes are desired, we do the wash without wetting the paper. Use the Flow brush to build a wide wall near the edge of scenery then fade the outer edge. Use the Wash Brush to cover a large area with horizontal strokes.

WASH BRUSH OR SPRAY BOTTLE

Excessive stroking with the Wash Brush may disturb detailed elements of the painting. We can use a spray bottle to spray these detailed areas instead of stroking over them.

While applying wash and shading mist, certain areas of the paper may become dry. Fine spray the drying areas so watermarks or hard edges do not form.

9) Guide to Symbols and Instructions

♌ indicates which brush to use.

❖ indicates which color to use or that it is time to load/change colors.

↖ arrows indicate where the brush tip is pointing when we begin a stroke. This is followed by instructions on the position of the brush handle and the motion of the stroke. For example, "↖ tilt and press moving downward."

"Color A + Color B" means load Color A 1/4" into the tip. Add Color B 1/8" into the tip. When loading multiple colors, each successive color covers a shorter length of the bristles. For instance "Color A + Color B + Color C," means we load Light Green 1/4", add Dark Green 1/6", then add Ink 1/8". Blend.

"Add Color D" means we still keep whatever colors are on the brush. If we are using similar colors, we do not need to clean the brush when we change or load additional colors especially when doing foliage, rocks, and mountains.

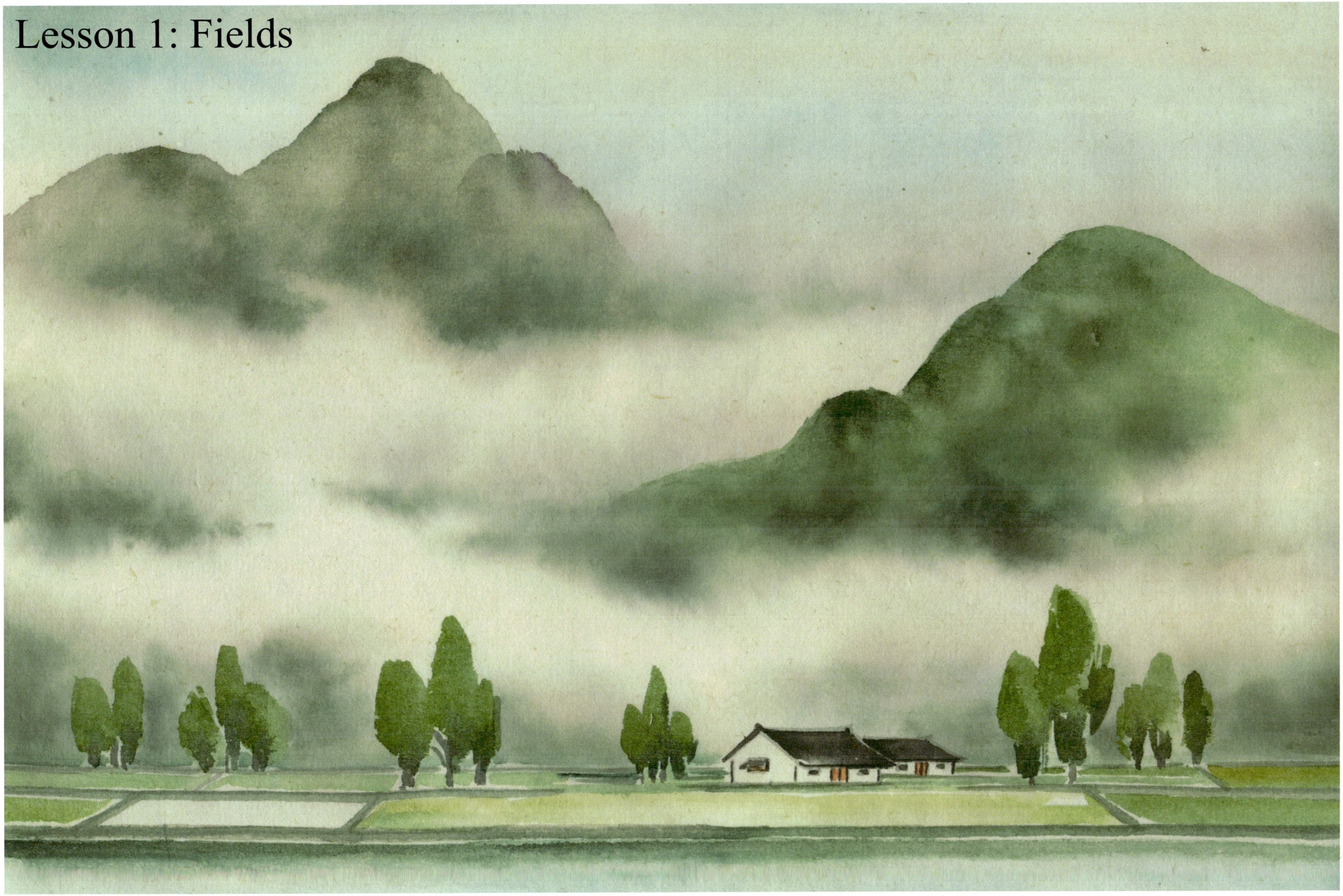
Lesson 1: Fields

Lesson 1: Fields

The goal of Chinese landscape painting is to express tranquility. Tranquility is the happy union of mountain and water. Plants and folks are the children of such union. Trees are clustered as happy dots. Houses are smiling. Mountains greet each other. Mist floats calmly. Fields are shimmering by the water.

In this lesson, we learn basic principles of perspective (e.g. fix eye level and vanishing point); develop horizontal layers of land elements; do simple structures and trees; learn to fade the base of mountains to integrate with layers of playful mist; and organize elements in "V" formation to lead the viewer to a focal point.

Step 1 (see diagram)

It is a good idea to work a draft of the composition on Pi paper with pencil outlines. Place the draft under our painting paper. It is not necessary to follow the draft all the time. It should be the same size as your painting paper, with a little extra edge to attach the painting paper on top with tape.

1. Fold the paper in half vertically and horizontally. Mark the folds (A, B). The eye level is at 1/4 height from the baseline. Eye level is not painted here, but it is an important suggestion. Below this invisible line the scenery moves inward. Above it, the scenery moves upward.

2. Do house C with a balanced A-frame. Run roof lines horizontally with sides parallel. Add wall lines (inside and under the A-frame and roof corner), a door and windows (windows do not show top). Make roofs larger and walls shorter. These treatments suggest that the houses are below eye level.

3. Do house D behind house C, with its roof line lower and eave line higher than house C.

4. Add baselines for both houses, extend the baseline of house D to both sides of house C.

5. Plant tree group E along the baseline of house C.

6. Run horizontal field lines F and G (Line G is discontinued in the middle to avoid monotony). Work field lines H, I, and J. Lead them to the middle (vanishing point). Outer ones tilt more (I and J).

7. Do bigger tree groups K and L. Plant their roots along line G.

8. Run a horizontal line M, leaping over trees and structures. The horizontal lines are closer together in the distance to project depth. Plant smaller tree groups N, O, and P on top.

9. Do mountains Q and R. Use dotted lines (as a reminder to fade) near the mountain base.

10. Add dotted lines S and T below the mountains to indicate mist.

11. Do dotted line U to show the area of shade behind the foreground scenery.

12. Add dotted lines V and W to show tapered triangles where the arms of the mist embrace the mountains.

13. Do dotted lines X and Y to show the dimples of clouds.

Step 1 (diagram)

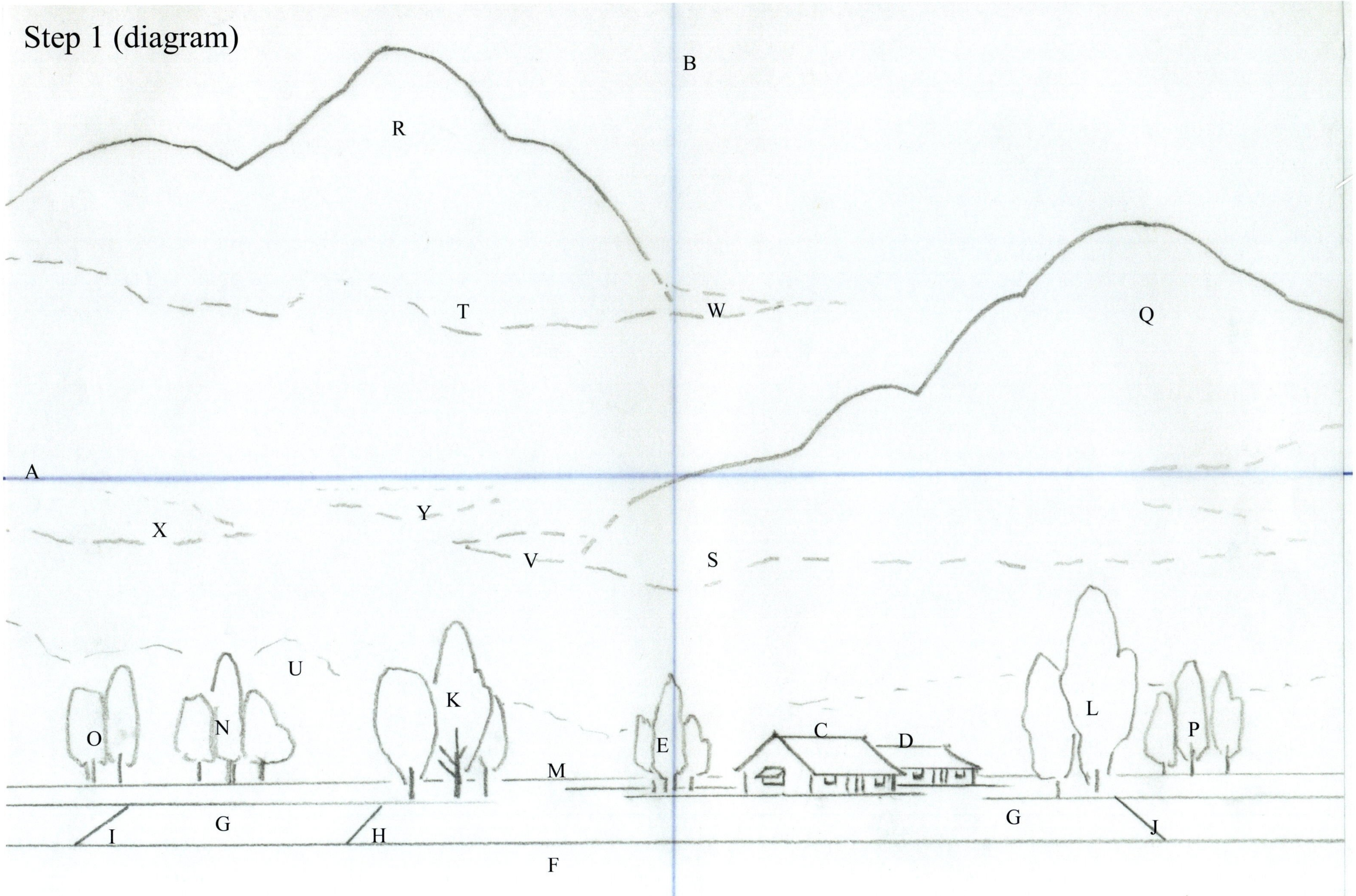

Step 2

1. Tree Dots

ℓ Flow, ❖ Light Green + Dark Green, ↖ tilt and press, moving downward.

❖ Shade, ↙ tilt and press, moving upward. Keep it simple, natural.

2. Lines for Houses, Fields, and Tree Trunks

ℓ Flow or Mt. Horse,

❖ Medium Ink (dry brush),

↓ vertical brush.

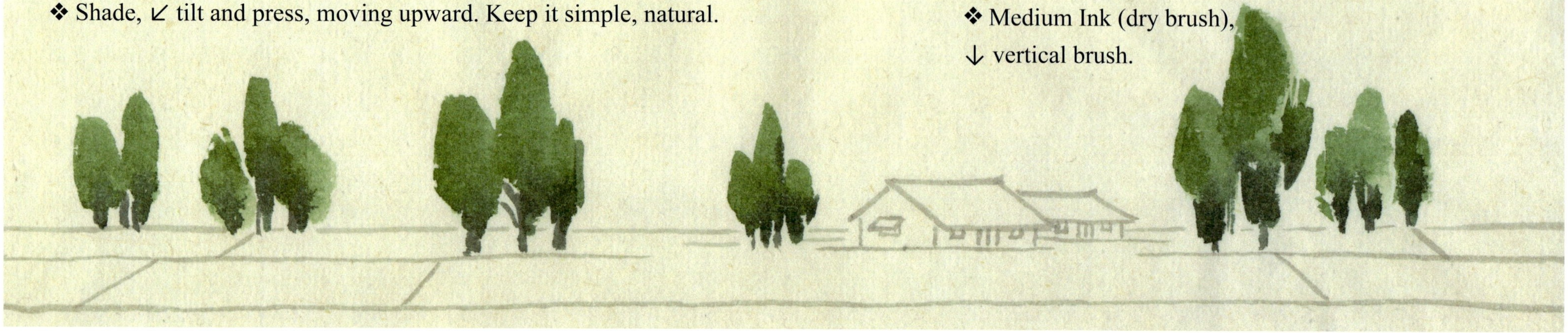

Step 3

1. Color for Houses

ℓ Flow, ❖ Ink (roof, windows) or ❖ Vermillion (doors and window) , ↖ tilt and press moving sideways.

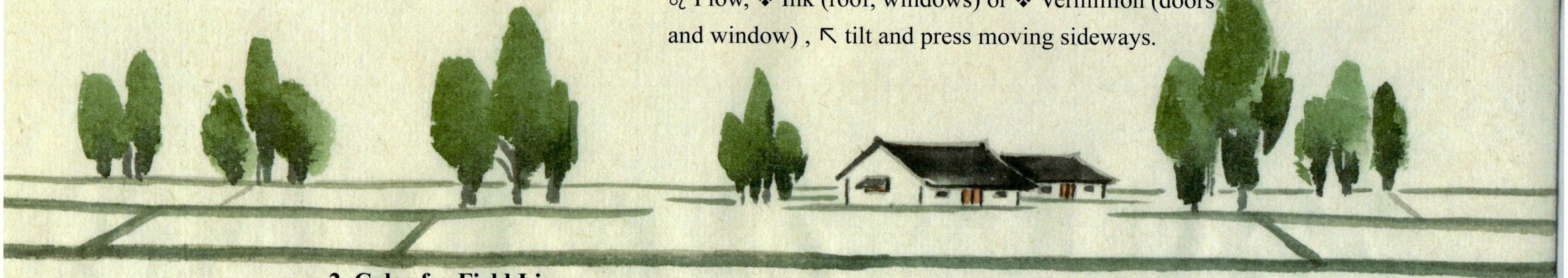

2. Color for Field Lines

ℓ Flow, ❖ Green, adding Shade occasionally while Green is still wet. ↓ vertical brush.

Step 4

1. Color for Fields (A-G)

ℓ Flow, ❖ Ochre + White Green, ↙ tilt with tip pointing at the corner of the field. Build a wall then press and move the brush sideways with broad strokes (A). Occasionally leave a hairline space between the field and path.

↘ Reverse the brush and do the other corner. Strokes should blend and fade naturally to fill the area.

❖ Ochre + White Green, do areas B and C.

❖ White Green, do D and E, leaping over tree trunks.

❖ Green, do F.

G is left uncolored to show water, so children can catch baby frogs.

2. Shade Above the Fields (H)

ℓ Flow, ❖ White Green + Shade, ↙ tilt and press, moving sideways. Strokes should fade naturally from the base up.

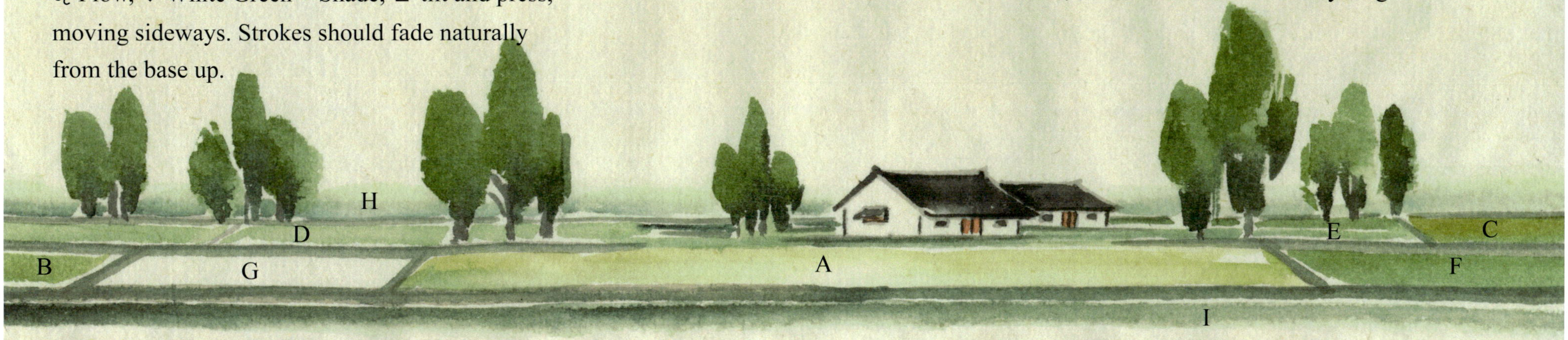

3. Shade Below the Fields (I)

ℓ Flow, ❖ White Green + Shade, ↖ tilt and press, moving sideways. Strokes should fade naturally from the top down.

Step 5

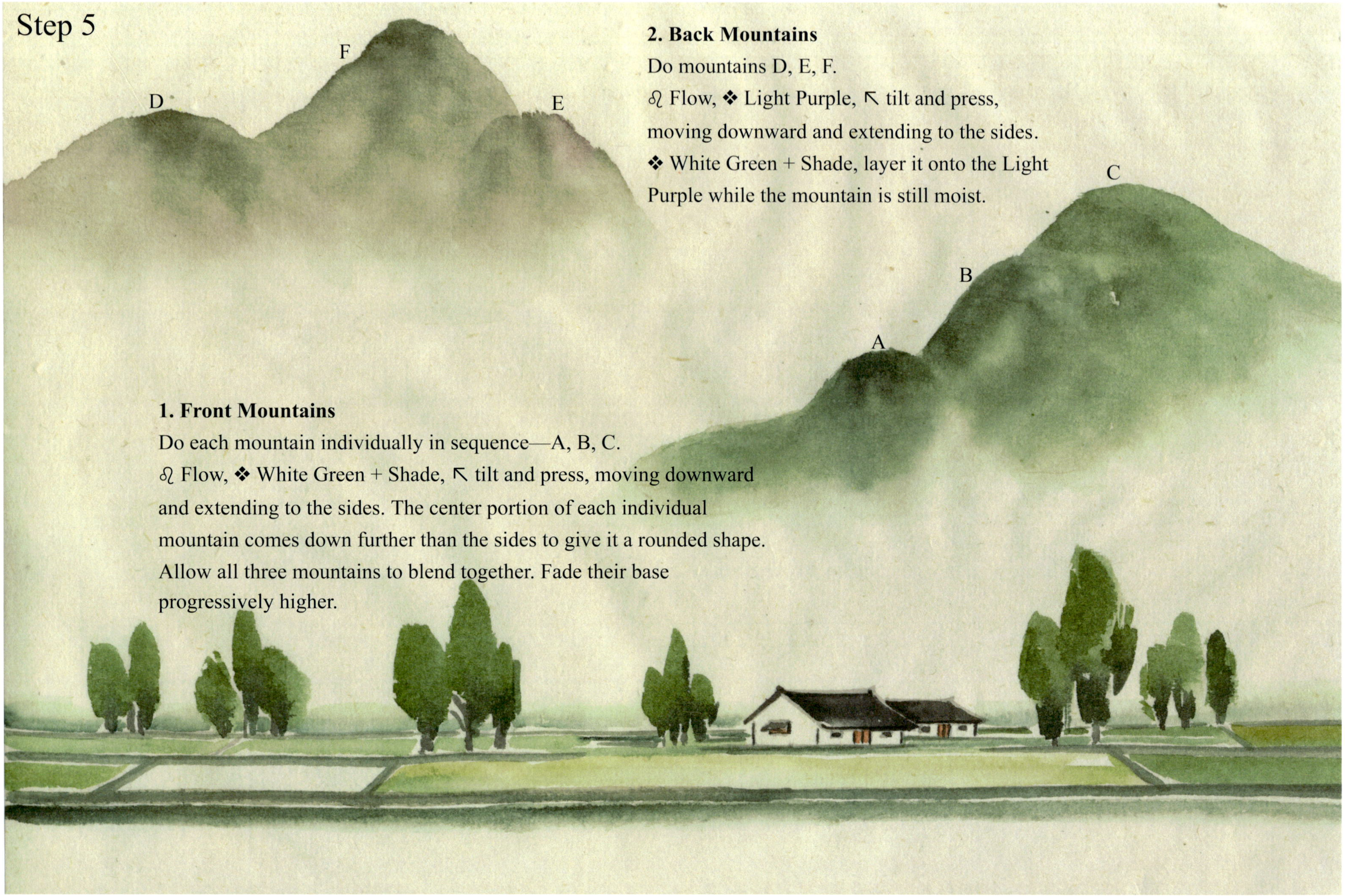

2. Back Mountains

Do mountains D, E, F.

ℓ Flow, ❖ Light Purple, ↖ tilt and press, moving downward and extending to the sides.

❖ White Green + Shade, layer it onto the Light Purple while the mountain is still moist.

1. Front Mountains

Do each mountain individually in sequence—A, B, C.

ℓ Flow, ❖ White Green + Shade, ↖ tilt and press, moving downward and extending to the sides. The center portion of each individual mountain comes down further than the sides to give it a rounded shape. Allow all three mountains to blend together. Fade their base progressively higher.

Step 6 (see diagram)

Sending in the mist is a uniquely exciting process in Chinese landscape painting. It is shaping the space, allowing the space to show meaning and movement.

Mist is the female gentle grace. It is playful, soft, illusive, rarely predictable. It is done by wetting the paper. We need to wait until all the painted elements are thoroughly dry before wetting the paper. Otherwise, everything starts to bleed.

Ironing or blow-drying can be a solution to speed up the drying.

1. Wet the paper.
ჲ Wash Brush
After the mountains dry, wet the whole painting with water using a wash brush. Apply strokes horizontally. Make sure the whole painting is wet. Use an absorbent paper towel to blot off the excess water.

Some colors may bleed even if we dry the painting. This could happen when colors are too thick. After loading a thick color, blend the tip to soften it a bit. By nature, some colors cannot hold still. Blot the runoff with an absorbent paper towel. Identify those unruly colors. Get rid of them, or apply them after the washes.

2. Add Shade at the root of the mountains (A, B).
ჲ Flow, ❖ Pasty Shade, blend and reload,
↙ tilt and press moving upward. Begin at the center (base of the mountain) then extend and taper to the sides. Make the Shade fade into the mountain upwards.

It is helpful to prepare a clean extra brush. Wet and dry the bristles. Use it to soften the edge of the shade to make it fade.

3. Add Shade as dimples in the cloud (C, D).
Do the center portion first, then extend and taper to the sides.

Mist is an illusion created by shade. We need to shape the space, rather than look at the shade. Shade alone does not mean anything. It is simply the shadow of something. It is important to make the shade fade and become part of mountain, water, or mist.

The mist (space) needs to be fluffy, relatively smooth and horizontally layered. No sharp points or too much rise and fall. It is the most important element to convey calmness and tranquility.

Apply thick Shade with relatively dry brush and while the paper is still damp. Apply Shade in one effort rather than going back again and again.

If Shade runs into the mist area, use an absorbent paper towel to blot the runoff. Do it right away. Diluted White (Sakura) can be added to force the runoff back. All these are done while the paper is still wet. Do not feel stressed if mist the disappears. It could be a sunny day.

4. Add Shade to the base of the mist to add volume and depth (E).

5. Add colors to the sky (F) and water (G)
ჲ Flow, ❖ Manganese Blue + light Shade, ↖ tilt and press, moving sideways.

It is important to keep the entire paper damp while rendering mist. Otherwise, undesirable hard edges may occur between the shade and other elements of the painting. Fine spray the drying areas every now and then.

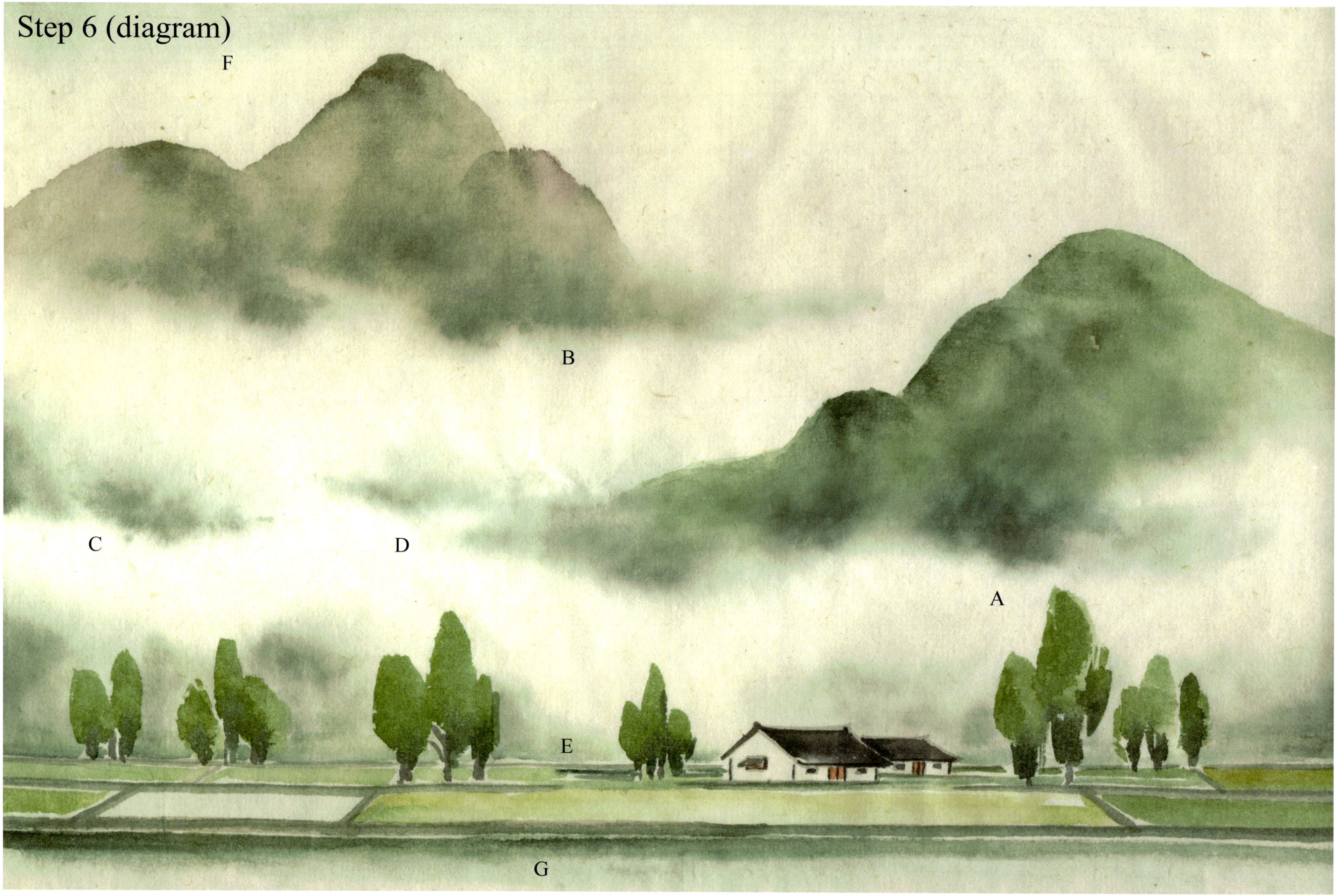
Step 6 (diagram)
F
B
C
D
A
E
G

Step 7 (see diagram)

After defining mist, let the painting dry. We will now apply the wash. We will need the Wash Brush and several flat saucers.

1. Wet the whole painting again

ꝺ Wash Brush

Using water, apply strokes horizontally. Make sure the whole painting is wet. Carry the strokes off the paper. Use an absorbent paper towel to blot off the excess water.

2. Blue wash

ꝺ Wash Brush

❖ Manganese Blue (diluted, in a flat saucer)

Wet and dry the brush. Load Manganese Blue on one corner of the brush, about 1" into the width. Blend.

Dip the colored edge in water to soften the color. This prevents the stroke from showing a hard edge.

Hold the brush vertically, colored corner up. Apply Manganese Blue wash across the top of the sky (A). Overlap the strokes to have smooth coverage of the area.

Brush another horizontal area as a guest element (B). Let the wash go through the back mountain.

Reverse the brush with the colored corner on the lower end. Wash across the bottom of the painting across to show the water (C).

Wash above the dimples and shade (D, E, F).

3. Purple wash

ꝺ Wash Brush

❖ Light Purple (diluted, in a flat saucer)

Load the brush the same way as the Manganese, colored corner down, add a Light Purple wash above the blue wash (D, E, F, and G).

4. Yellow-Vermillion highlights

ꝺ Flow

❖ Yellow + Vermillion (diluted, in a flat saucer)

Load the Flow brush with some Light Yellow Vermillion and add across area H and above the light Purple areas.

Congratulations, we now have a masterpiece and many neat tricks to enjoy our journey into Chinese landscape painting.

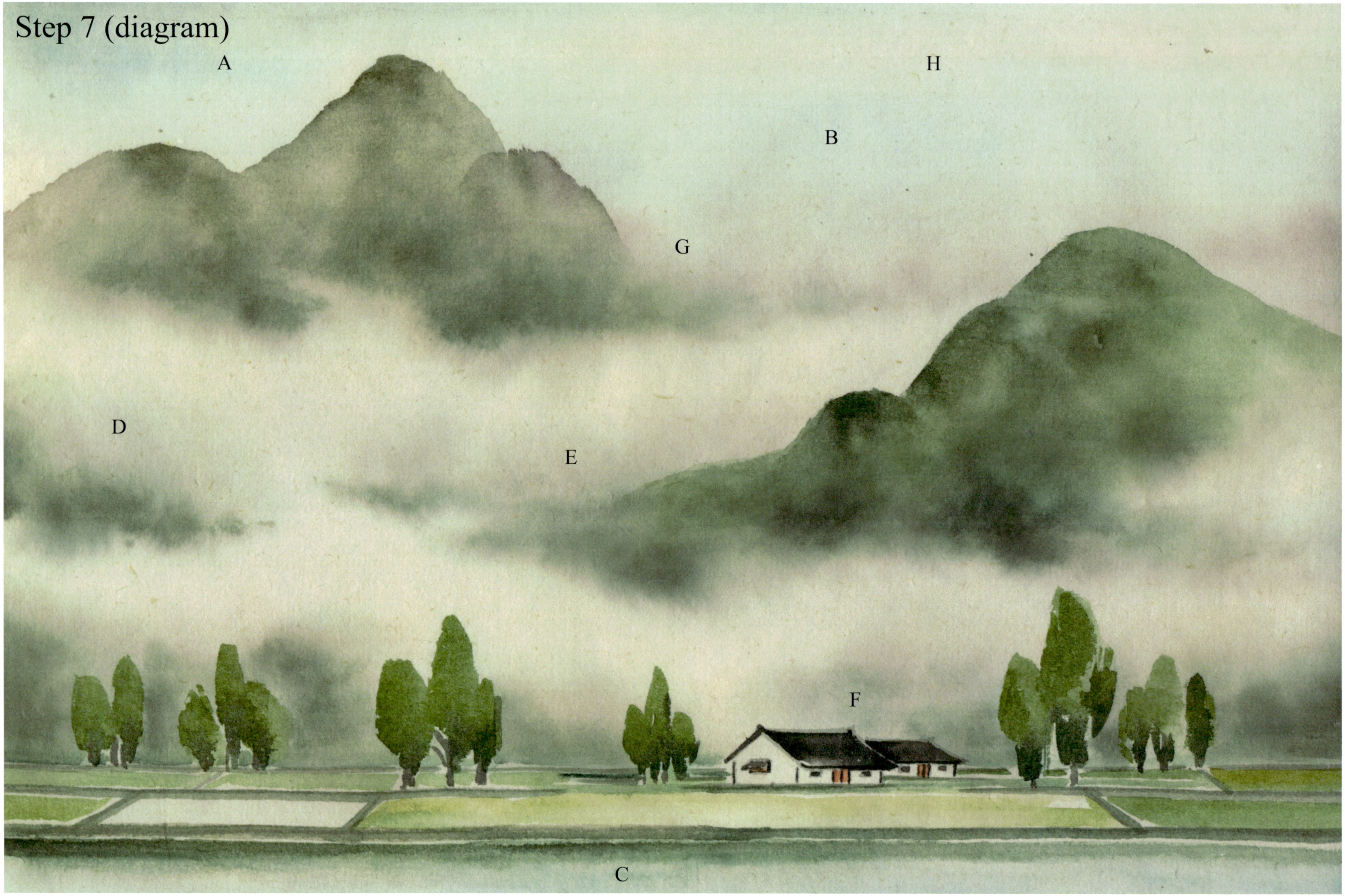

Step 7 (diagram)

Lesson 2: Sunset

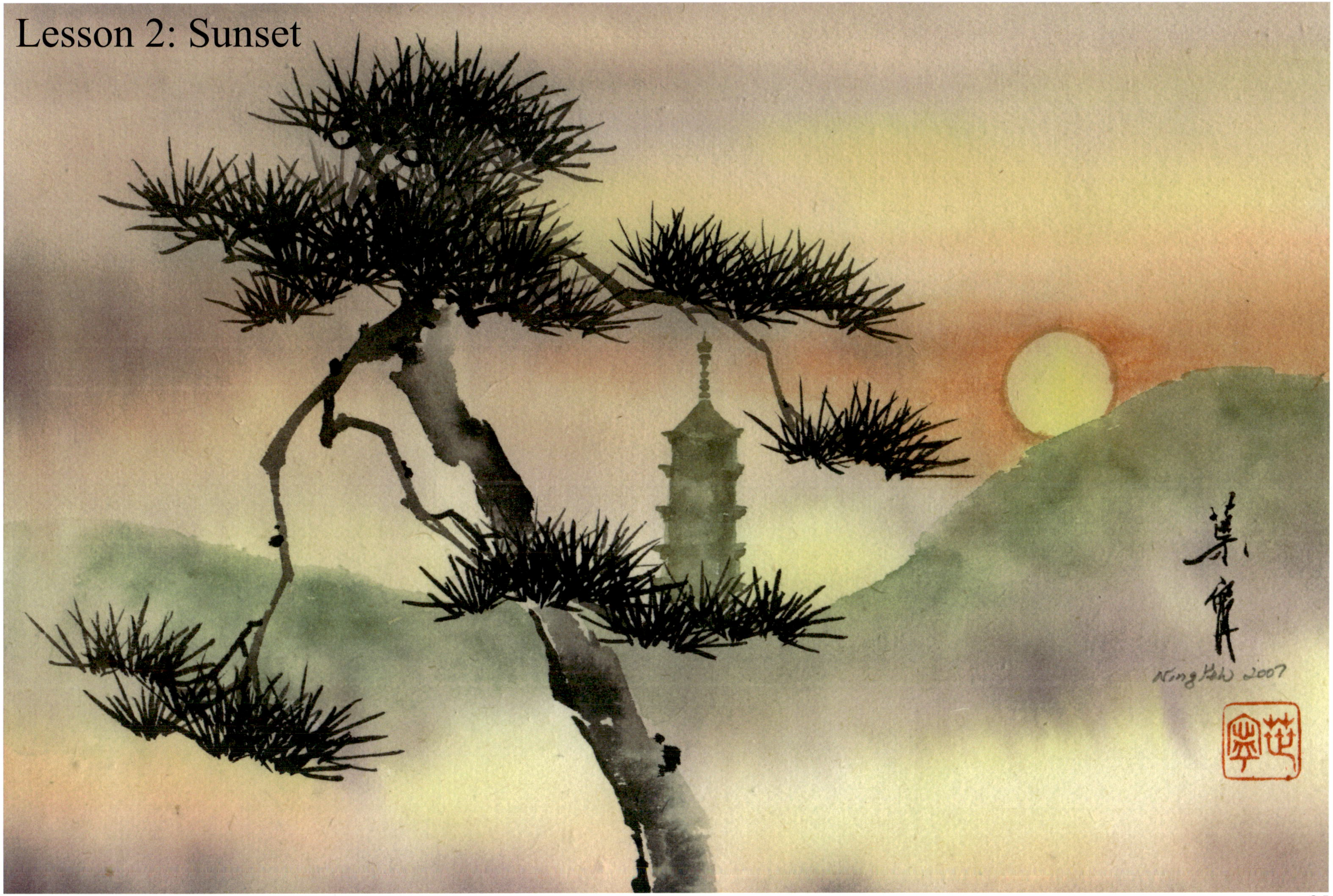

Lesson 2: Sunset

In the winter of 1991, we traveled north in China to Chengde, the origin of the Manchu Empire. The town is located in a small basin 400 miles northeast of Beijing. I rank the scenery of Chengde to be among the top ten sights in China.

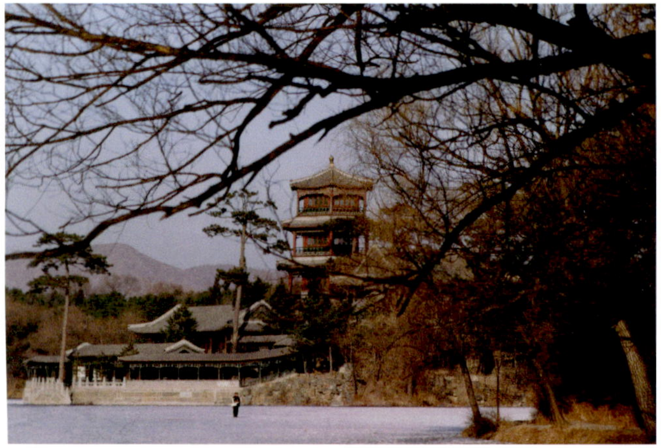

The early emperors of Qing were people with great taste. They traveled to South China, and wherever the scenery pleased them, they ordered a replica to be built here. Pavilions and towers dot the many islets linked by causeways. A stroll along these paths is reminiscent of a walk through the garden cities of south China.
It is a miniature south China, well blended with the surrounding north China scenery.

Outside the Emperor's Mountain Retreat, there are eight temples built on the surrounding hill slopes. The temples represent the major religions of the outlying minorities of China.

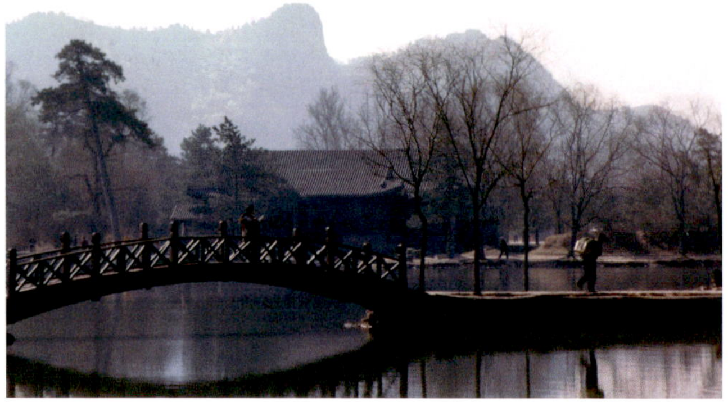

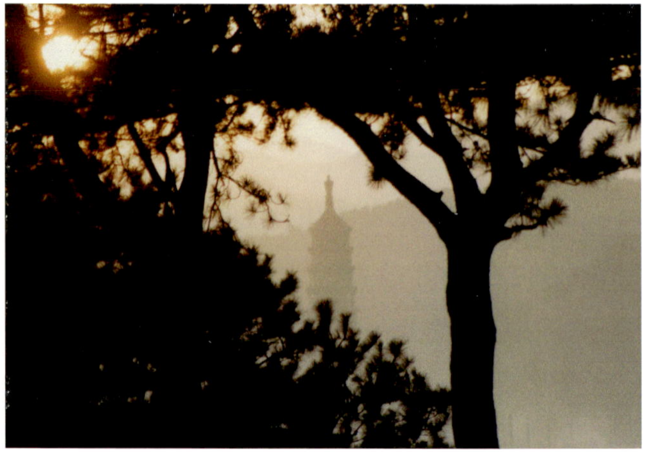

This was the birthplace of an empire. There still exists a celestial regal spirit today.

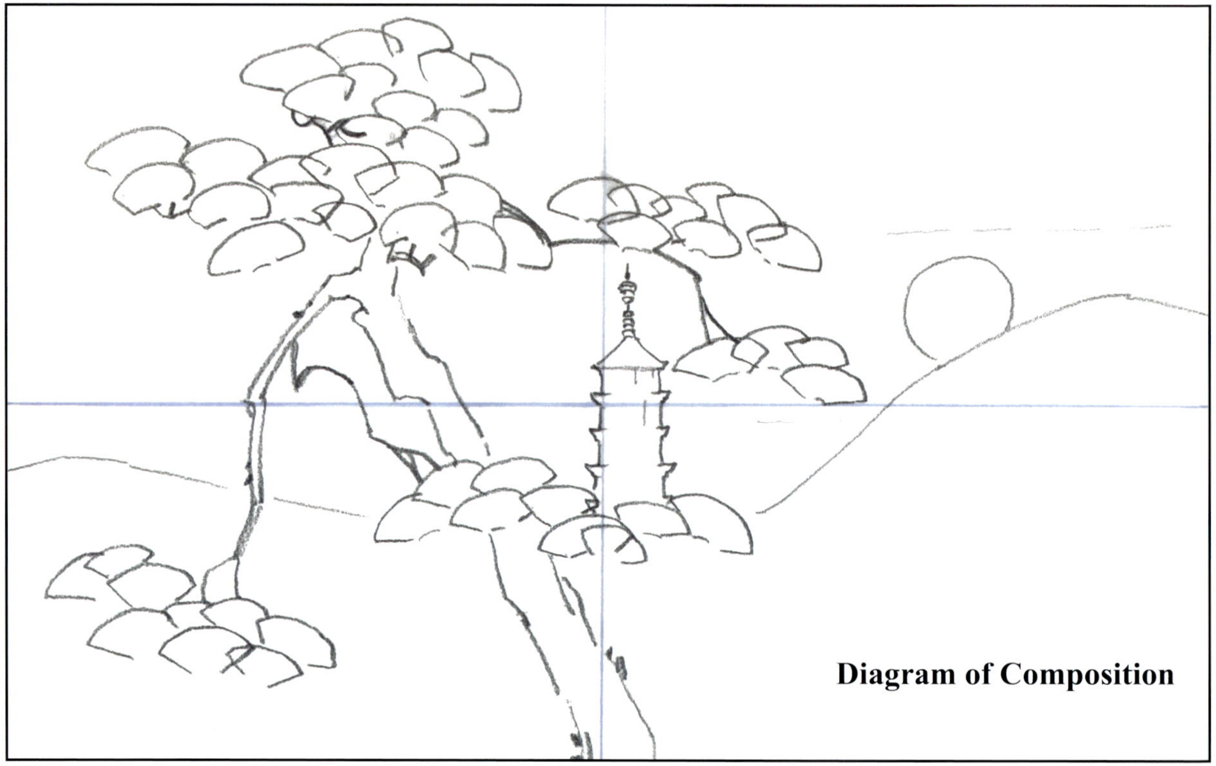

Diagram of Composition

Step 1

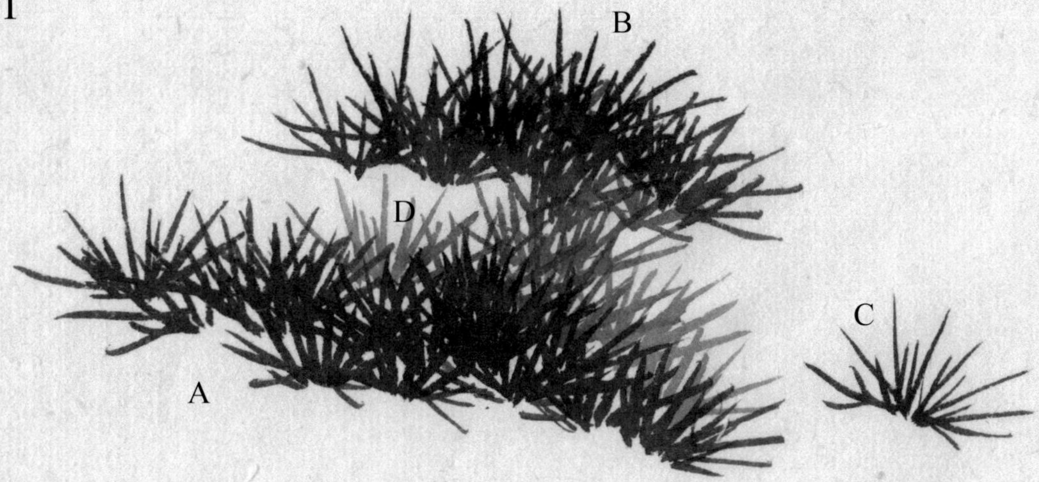

Pine Needle Clusters

ℓ Happy Dot or Small Mt. Horse, ❖ Ink (generous amount, almost dripping) , ↓ vertical strokes, moving the brush with arm.

Work needles from outside to the center. Long with short, crossing at times. Arrange the needle cluster into a horizontal fan shape with side ones curving (embracing) and front ones foreshortened (C).

Do a host group (A) and guest group (B). Overlap the fans into waving horizontal layers (see diagram).

❖ Medium Ink. Add a lighter cluster (D) as a go-between. Do more needles to thicken the clusters and reduce the spaces.

Pine needles can be addictive. Try to get a hold of yourselves. Leave room for other things to come.

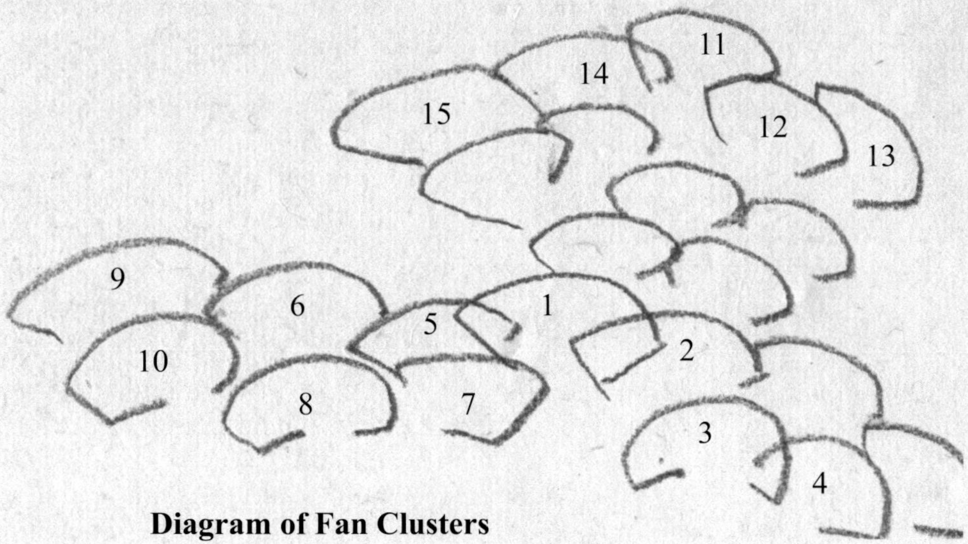

Diagram of Fan Clusters

Build up the pine needle fan clusters in the layout and sequence shown above (1-15).

Step 2

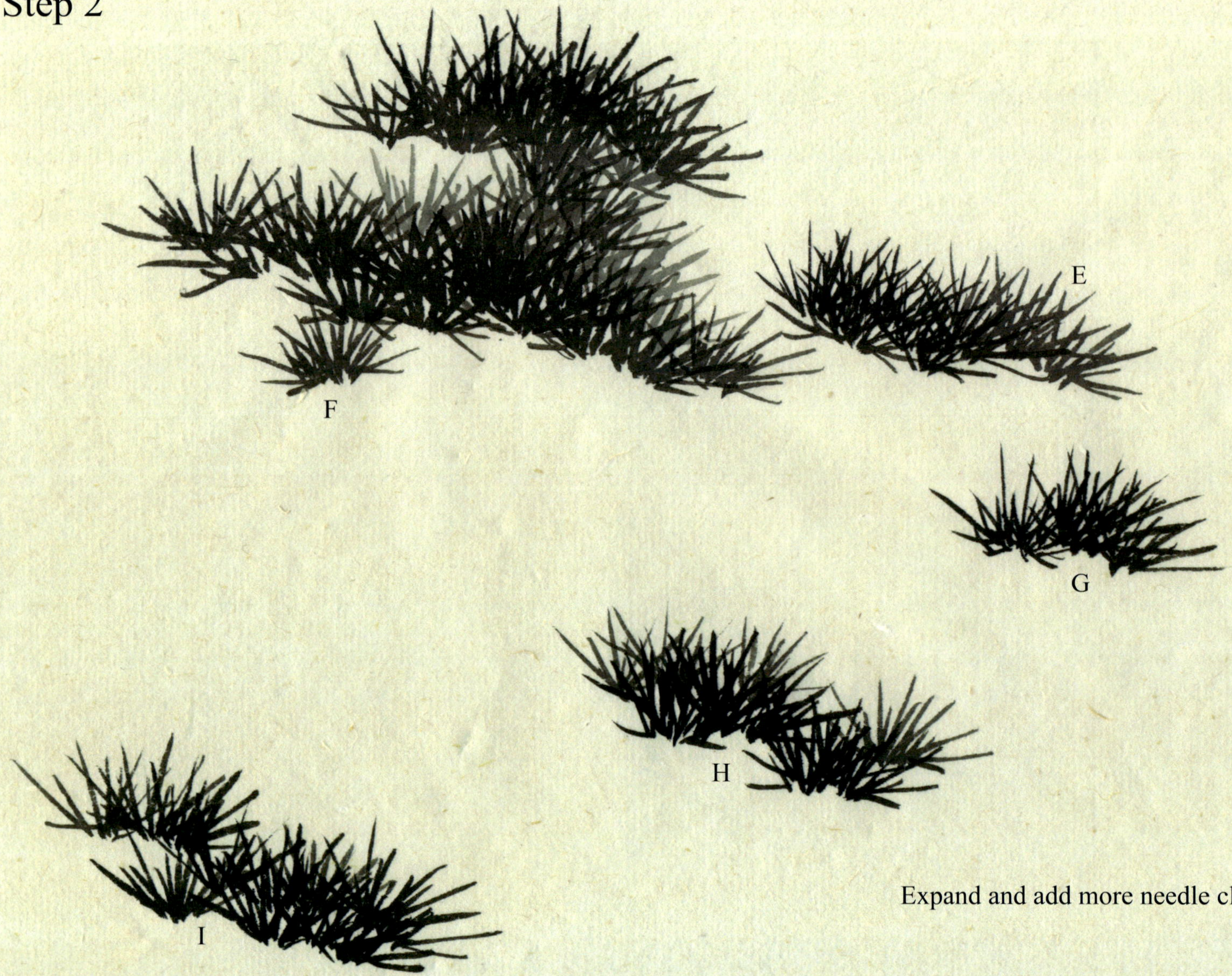

Expand and add more needle clusters (E-I).

Step 3

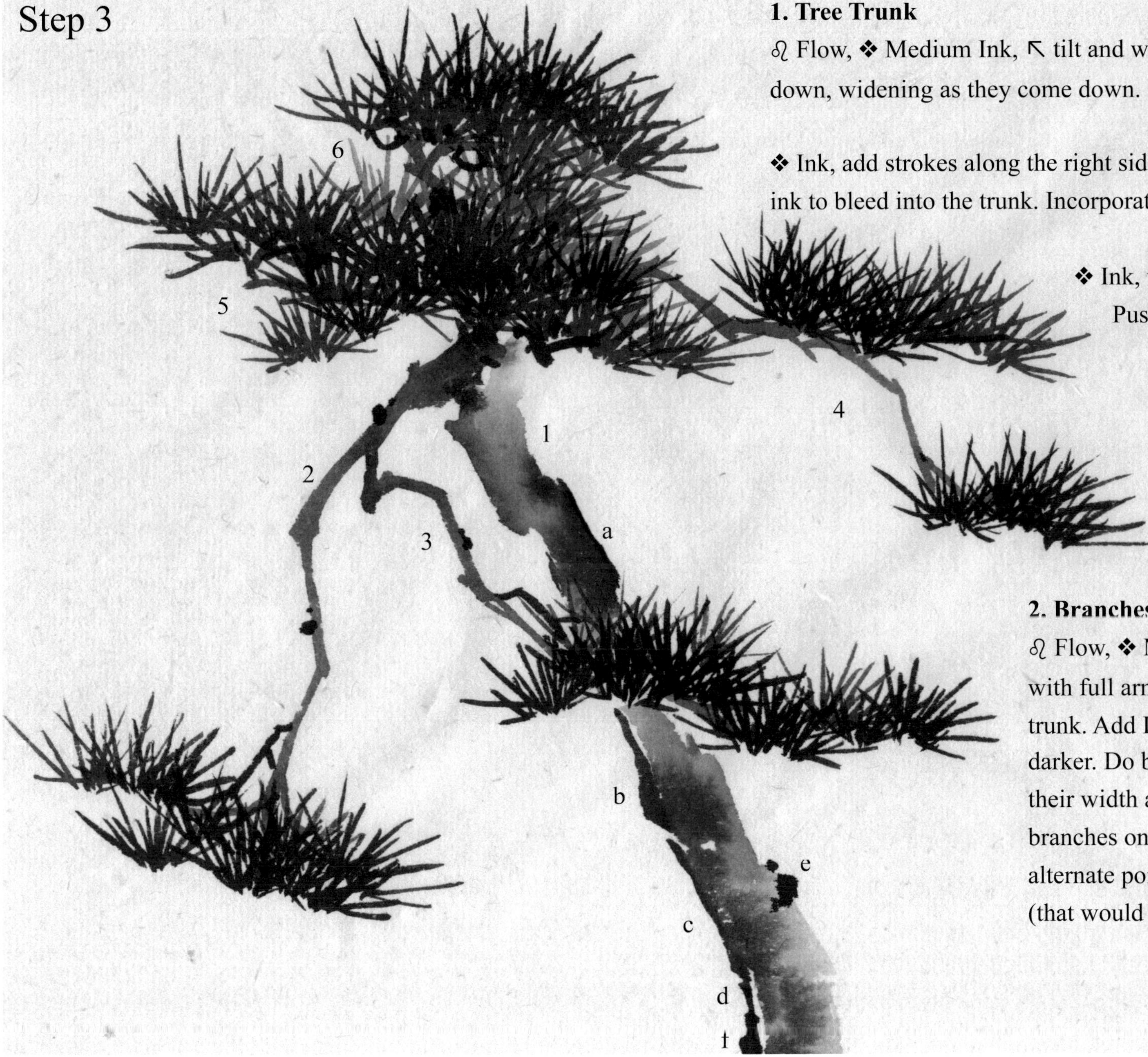

1. Tree Trunk

♌ Flow, ❖ Medium Ink, ↖ tilt and work overlapping strokes from the top down, widening as they come down.

❖ Ink, add strokes along the right side (a) and left side (b, c, d). Allow some ink to bleed into the trunk. Incorporate occasional spaces.

❖ Ink, work happy dots in clusters. Push them from outside in (e, f).

2. Branches

♌ Flow, ❖ Medium Ink, ↓ vertical brush moving with full arm. Branches should be darker than the trunk. Add Ink to make the smaller ones even darker. Do branches from the trunk out. Reduce their width as they move out (2-6). Attach the branches onto the trunk. Branches come out from alternate points. Do not grow them from one point (that would be the dreaded chicken foot).

Step 4

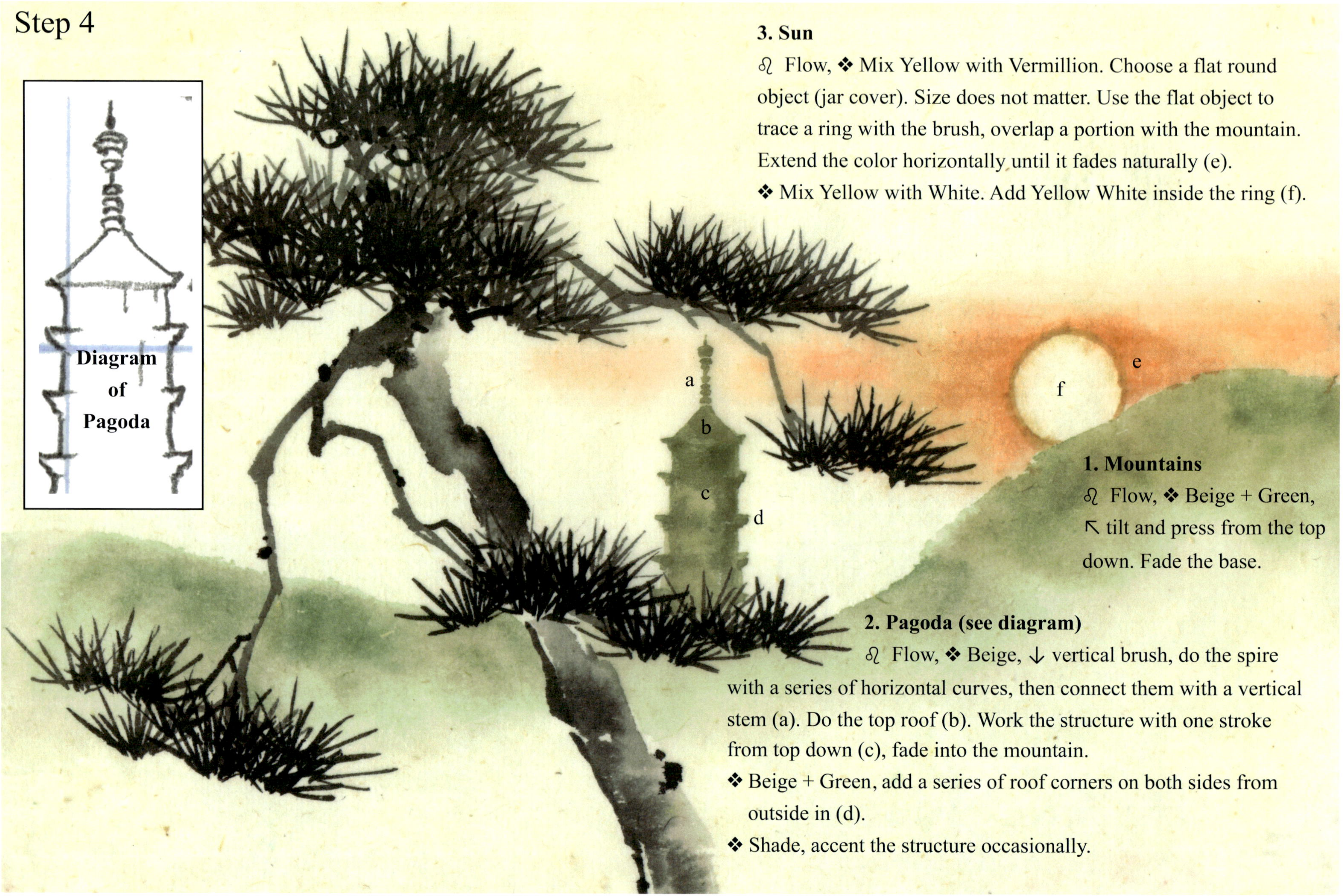

3. Sun

ℓ Flow, ❖ Mix Yellow with Vermillion. Choose a flat round object (jar cover). Size does not matter. Use the flat object to trace a ring with the brush, overlap a portion with the mountain. Extend the color horizontally until it fades naturally (e).

❖ Mix Yellow with White. Add Yellow White inside the ring (f).

1. Mountains

ℓ Flow, ❖ Beige + Green, ↖ tilt and press from the top down. Fade the base.

2. Pagoda (see diagram)

ℓ Flow, ❖ Beige, ↓ vertical brush, do the spire with a series of horizontal curves, then connect them with a vertical stem (a). Do the top roof (b). Work the structure with one stroke from top down (c), fade into the mountain.

❖ Beige + Green, add a series of roof corners on both sides from outside in (d).

❖ Shade, accent the structure occasionally.

Step 5 (see diagram)

Wait until the painting dries. We will now apply the wash. We will need a Wash Brush and several flat saucers.

Prepare the following colors in flat saucers:

❖ White Yellow: Mix Yellow with White, dilute into a light wash

❖ Yellow Vermillion: Mix Yellow with Vermillion, dilute to medium

❖ Purple: Watery but strong

❖ Pink: Watery

♌ Wash Brush

Using water, apply stroke horizontally. Wet the entire painting.

❖ White Yellow

Load the bristles with White Yellow then dip both ends of the Wash Brush into water so the strokes do not show hard edges. Apply across areas A and B.

❖ Yellow Vermillion

Do areas C and D the same way.

❖ Purple

Load one corner of the brush about 1" into the width. Blend. Dip the colored edge in water to soften the color so the strokes do not show hard edges.

Hold the brush vertically, colored corner up. Apply Purple across the top and middle of the sky (E and F). Overlap the strokes to have smooth coverage of the area.

Reverse the brush with the colored corner now on the lower end.

Work along the lower edge of the painting across (G) and the base of the mountain (H).

❖ Pink

Add Pink into the Purple and Yellow Vermillion areas.

Blend the various colors into one another. Do not make them spotty. Let these washes go through the painted elements (tree, pagoda, etc.)

In Chinese culture, pine is the symbol of longevity. Its movement reflects the spirit of a royal dragon. In this lesson, we practiced line work through pine needles, dashing branches, and a bold trunk. We learned how to cluster foliage into host and guest shapes. We studied the intriguing pattern of the simple pagoda. Of course, we immersed ourselves in the glorious colors of the sunset.

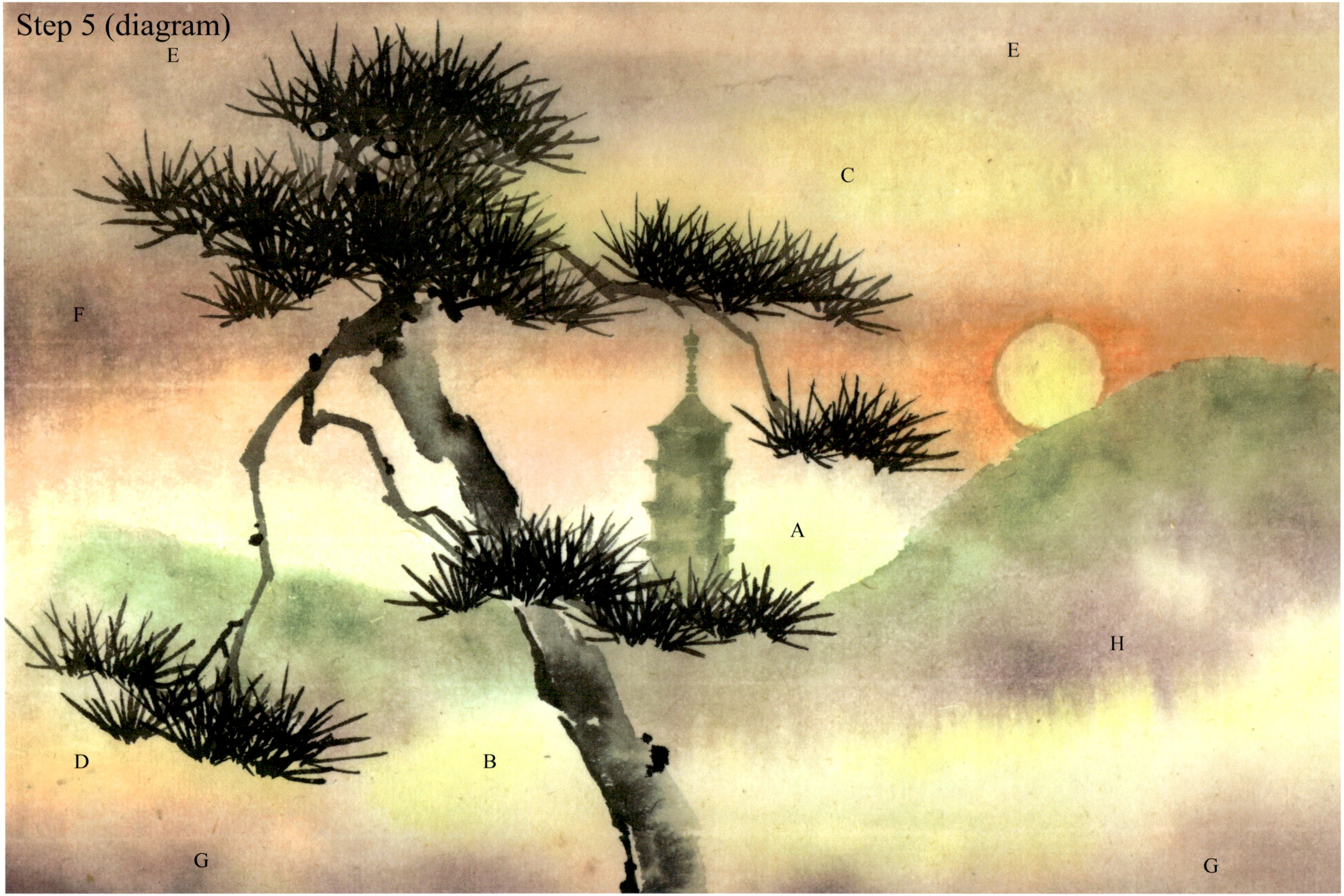

Step 5 (diagram)

Lesson 3: Reflections

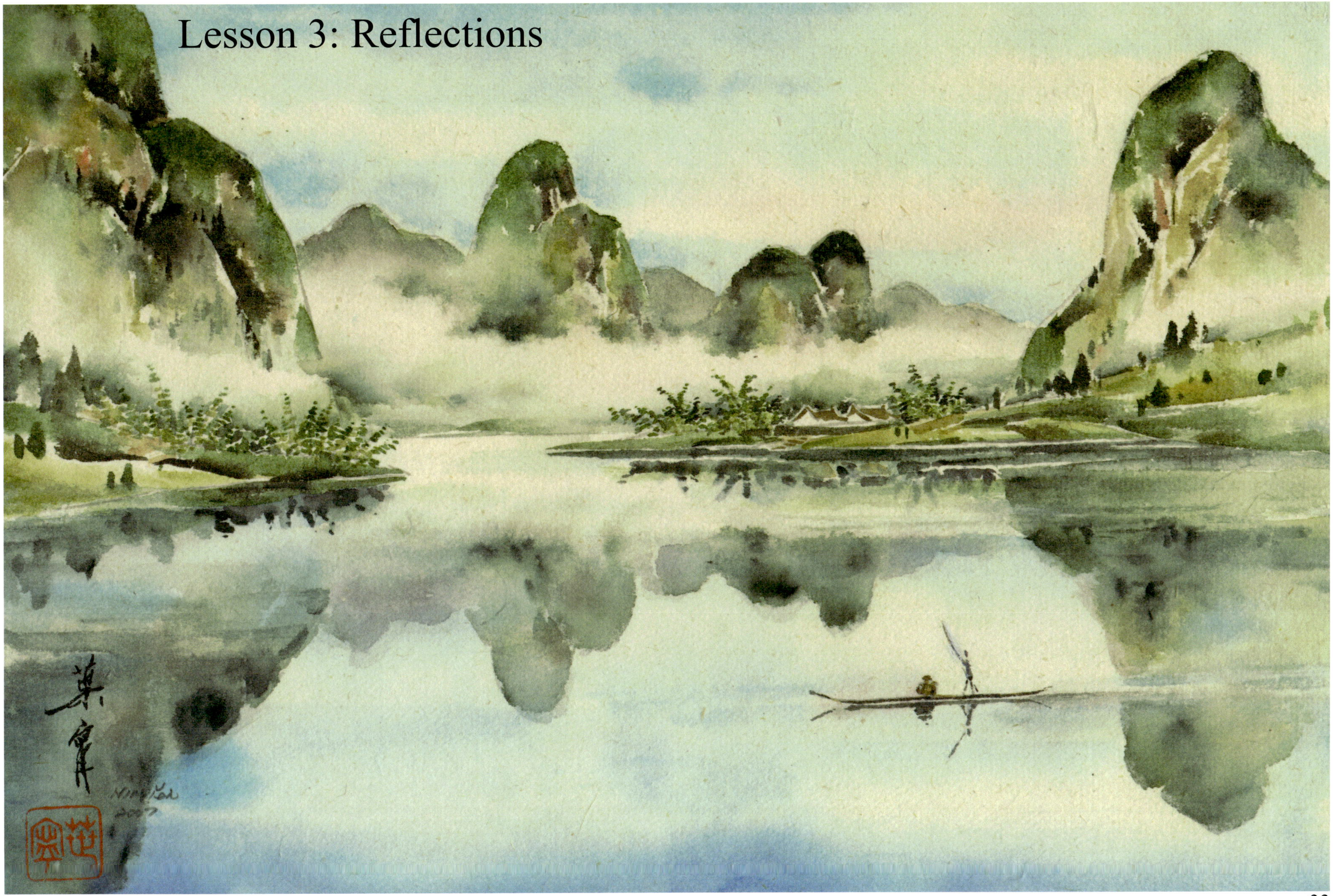

Lesson 3: Reflections

Shan shui is the Chinese word for landscape. Shan is mountain, the land and its elements. Grand and massive, it represents nature's constancy and strength. Shui is water, with its ever-changing faces: mist, river, lake, waterfall. Soft and graceful, it represents nature's fluidity and changes. When mountain meets water in harmony, one finds all the abundance nature has to offer—flowers bloom, trees grow, and people develop literature and art.

Nowhere on earth, is this perfect union more evident than at the Li River in Guilin. Covered with foliage, Guilin's colorful limestone pinnacles are not tall. Friendly and approachable, they lean towards the water, greeting guests and one another. On a clear day, beautiful reflections take place.

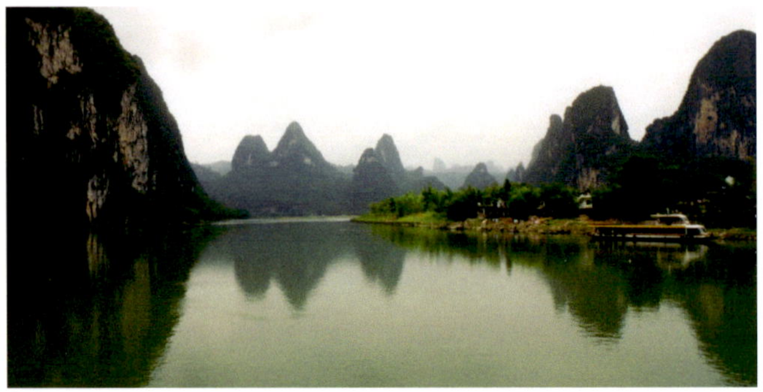

Step 1 (see diagram)

In this lesson, we will take advantage of rice paper's unique qualities to enjoy a perfect reflection. We begin by preparing a draft.

1. Do river bank A. Keep the baseline horizontal then gradually moving downward as it moves out. Do the top of bank A tapering down toward the river with a sharp tip and rising up as it moves inland.

2. Do the baseline of bank B a little higher then bank A, also keeping it horizontal. Do the top of bank B flat to settle houses. Do bank C.

3. Add the nose of the river banks coming forward (a, b, c). Do a few flat steps (d), with the lower ones longer. Show flat house roofs (e). Add clusters of bamboo trunks (f).

4 Do mountain D from the top. Make the left edge more vertical so the mountain faces inward. Big mountains show extra sets of nose lines (g, h). Use dotted lines at their roots as a reminder to fade. Show "Y" (i, j) to reveal some armpits of the mountain. Everything is personified. This is how Chinese relate to scenery.

6. Do mountain E. Overlap the lines. Define the nose and armpit. Fade the base.

7. Do mountain group F and G as a liaison between the two sides. Make their roots end higher. There is an invisible horizontal layer of mist below. We can use a red dotted line for the mist line, reminding us to fade the mountain roots and leave space open below. We do not go into this a Red Light District. (In China, such place is called the Green Light District, a difference of culture.) I do not use the dotted line because students inadvertently painted these dots and had to turn them into a flock of geese.

8. Work the distant hills (H, I, J) with no detail. End them higher. Mark horizontal line K to show a distant bank.

9. Do the lady then the boat. Do the head dot, upper body, arms and legs (L). Run a horizontal line for the bamboo boat, gently tilting the ends upward (M).

10. Run a pole through her hands. Do not run the pole past the boat, it is behind. Add a basket (N). The cormorants are fishing in the water.

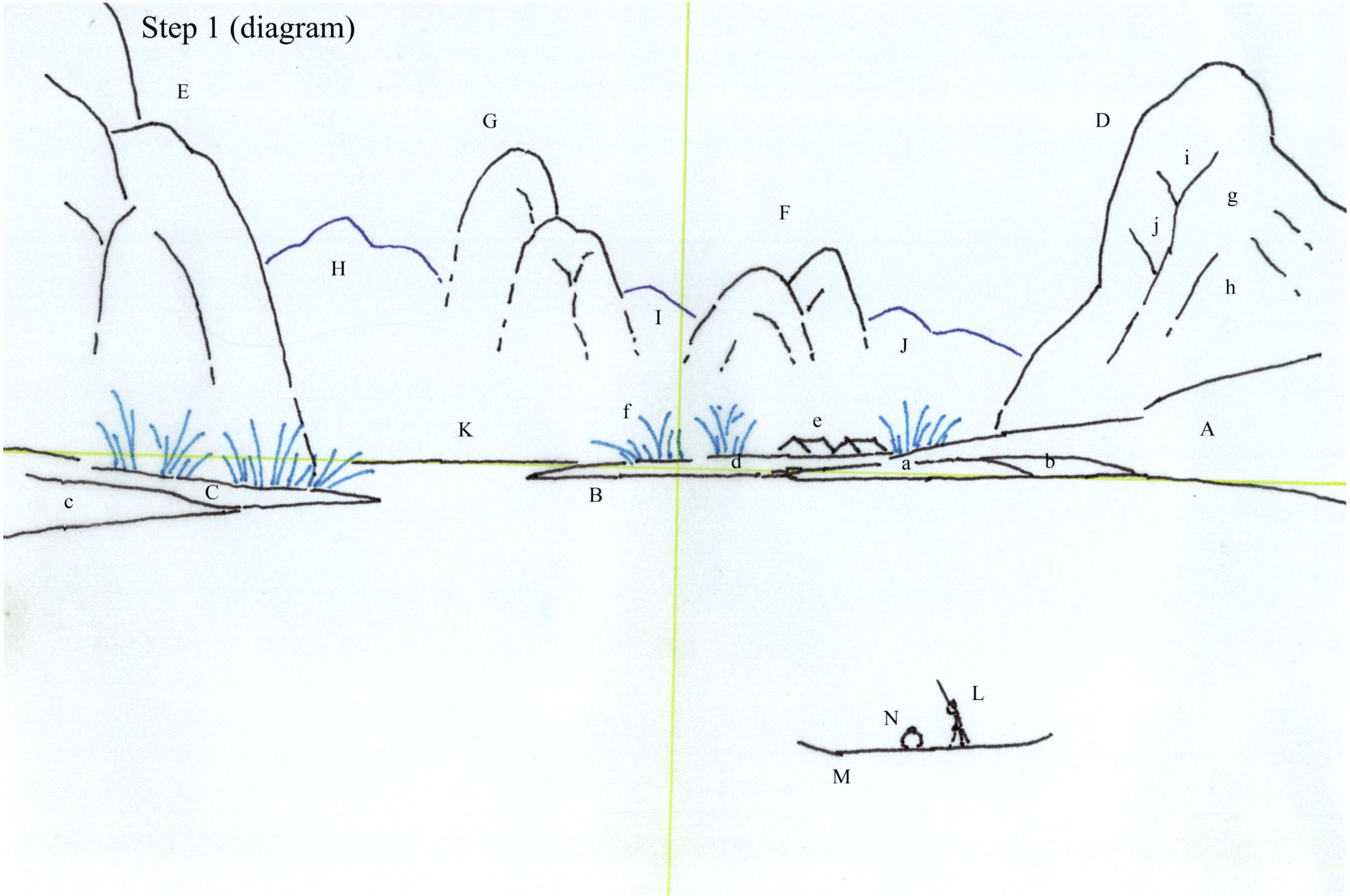

Step 1 (diagram)
E
G
D
i
g
F
j
H
h
I
J
f
e
K
A
d
a
b
c
C
B
L
N
M

Step 2

Coloring: ♌ Flow brush throughout. Load colors only at the tip from light to dark (see "Brush Fundamentals"). Tilt and press to fade, move from the edge of the shape inward. Apply light colors from one direction, dark colors from the opposite direction, and blend in the middle. Leave a hairline space between elements to avoid bleeding. In landscape, bleeding is never a problem. Mother Nature does it all the time. This diagram helps identify color groups.

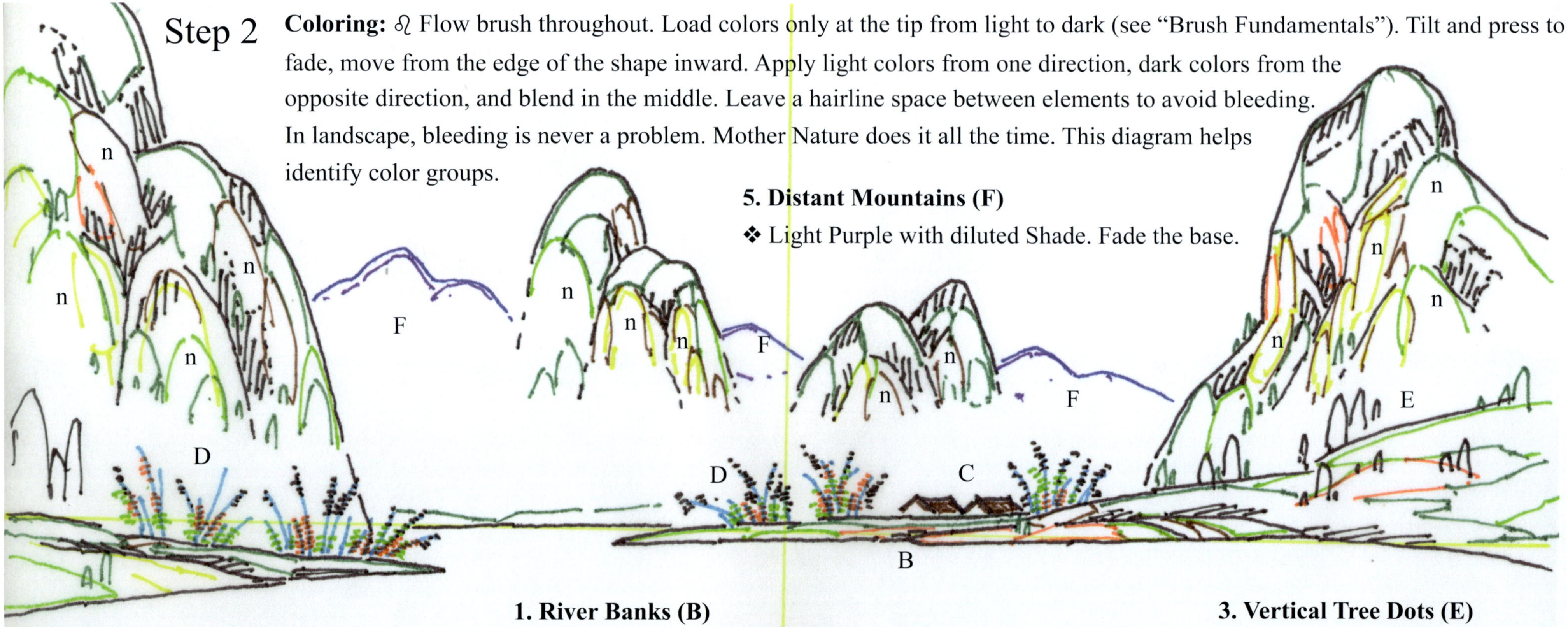

5. Distant Mountains (F)

❖ Light Purple with diluted Shade. Fade the base.

1. River Banks (B)

❖ Ochre, Light Green, or Ochre + Light Green, color the tip and nose of the banks. ❖ Dark Green, Shade, and Ink to add shadows.

3. Vertical Tree Dots (E)

❖ Dark Green + Shade + Ink
Work dots from top down.

4. Front Mountains

❖ Ochre, Light Green, Beige, and occasional Vermillion to color the nose areas (n). Use colors individually or load multiple colors from light to dark but only at the tip and blend (see "Brush Fundamentals"). Streaks of space adds texture to rocky elements.

❖ Dark Green, Shade, and Ink to add shadows. Fade the base.

2. Bamboo Groves (D)

Use horizontal dots overlapping along the trunks. ❖ Ochre, Light Green for lower center ones. ❖ Dark Green, Shade, and Ink for tips and shadow areas.

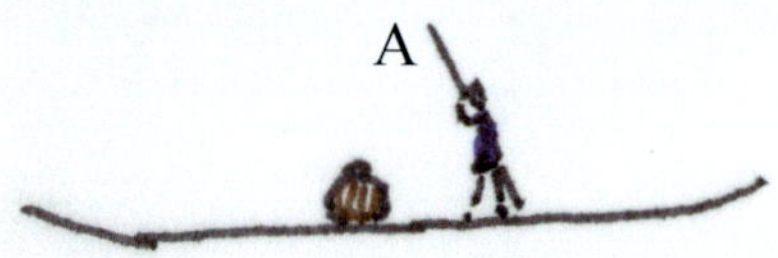

6. Other Elements

❖ Brown for the roof (C), boat, basket (A)
❖ Sky Blue for the lady's upper body

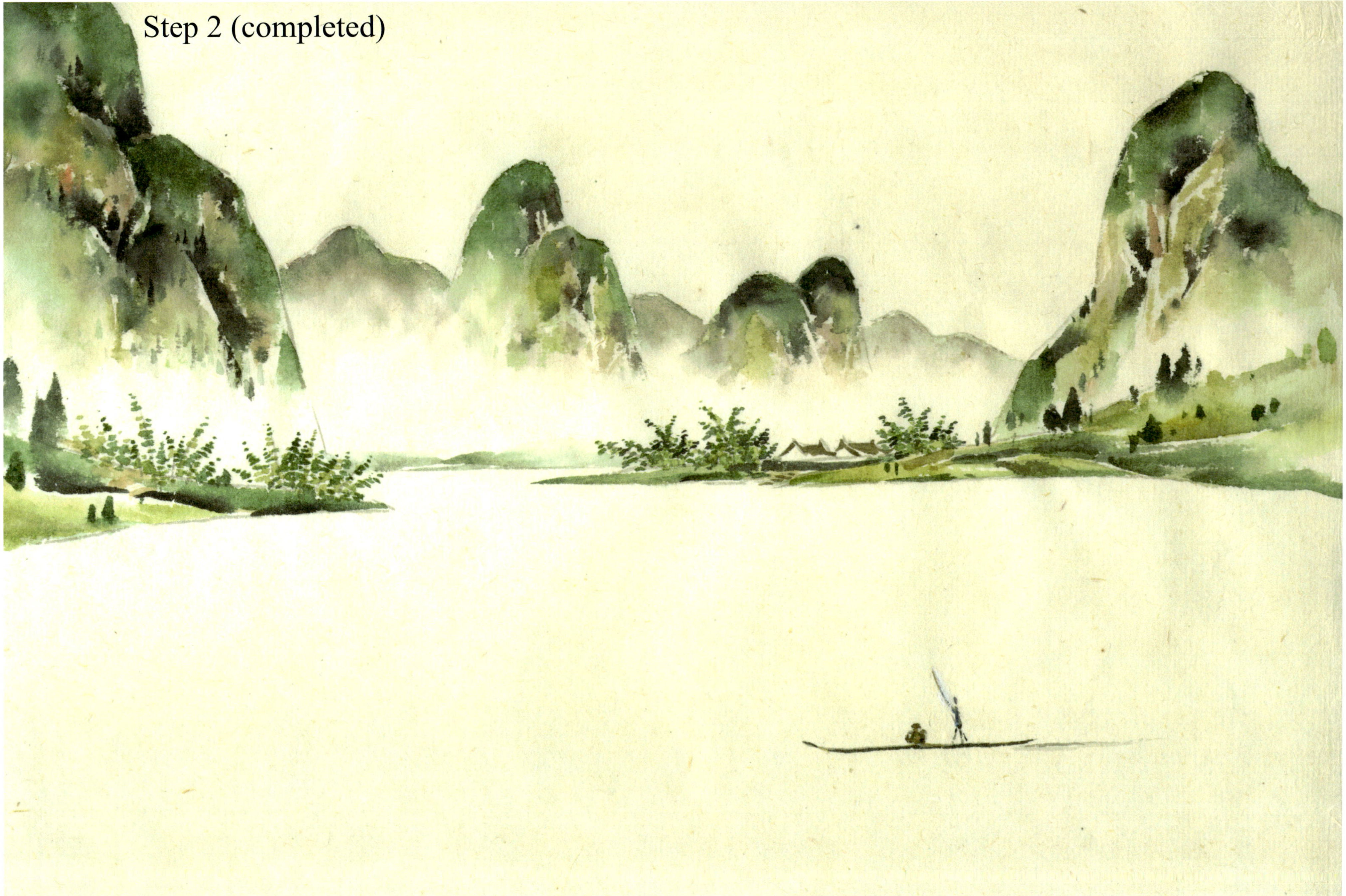
Step 2 (completed)

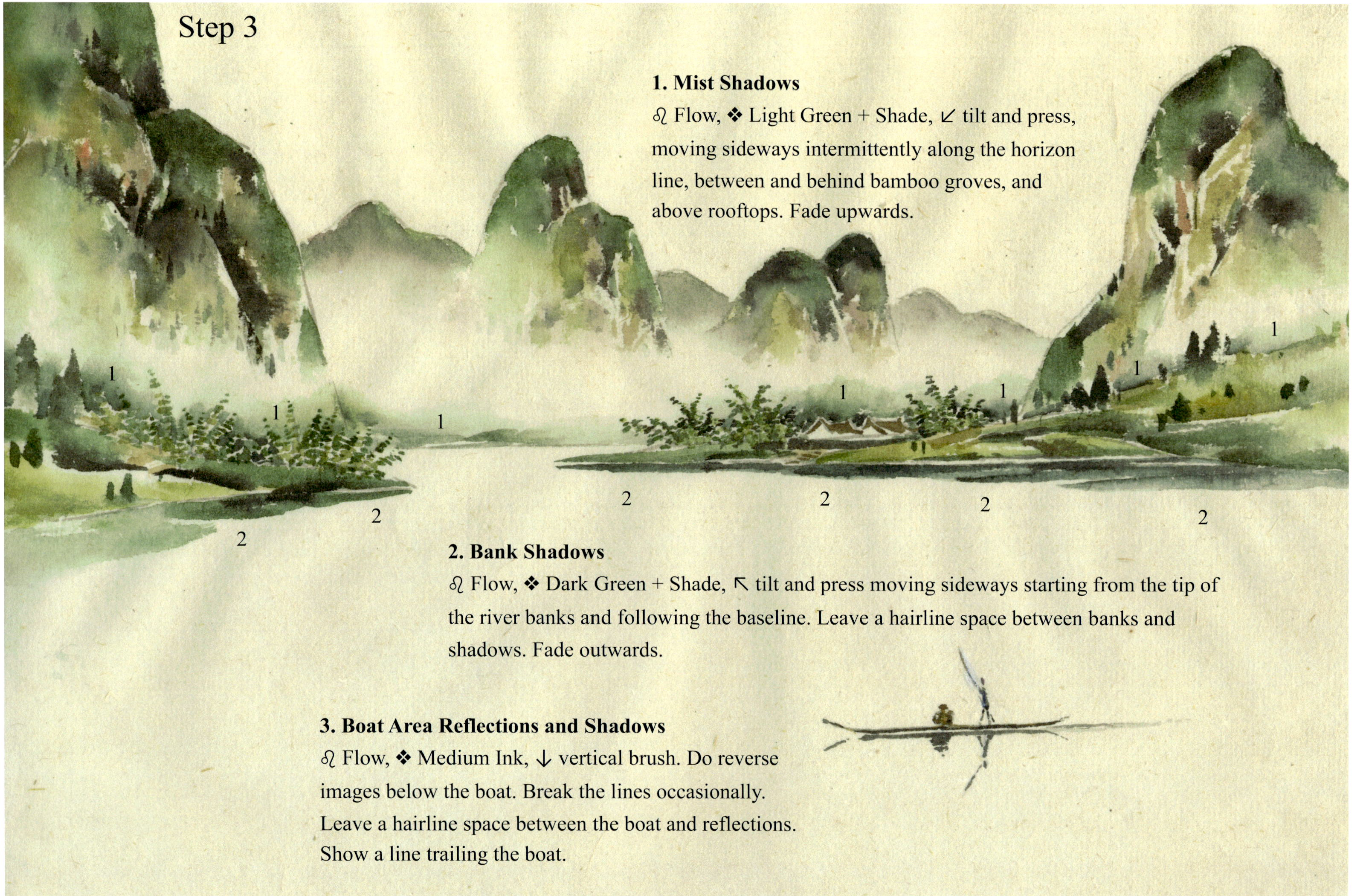

Step 3

1. Mist Shadows

ᘓ Flow, ❖ Light Green + Shade, ↙ tilt and press, moving sideways intermittently along the horizon line, between and behind bamboo groves, and above rooftops. Fade upwards.

2. Bank Shadows

ᘓ Flow, ❖ Dark Green + Shade, ↖ tilt and press moving sideways starting from the tip of the river banks and following the baseline. Leave a hairline space between banks and shadows. Fade outwards.

3. Boat Area Reflections and Shadows

ᘓ Flow, ❖ Medium Ink, ↓ vertical brush. Do reverse images below the boat. Break the lines occasionally. Leave a hairline space between the boat and reflections. Show a line trailing the boat.

Step 4 Reflections (see p.39)

We can take advantage rice paper's see-through quality to produce a mirror image. After mounting, all the folds disappear. How exciting.

1. Mountain and River Bank on the Right

From the boat area reflection, we learned that the reflection starts from the baseline of the object. Fold the paper up horizontally along the baseline of the mountain and river bank 1 (dashed line). ℓ Flow, ❖ Diluted Light Green + Shade, ← Tilt and press moving sideways. Using broad horizontal strokes, do the shape of the mountain on the back of the paper (1a). Leave streaks of space (one in line with the boat). ❖ Add a few colors used on the mountain here too. While wet, work the reflected shape on the front side creating a blurry, soft edge. Perfect for reflection.

2. Distant Bank with Houses

Fold along the baseline of river bank 2. Trace the the foliage and the houses on the back using matching colors (2a). Work them on the front too.

3. Left Bank and Mountain

Fold along baseline 3 and work the left side (3a).

4. River Horizon Line

Fold along baseline 4. Work the reflections of the mountains in the middle and in distance (4a).

Step 5 Mist and Wash (see p.40)

5. Mist at the Mountain Base

ℓ Flow, ❖ Pasty Shade, blend and reload. ↙ tilt and press at the root of the mountains.

6. Wash the Sky

Let the painting dry. Rewet the whole painting. Use flat saucers for Manganese and Light Purple. ℓ Wash Brush ❖ Manganese Blue (diluted), load one corner of the brush, about 1" into the width. Blend. Dip the colored edge in water so the stroke will not show a hard edge. Hold the brush vertically, colored corner up. Apply overlapping strokes smoothly across the sky.

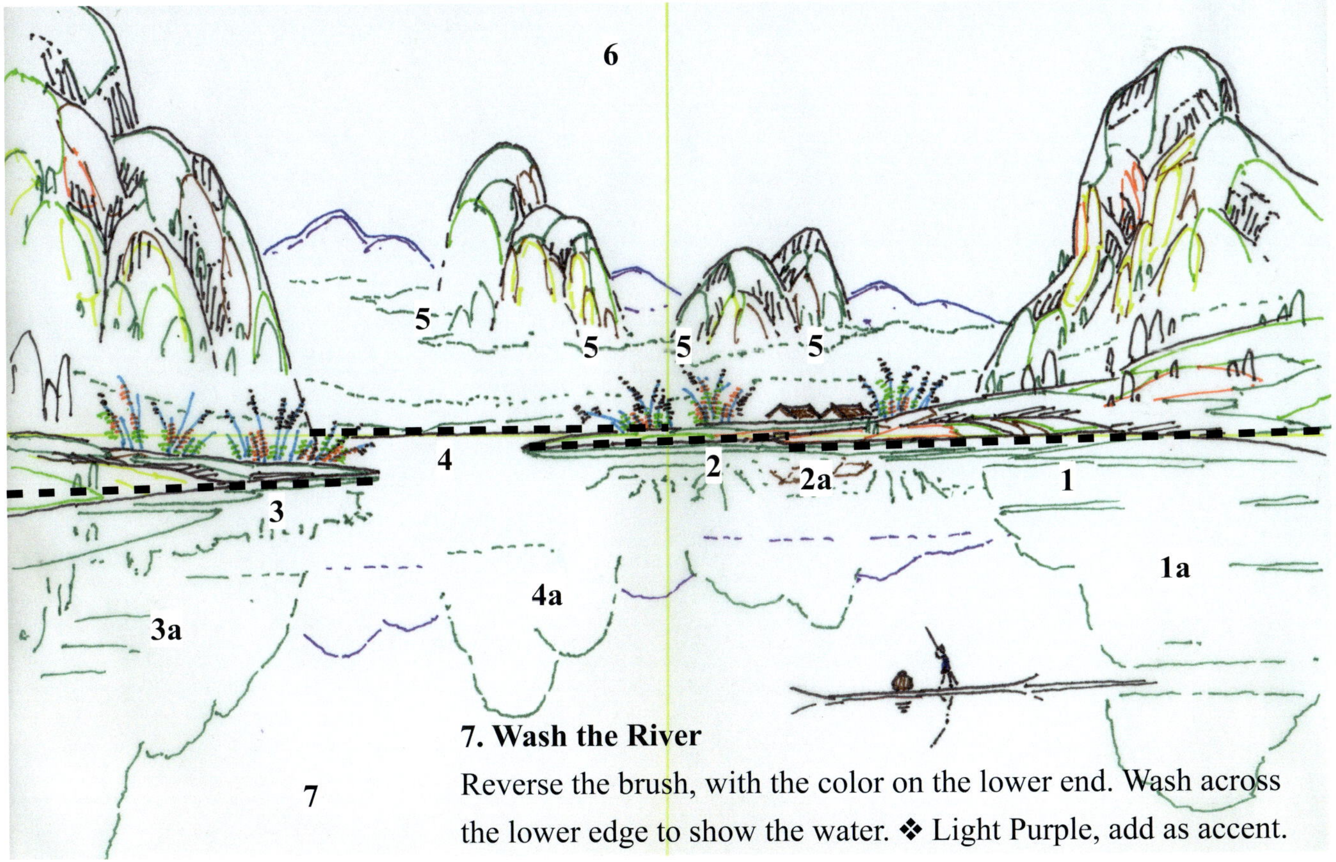

7. Wash the River

Reverse the brush, with the color on the lower end. Wash across the lower edge to show the water. ❖ Light Purple, add as accent.

Step 4 Reflections

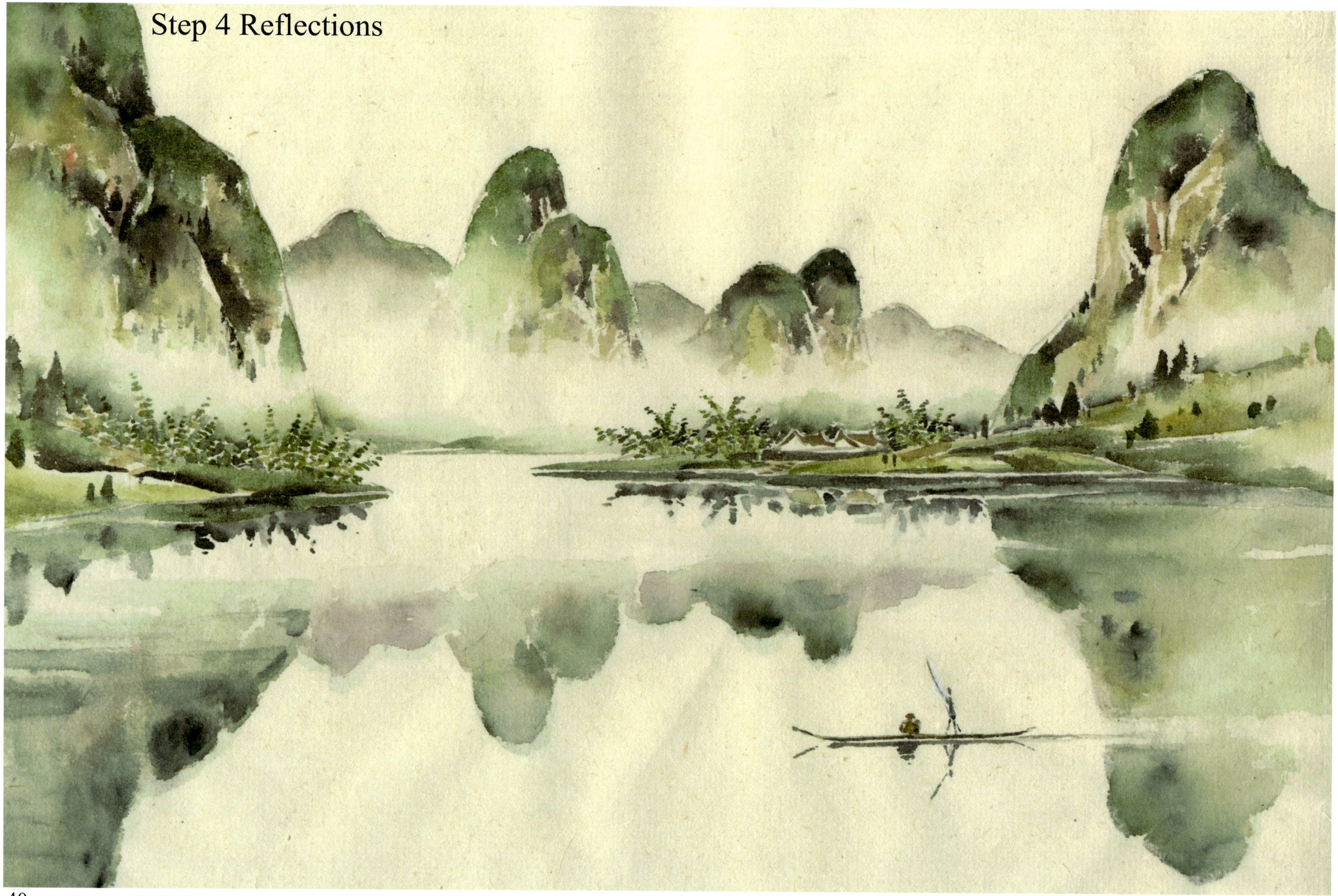

Step 5 Mist and Wash

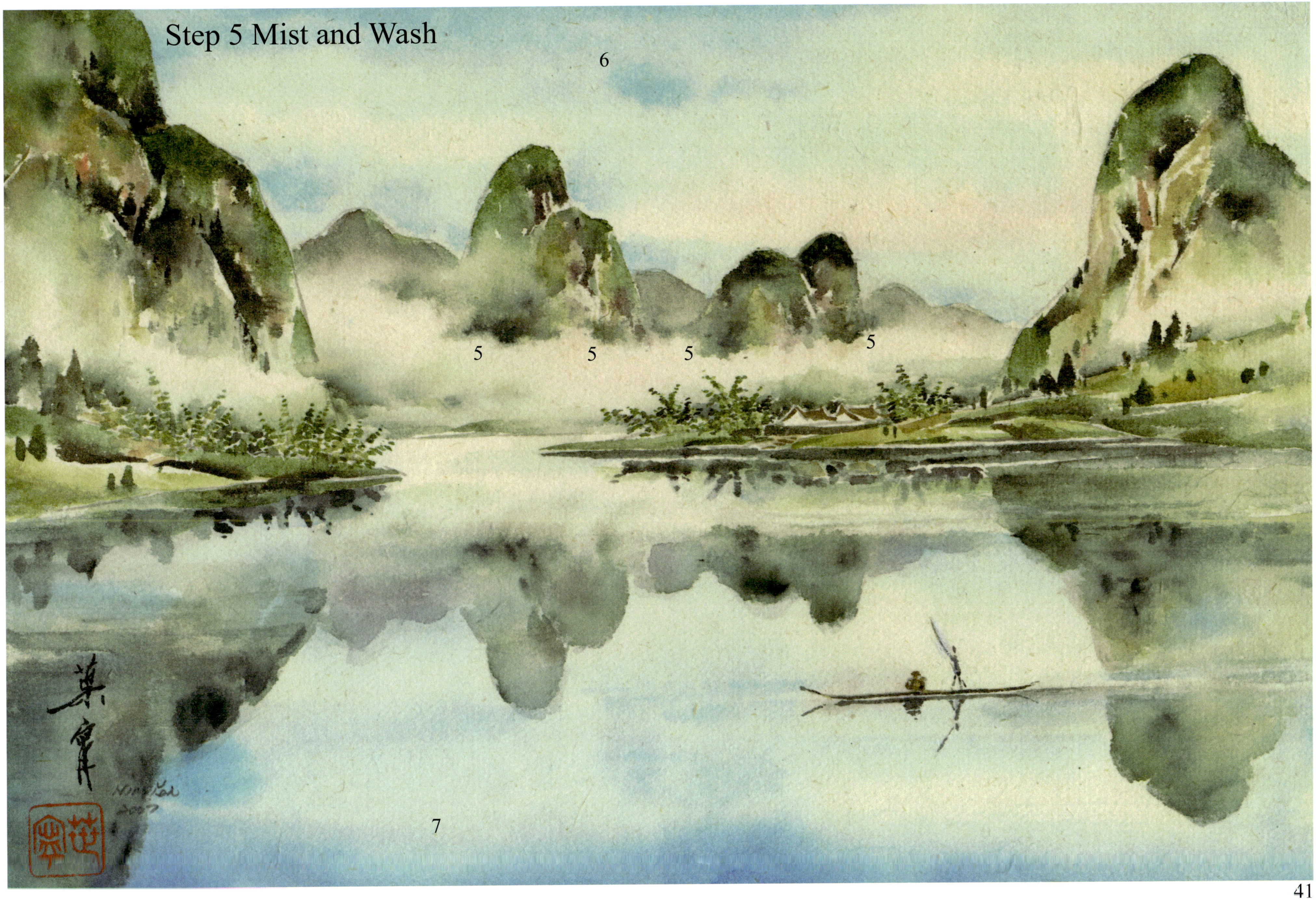

Lesson 4: Village

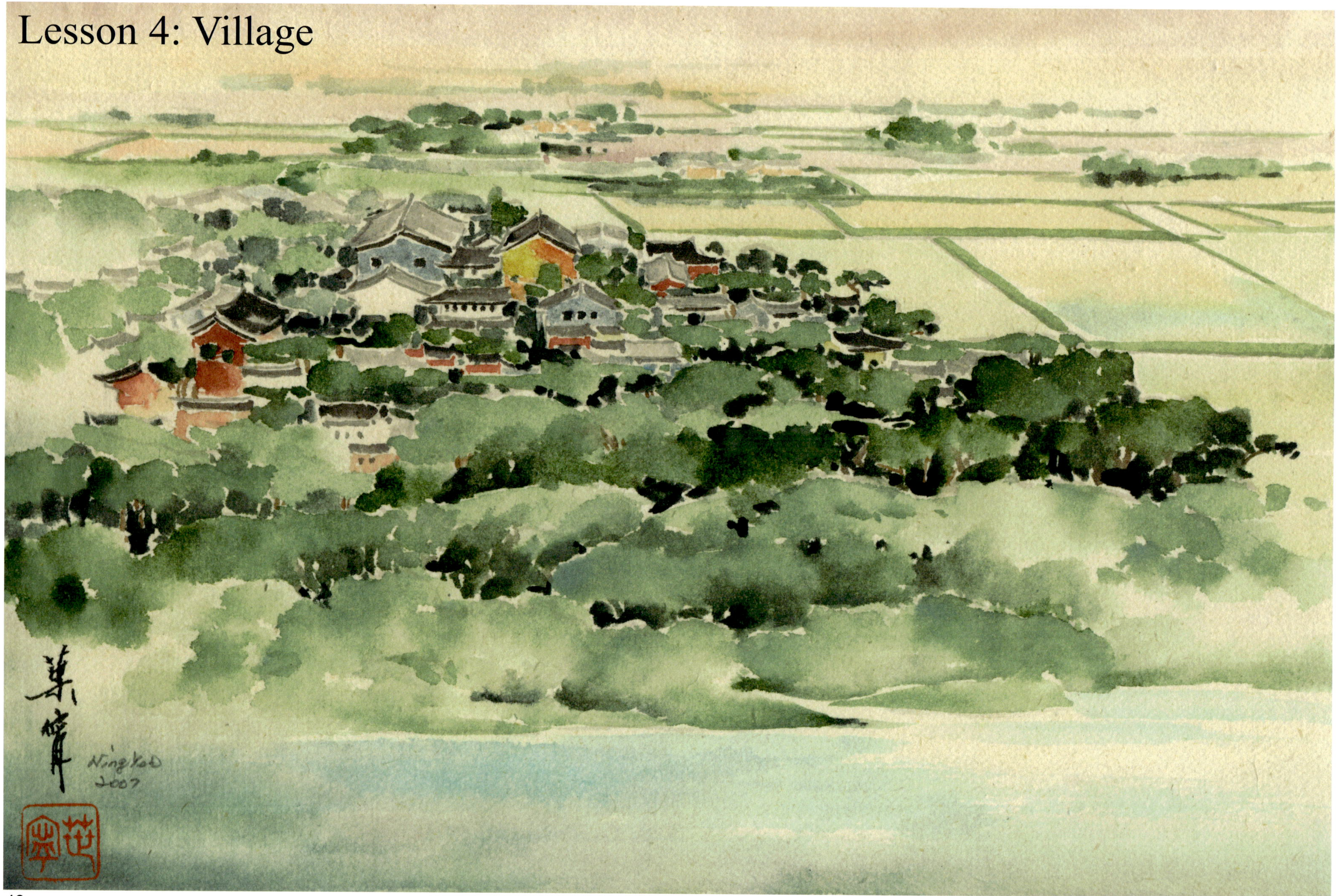

Lesson 4: Village

This painting is based on a photo I took of Yangzhou when I first visited the town on a rainy summer day in 1996.

Yangzhou is in the middle of the lower Yangtze delta, a flat, fertile land without mountains. It was everything I dreamed of—a beautiful small town that still possessed all the charm Suzhou and Hangzhou used to have: exquisite pavilions, streets shaded with lush foliage, stone covered alleyways filled with life and vitality.

I went alone to neighboring Ping Shan town, north west of Yangzhou. Located on a small hill, Ping Shan is the home of Sung scholar Ouyang Xiu, the teacher of the great poet Su Tung-po. After climbing up to the third floor of the town's pagoda, I felt like I'd seen enough. I looked up at the Buddha, he had his middle finger stuck out at me. I decided to climb to the top.

Life is like this. One climbs up to enjoy the view. Each climb adds a bit more experience, and each gives a bit more confidence. Reaching the top, the satisfaction is intensified. One climbs down with care, so as not to lose one's footing.
In the old days, a pagoda was usually the tallest structure and focal point of the town, giving people a bird's eye view of the best scenery.

I could see the Slim West Lake, the entire town of Yangzhou beyond, and the whole complex of Ping Shan Town. There were a huge flock of beautiful egrets perched on tall, old trees.

On the next hill, Guanyin Shan (Goddess of Mercy Mountain), was a beautiful group of temples. The closeness of the two hills enhanced the scenery of both. One accompanies and looks over the other. Chinese buildings incorporate their surrounding elements, thereby enhancing each other's beauty. In this painting, we learn more about perspectives.

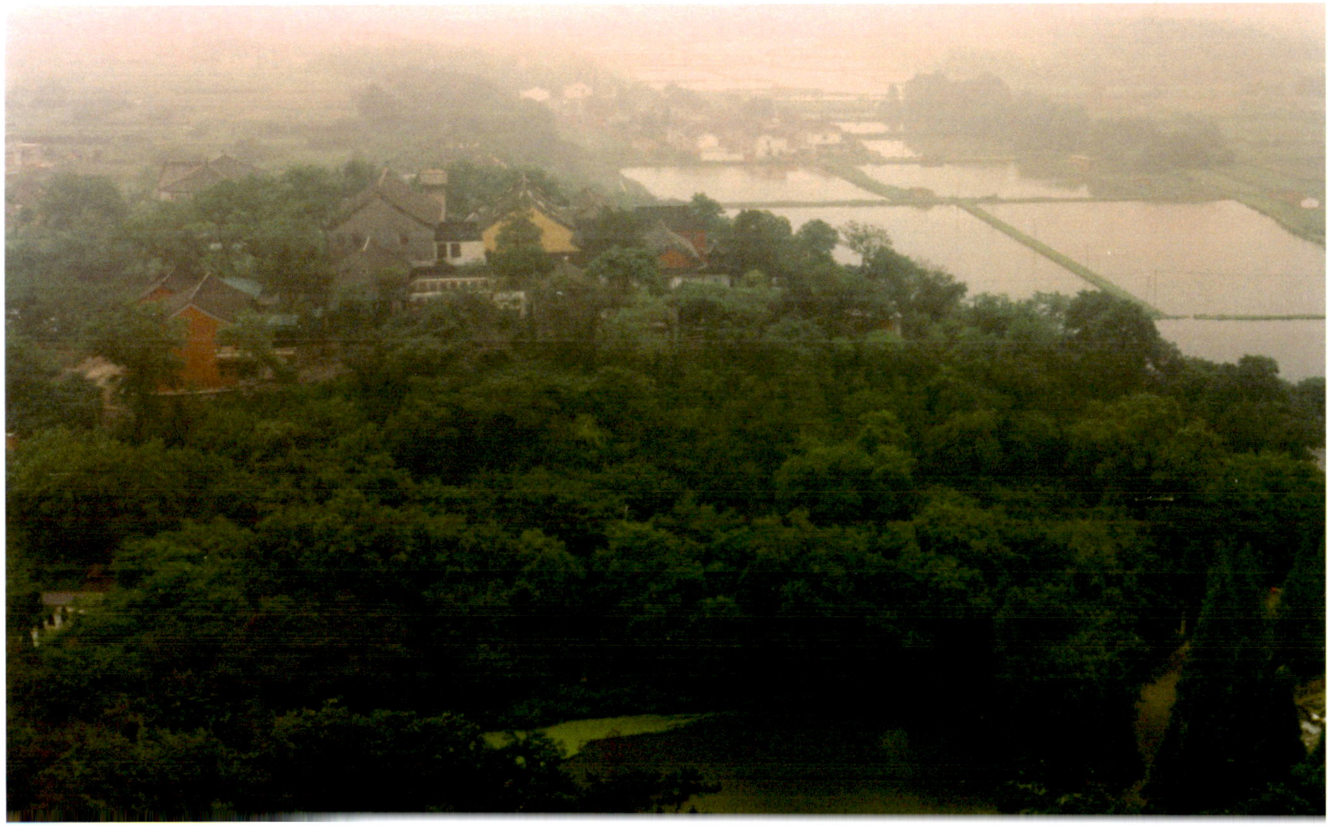

Step 1 Draft

Prepare a draft. Most of the horizontal lines are kept flat and progressively closer together as they move up. The vertical lines converge toward the middle. Draw houses (1). Show banks (2) to define the pond (3). Do groves of foliage, some lighter (4) and some darker (5), getting smaller with distance. Mark shadow areas (dark dotted lines 6). Add tree trunks (7) in the gaps between foliage. Do field lines (8), distant houses and groves with reflections.

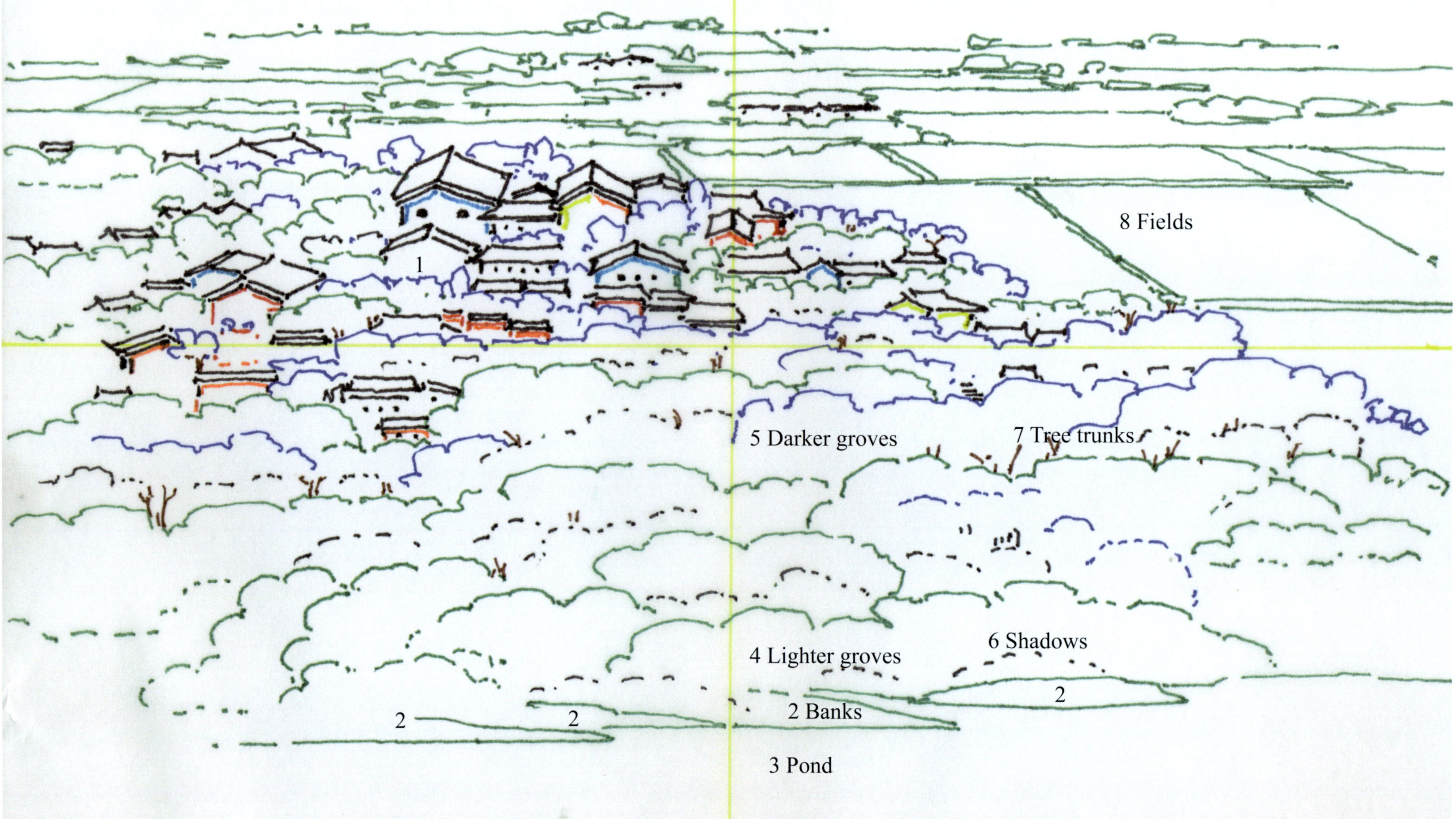

Step 2 Outlines and Foliage

Outlines: ꩜ Flow or Mt. Horse, ❖ Light Ink (dry brush), ↓ vertical brush, do lines for houses, fields, and groves. ❖ Ink, add shadows on houses.

Foliage: ꩜ Flow, ↖ tilt and press the brush moving more than halfway down the grove foliage. ❖ Light Green for lighter groves. ❖ Green (at the tip) for darker groves. ❖ Shade + Ink, ↙ tilt and press the brush upward, blending into the upper strokes to complete the lower part of the grove foliage.

Tree Trunks: ꩜ Flow, ❖ Brown or Ink, ↑ vertical brush moving downward, add tree trunks in the gaps between groves.

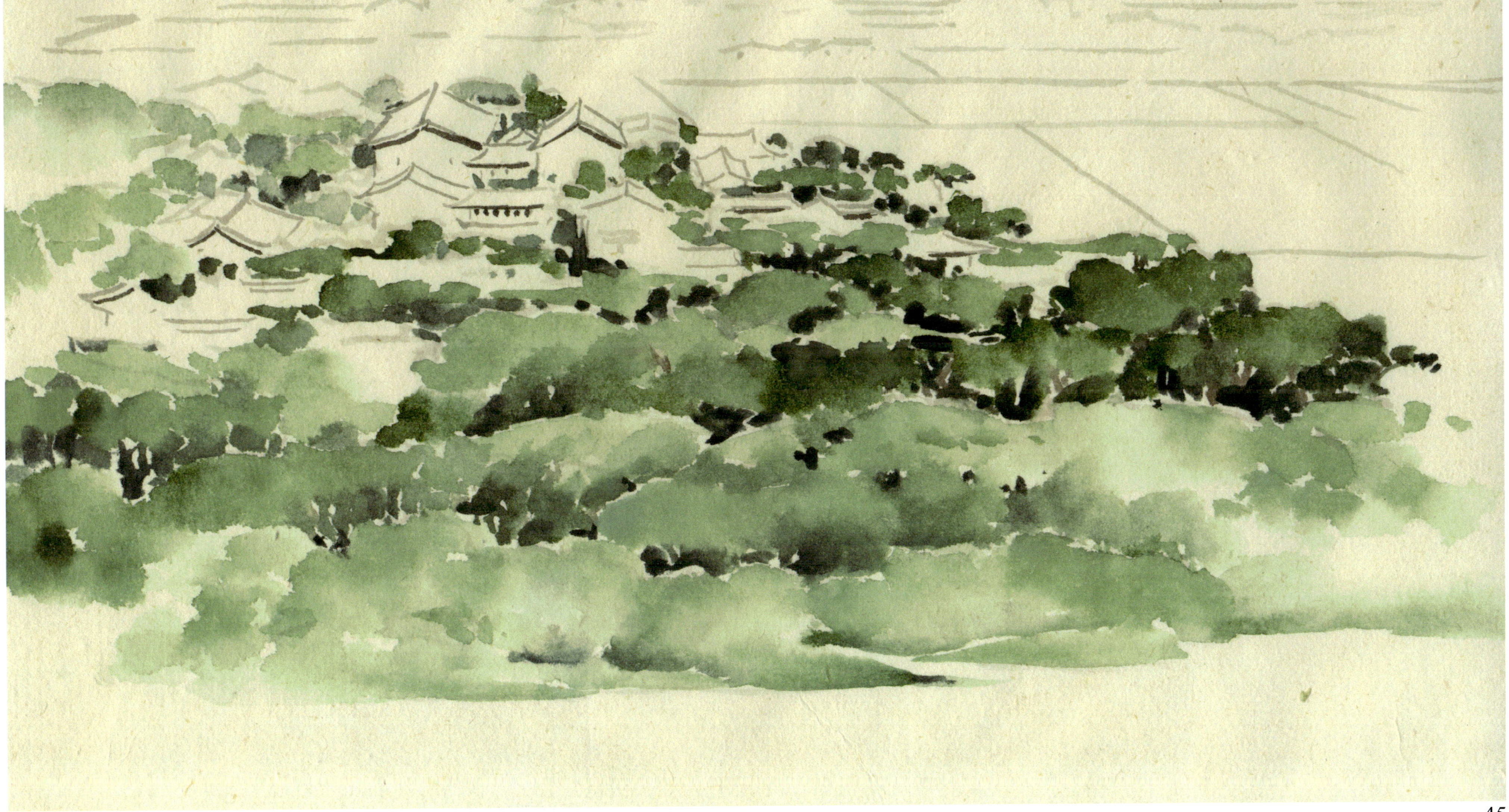

Step 3 Houses

ℓ Flow. Occasionally leave hairline spaces between the shapes.

Roofs

Mix Ink and White to make a Dark Gray and a Light Gray. Do roofs with different tones of gray.

❖ Light Gray (1)

❖ Light Gray + Dark Gray (2)

❖ Ink (3).

Walls

❖ Red walls: Red + Dark Red (4).

❖ Peach walls: make Peach by mixing Vermillion with White. Peach + Vermillion (5).

❖ Blue walls: mix Light Gray with Manganese Blue (6).

❖ Yellow Walls: mix White with Yellow (7).

Yellow Vermillion wall: we need not premix colors all the time. Sometimes, it is more exciting to load colors from light to dark and watch the spontaneous blending on the rice paper.

❖ Yellow, ↖ tilt and press the brush from one side. ❖ Vermillion, ↖ tilt and press the brush from the other side (8).

White Walls: leave them unpainted (9).

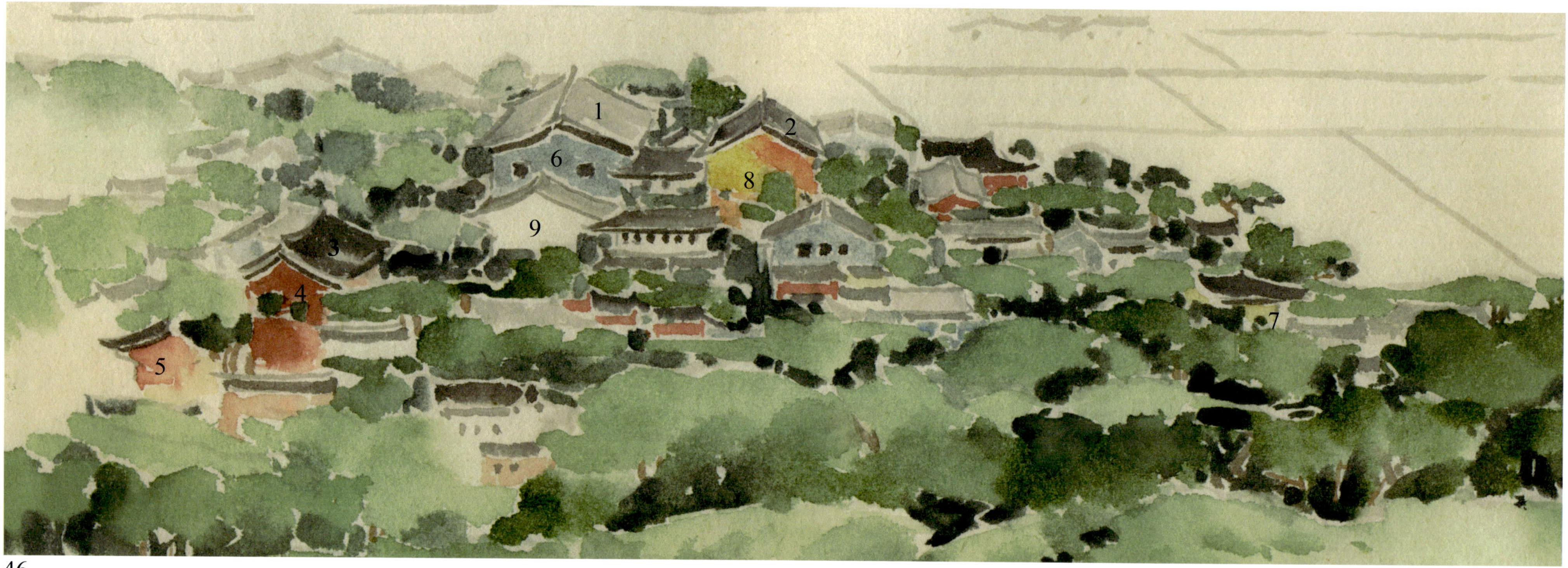

Step 4 Distant Scenery

Roofs: ẟ Flow, ❖ Light Gray. **Walls:** mix diluted Yellow and Vermillion. **Groves and Reflections:** ❖ Light Green, Green and Shade. Do them lighter as they move up. **Field Lines:** ❖ Light Green (above the Ink lines) Do them thinner and lighter as they move up.

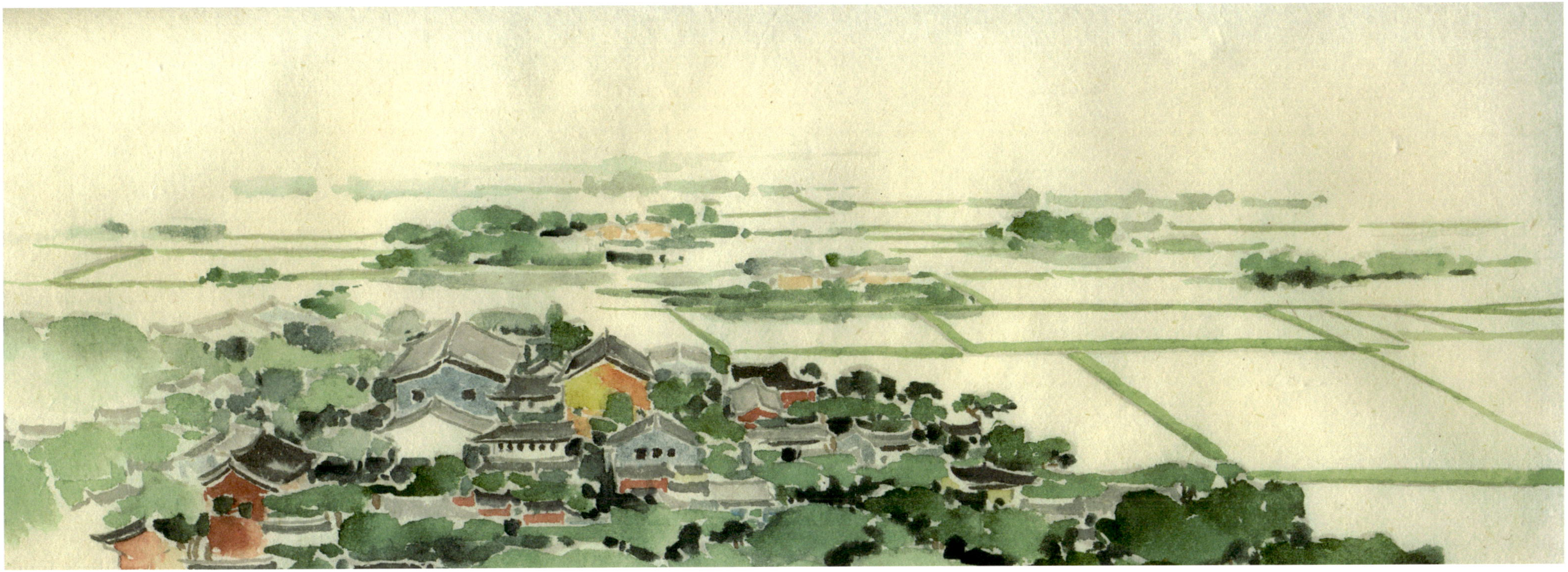

Step 5 (see diagram on p.48)

Pond and Fields: ẟ Flow, ❖ Diluted Manganese Blue. Work horizontal strokes to color the pond and some areas of the fields. Fade naturally to the right (1, 2, 3). ❖ Diluted White Yellow (4, 5, 6, 7, 8, 9). ❖ Diluted Light Purple (10, 11, 12, 13). Fade outwards.

Wash: Let the painting dry then rewet the whole painting. ẟ Wash Brush, ❖ Shade, load on one corner of the brush (about 1" into the width) then blend. Hold the brush vertically, colored corner down. Apply Shade across the lower edge of the painting, fading to the right (14). ❖ Light Purple, colored corner up. Apply across top of the sky (15). Overlap the strokes to have smooth coverage of the area.

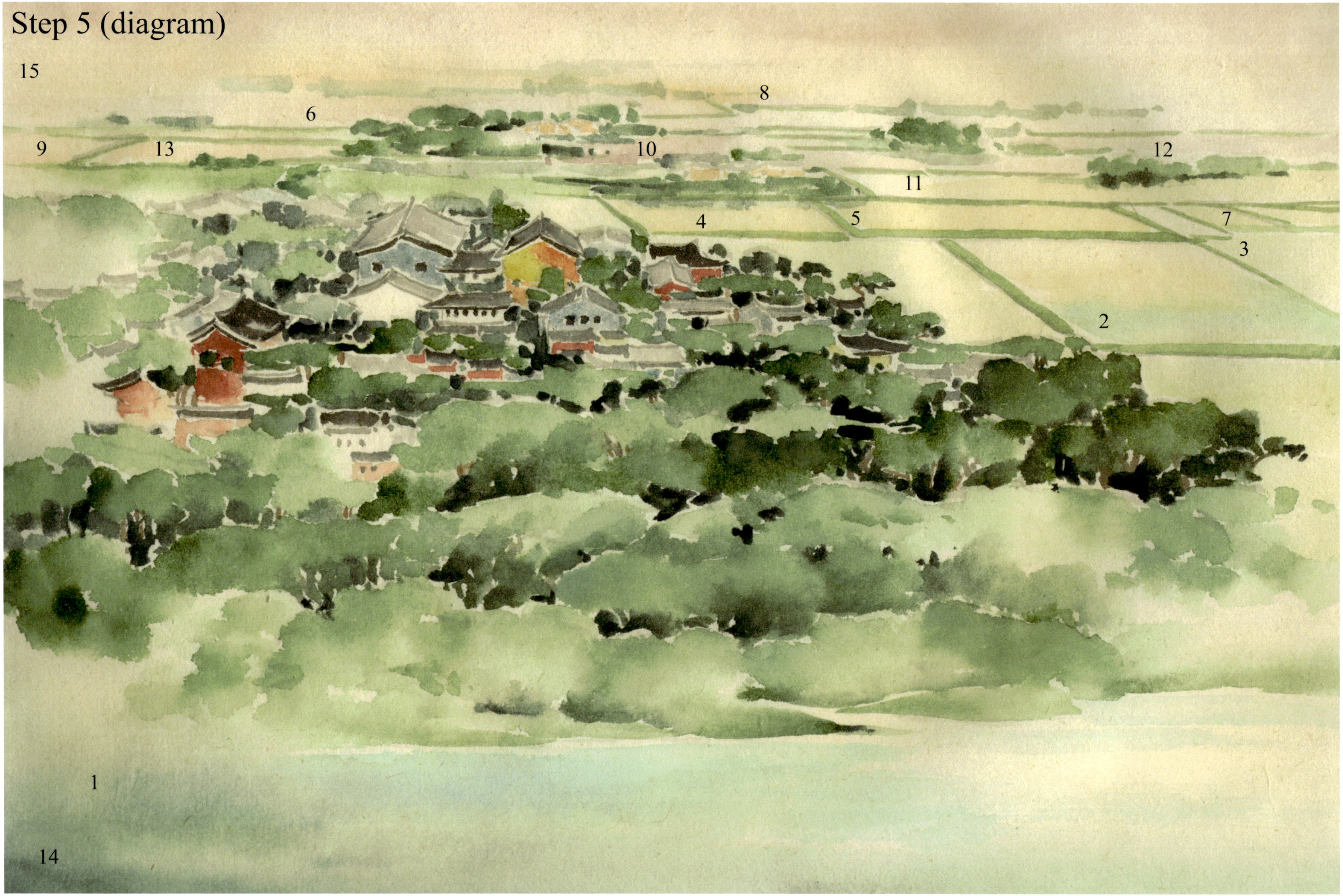
Step 5 (diagram)
15
8
6
9
13
10
12
11
4
5
7
3
2
1
14

Lesson 5: Snow Scene

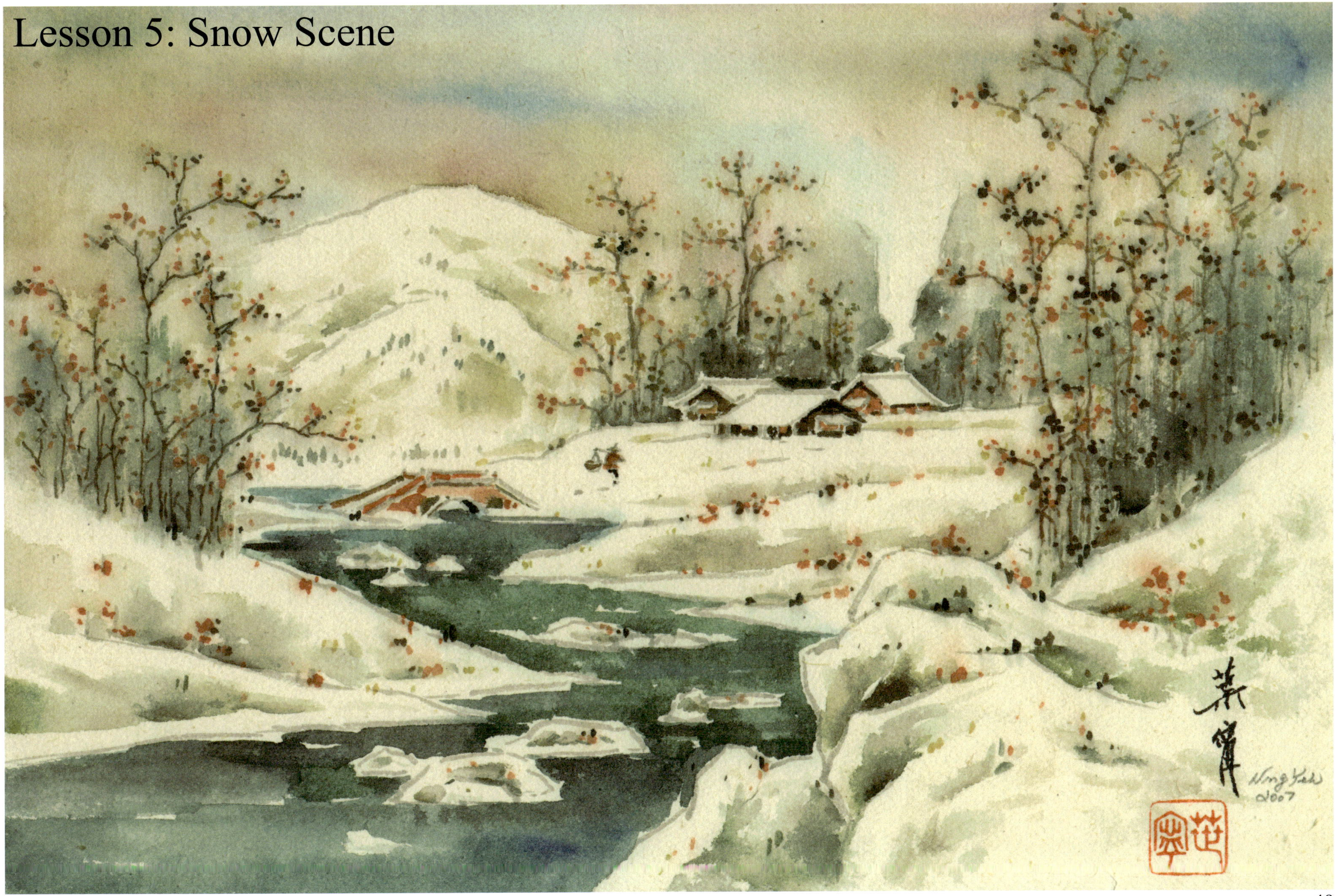

Lesson 5: Snow Scene

I came to the U.S. in 1969 for post graduate studies. It took me a long time to get my Ph.D. In 1978, I returned to Taiwan with my family, accompanied by 40 American artists. The Pacific Cultural Foundation sponsored our exhibition. My homecoming was an extraordinary event. That year, I also published my first painting album. This composition is featured in the album.

Many men in farm villages throughout China go to faraway cities to find work. They come home at yearend bearing gifts. It is gratifying to see the warm light and smoke from the kitchen chimney awaiting the man wading through the snow.

Step 1 Line Work (see diagram)

ℓ Flow or Mountain Horse, ❖ Medium Ink
Before doing the line work, prepare a draft on a separate sheet. Put the draft underneath the painting paper as a guide for the line work.

1. Foreground Rock
Do thin lines with occasional breaks for the top of the rock. Since snow is not painted, suggest it with soft turns and tapered lines. Add bushes.

2. Lower Right Bank
Work a small rock with shoulders.

3. Right Slope
Do the slope to the right of the foreground rock.

4. Right Forest
Do short, tall, and side trees from the top down. Branches need not join (to suggest snow). Add low bushes and the slope behind the forest.

5. Lower Left Banks
Starting from the tip, move the baseline gradually downward. Slope the top line upward, with occasional breaks (5a). Add bushes. Work a second bank higher (5b).

6. Left Forest
Do trees. Show a "Welcome Guest" tree reaching to the bridge (a).

7. Upper Right Bank
From the tip, keep the baseline flat and slope the top line upward. Add bushes. Finish with b and c.

8. Bridge
Show a bank on the left (d). Work a balanced arch (e). Add three lines to build the bridge (f). Run parallel lines above to show the railing. Add the other side (g, h). Define the river edge (i, j).

9. Man (smaller that bridge)
Do the hat. Show a wider body and short arms for heavy clothing. Do short legs to show him in the snow. Run a pole through his hand with a basket. Show his tracks with horizontal dots.

10. Houses (keep all horizontal lines flat)
Do the center house (k). Start with the A-frame and work the roof. Do walls with short vertical lines. Add a door and windows. Extend the baseline on both sides. Add flat dots for a path. Do house (l). Add a chimney. Show smoke lines coming out sideways then rising and dissipating (m). Extend the baseline (n). Do house (o). Extend the baseline to the bridge (p).

11. Back Forest
Embrace the houses with a forest. Leave the smoke area alone.

12. Mountain
Add a mountain with a soft slope. Show the nose.

13. Rocks in the River
Cluster flat bottomed rocks in the river.

Step 1 Line Work (diagram)

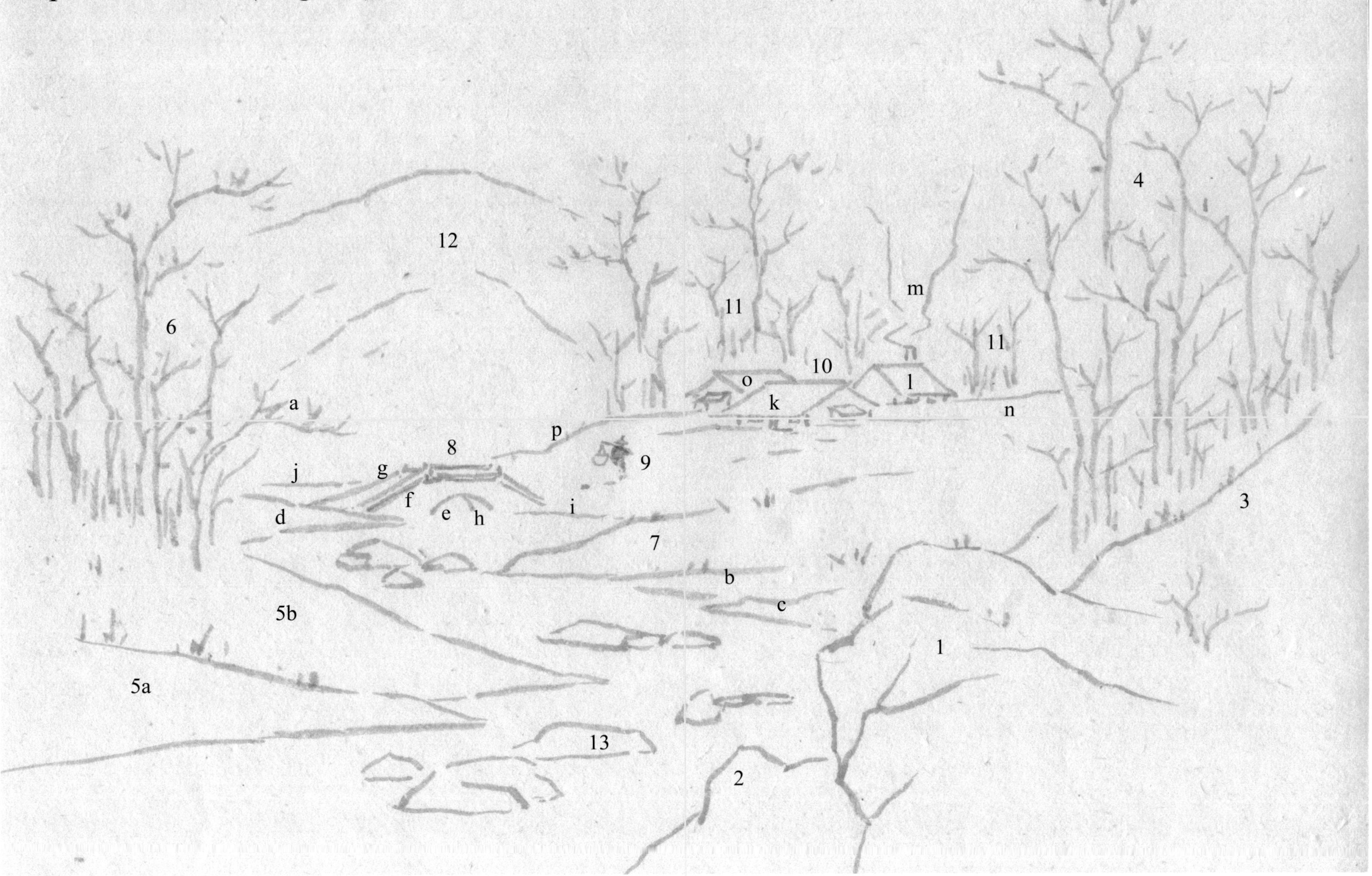

Step 2 Coloring

ᔑ Flow

Do not allow the brush body to get too wet. Show texture (dry spots). Use the idea of host and guest. Change stroke patterns and direction. Alternate wet and dry; dark and light; warm and cool colors. Shadows are applied to show space and snow. Pay attention to the shapes of space. Shadows are not solid objects. They should fade and integrate with space.

Houses: ❖ Vermillion for door, windows, and chimney. ❖ Ink for shadows under A-frame. ❖ Brown + Ink for walls of two houses. ❖ Vermillion + Brown for the house on the right.

Bridge: ❖ Vermillion for center. ❖ Vermillion, Brown, and Ink for selected areas. Leave white spaces to show snow.

Man: ❖ Brown for body and basket.

Rock Shadows: ❖ Mix Shade with Brown and dilute into a Light Shade. Load Light Shade + Shade, ↙ tilt position and press from the crevice upwards. ❖ Mix Ochre with Beige and dilute into a light wash. Load Ochre Beige wash. Brush into the shaded area and extend further. Keep areas open on top of the rocks and along the river to show snow. Accent the base of the shadow occasionally with Ink.

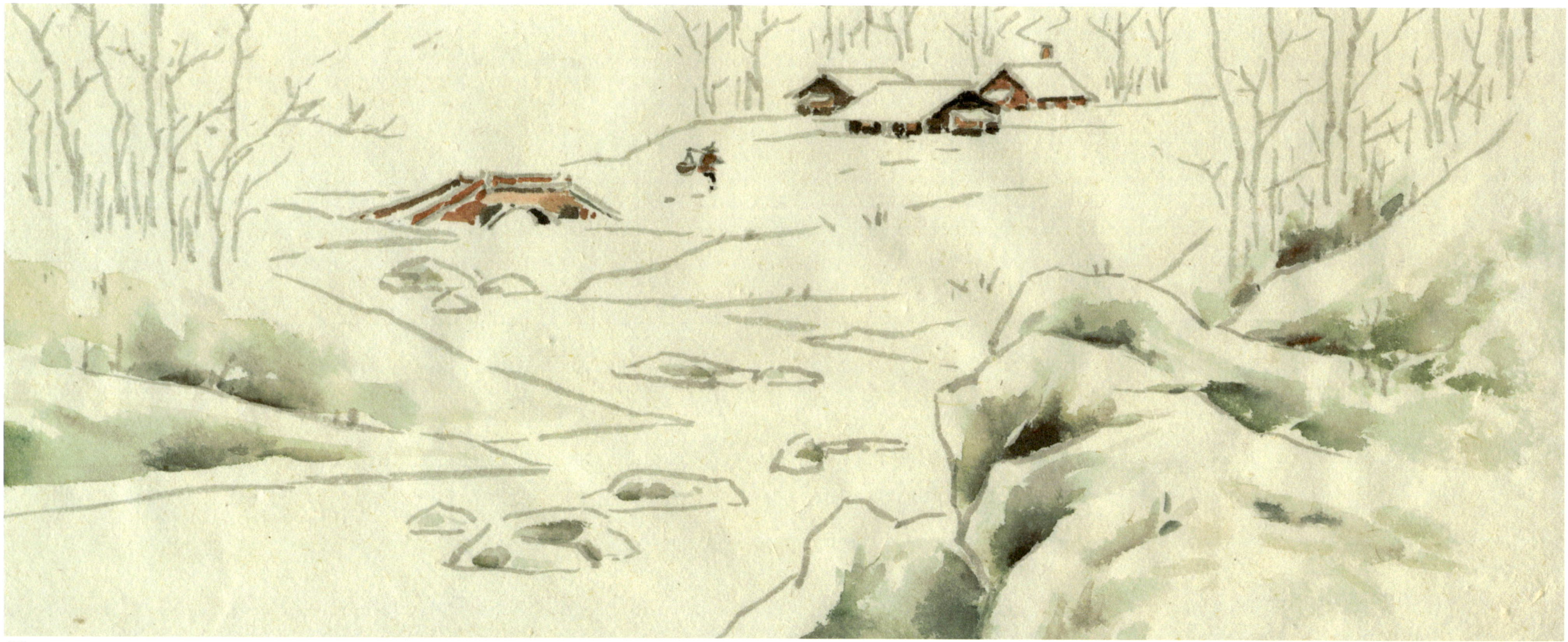

Step 3 More Coloring

Tree Shadows: Wet and dry the brush. Apply the leftover moisture on lower sections of the forest. ❖ Light Shade, dip the tip in water to soften the colors. Tilt brush sideways, apply vertical strokes in middle sections of the forest. ❖ Add Shade in lower area. ❖ Diluted Ochre Beige mixture, add spotty warm colors at top area of the forest. ❖ Light Shade then accent with Dark Shade above the roofs and along both sides of the smoke. Leave a little space above the roofs and along the smoke line to avoid bleeding.

Banks and Mountains: ❖ Light Shade, add along crevices. ❖ Add diluted Ochre Beige. Fade colors at the foot of the mountain. Leave space along the river.

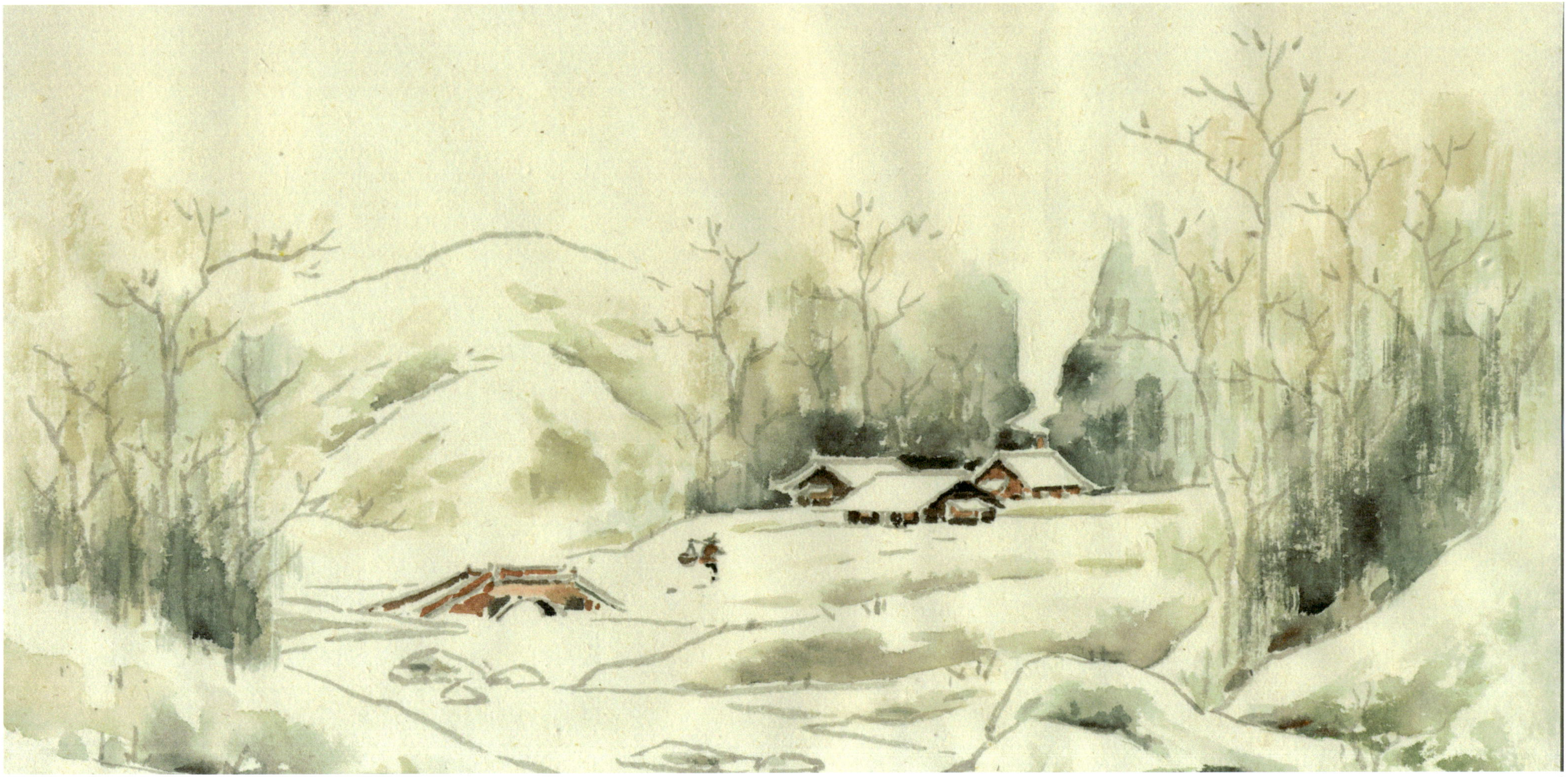

Step 4 Sky and Water

Flow or Large Flow. Load diluted colors about 1/2" on the tip. Apply colors with horizontal strokes. Overlap the colors.

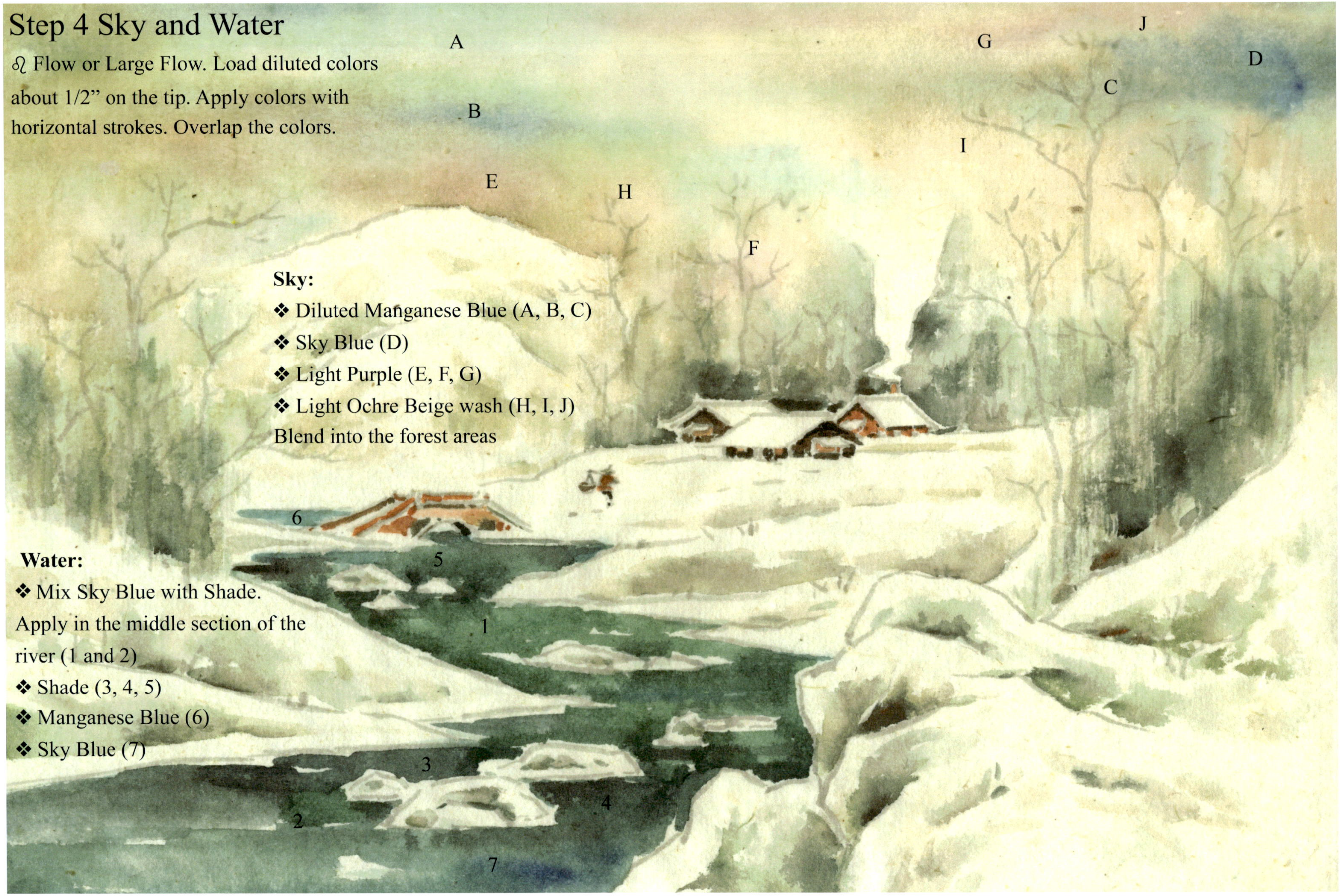

Sky:

- ❖ Diluted Manganese Blue (A, B, C)
- ❖ Sky Blue (D)
- ❖ Light Purple (E, F, G)
- ❖ Light Ochre Beige wash (H, I, J)

Blend into the forest areas

Water:

- ❖ Mix Sky Blue with Shade. Apply in the middle section of the river (1 and 2)
- ❖ Shade (3, 4, 5)
- ❖ Manganese Blue (6)
- ❖ Sky Blue (7)

Step 5 Happy Dots

♌ Flow, ❖ Ochre, Vermillion, Brown, and Shade, apply dots on the ground and branches. Do the closer (lower) dots brighter and larger. ❖ Light Shade, add vertical dots on the mountains to show evergreens.

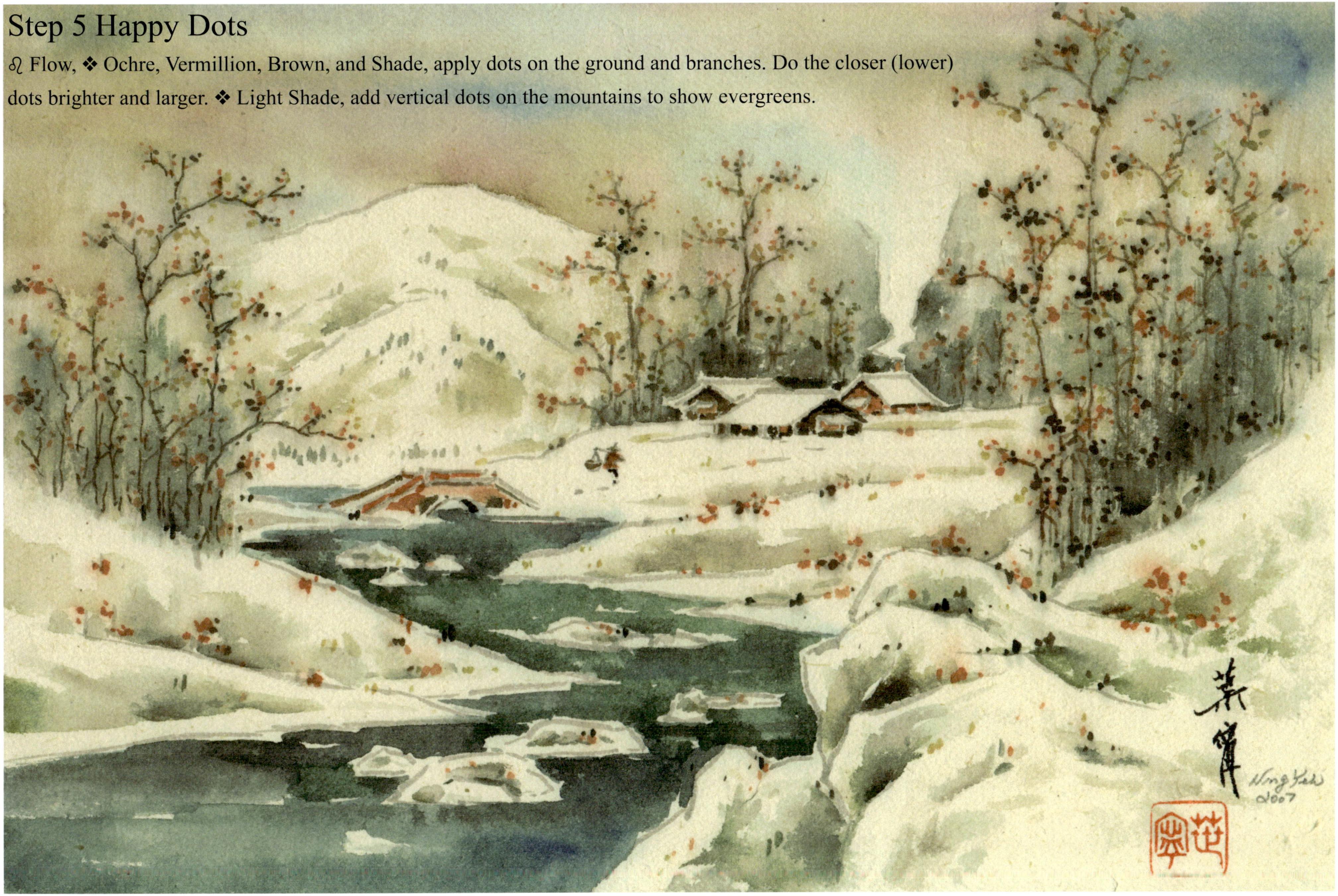

Lesson 6: Waterfalls

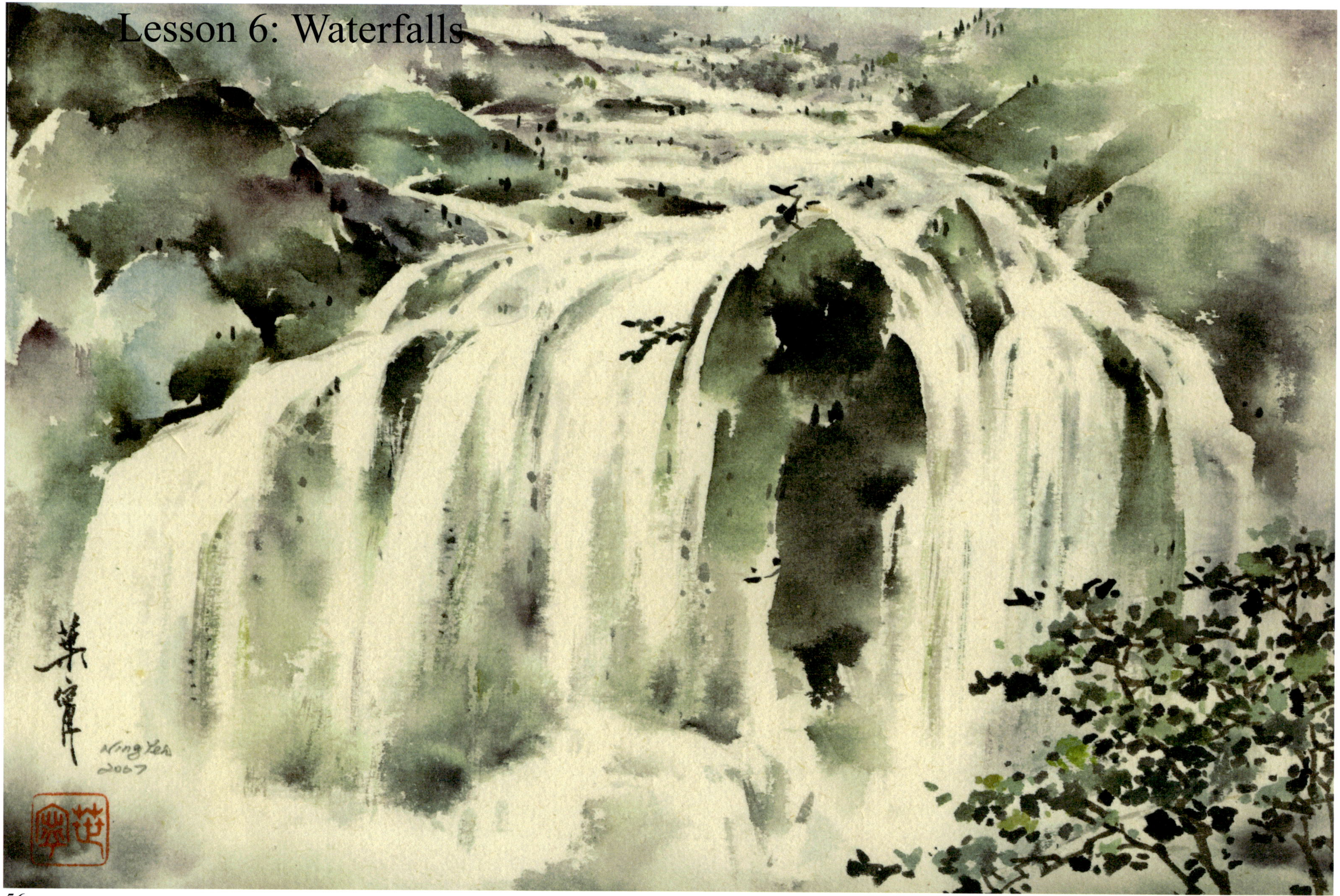

Lesson 6: Waterfalls

Waterfalls are the most exciting playground for mountains and water. It is the ideal subject for exercising an artist's power of suggestion, spontaneity, and imagination.

In the early 80s, a gallery in Beverly Hills used a waterfall painting on the invitation for my show. An Arab royal sent his staff to purchase the painting. The excited gallery owner called me. "Ning, his majesty wants the painting, but he insists the painting is an exotic dancer. Is it OK?" Of course, waterfall is nature's exotic dancer. The painting was sold.

I have visited magnificent waterfalls in China including Guizhou's Huangguoshu, Sichuan's Jiuzhaigou Pearl, and Lu Mountain's Three Layers. Today's lesson, however, is imaginary.

Step 1 Draft (see p.57)

We begin by preparing a draft on a separate sheet of paper and placing it underneath the painting paper. The composition consists of two waterfall groupings divided by the rock group in the center. The falls cascade with multiple layers. It is important to picture the invisible definition of the layers (shown in dotted yellow lines).

The water is not painted—it is left as the space between landforms. Its flow is suggested by the rocks next to it. The suggestion is more vivid if the space is not too wide. We use dividers (small rocks inside the waterfalls) and shadows to streamline the falls.

Water squeezes through the rocks. The initial phase is left blank to show white water jet streaming. As the water falls, it thins out into a transparent screen. Shadows begin to occur. When water hits the base, mist takes place.

Waterfalls originate from a river at the top. Therefore, there is a change in plane from the horizontal river to the vertical falls. Within the falls, such change may also take place. It is like water stepping downstairs in layers. Shadows may help to show the layers. Like running a hose, water comes out sideways, then downward. There is a curve that shows this transition.
Do rocks on both sides to shape the space for the water. Draft the layer lines like stairs—they need not be flat. Water cascades down. Do not turn the flow direction upward. Place rocks in the middle with their roots pointing to the layer lines. Sometimes, rocks may hide portions of the waterfall.

Add a zig-zagging river above the falls. Indicate the mist line below on your draft. Use this as a guide for working the mist but do not paint this line on your final painting. We have a magnificent waterfall.

Step 2 Rock Texture (See p.58)

❖ Mt. Horse or Flow, ❖ Light or Medium Ink, split brush tip open, very dry. After loading, wipe off the moisture. Work the center rocks from top down (1, 2). Their sides show the flow of water. Do the right side of the falls (3, 4), the left side (5-10), and the top (11, 12). Add rocks and shadows to divide the falls (a, b, c on the right; d-h on the left). Do some lower ones to show layers (i-m). Pay attention to the space. Make each space show the flow of water. Most of them show a slight curve on top. Fade each rock at the tip as well as the base. Show less solid borders. Less is better.

Step 1 Draft

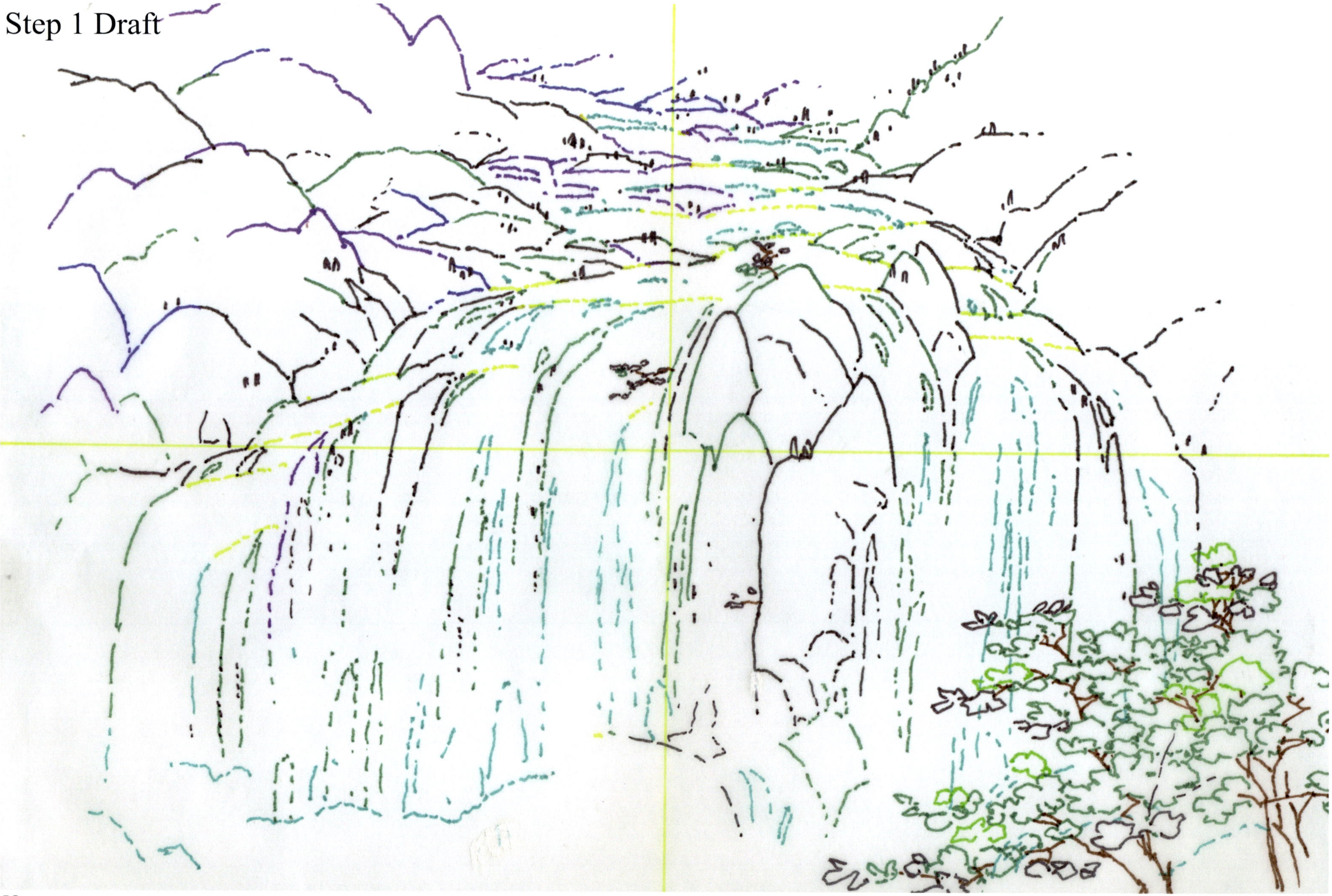

Step 2 Rock Texture (diagram)

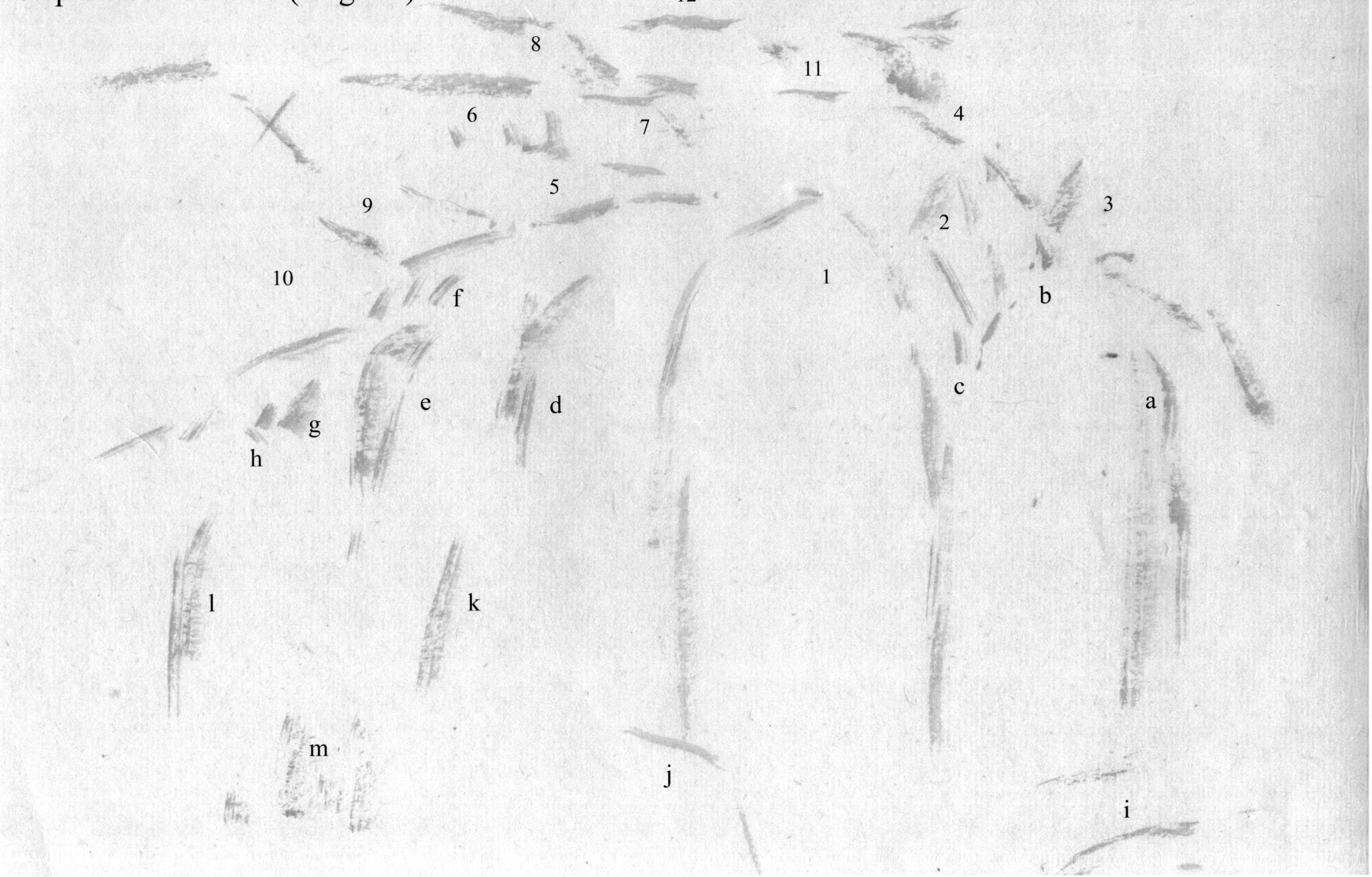

Step 3 Coloring (see diagram)

Closer elements are darker with more green and warm colors. Distant scenery is lighter and has more blue and purple.

Arrange each color group in host and guest clusters. Integrate them freely. No color should stand out.

ᘊ Flow, ❖ Prepare Light Green, Dark Green, Shade, Ink, Light Purple, Purple (add a touch of Shade), diluted Manganese (add a touch of Shade).

Center Rocks

↖ Tilt and press strokes downward, end with fading.

Rocks (1-5): ❖ Dark Green + Shade + Ink

Rocks (6-9): ❖ Light Green + Dark Green, accent some base areas with Ink.

Dividers (a-k): ❖ Light Green + Dark Green.

❖ Ink and Medium Ink, accent some areas. Hide the tip inside the shape, move some strokes up and move some down, so the colors can fade on both ends of the shape. There are a lot more (as shown) than indicated with letters. Use these divider rocks to shape the space and define the flow of water.

Right Side

Use more green for areas that are closer to us. Work the rocks from the water's edge, fading as the stroke moves outward.

Rocks A-E: ❖ Light Green + Dark Green + Shade + Ink.

Left Side and Top

Distant scenery uses more blue and purple.

Rocks F-J: ❖ Light Green + Dark Green + Shade + Ink, do I and J from top down.

Rock K: ❖ Manganese

Rocks L and M: ❖ Manganese with Green (Sky Blue with Green is pretty too).

Rocks N - Q: ❖ Light Purple + Purple.

Rocks R and S: ❖ Manganese

❖ Shade and Ink, add shadows and unify the colors.

Keep a spare brush. Wet and dry it. If necessary, use it to brush hard edges to let them fade. Softening hard edges along the waterfall to add a feel of water.

Step 3 Coloring (Diagram)

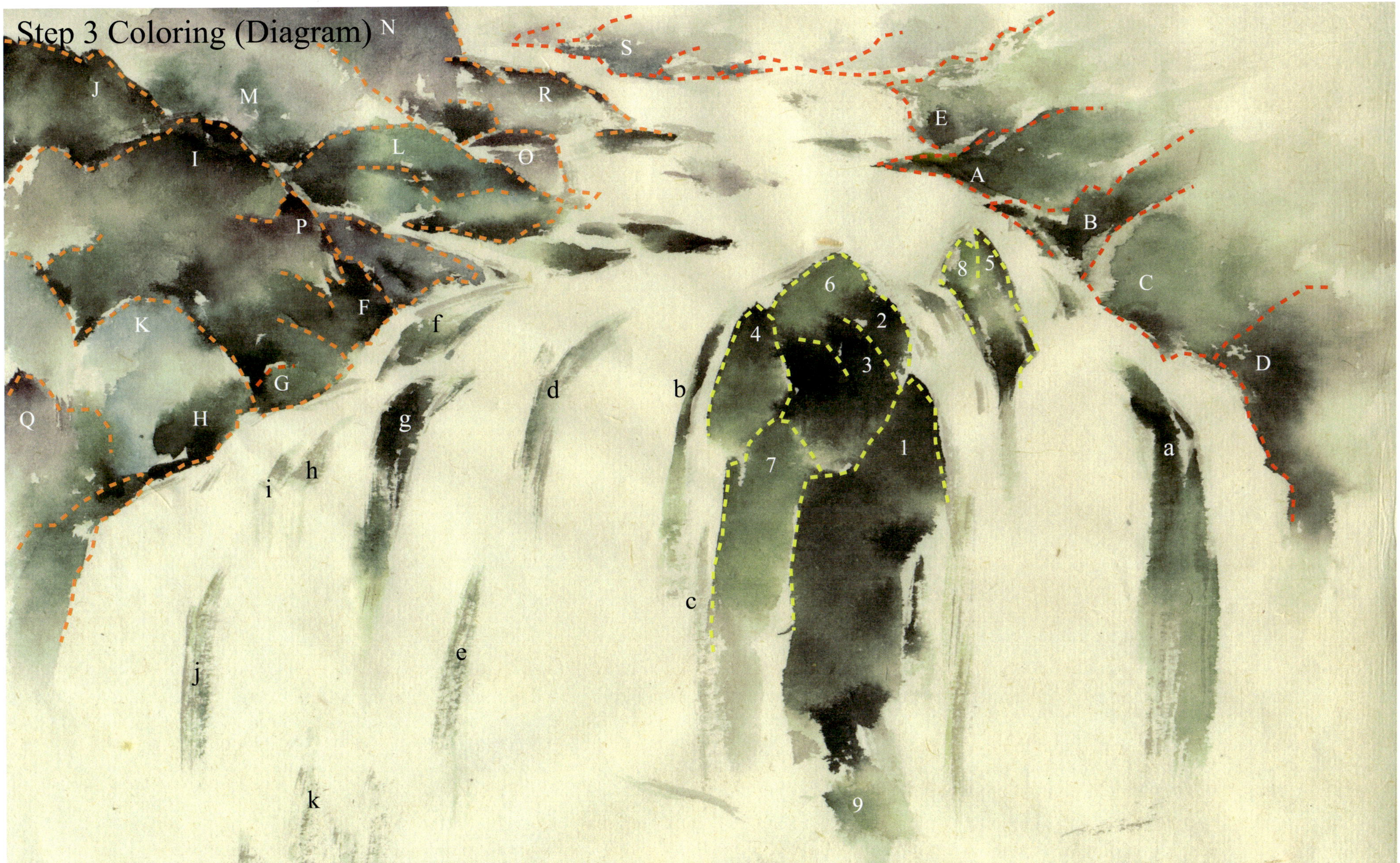

The dashed lines indicate the general shape of the rock formations. These lines are only intended as a reference. The draft you prepared underneath your painting already has these lines to guide you. Do not paint the dashed lines on your painting.

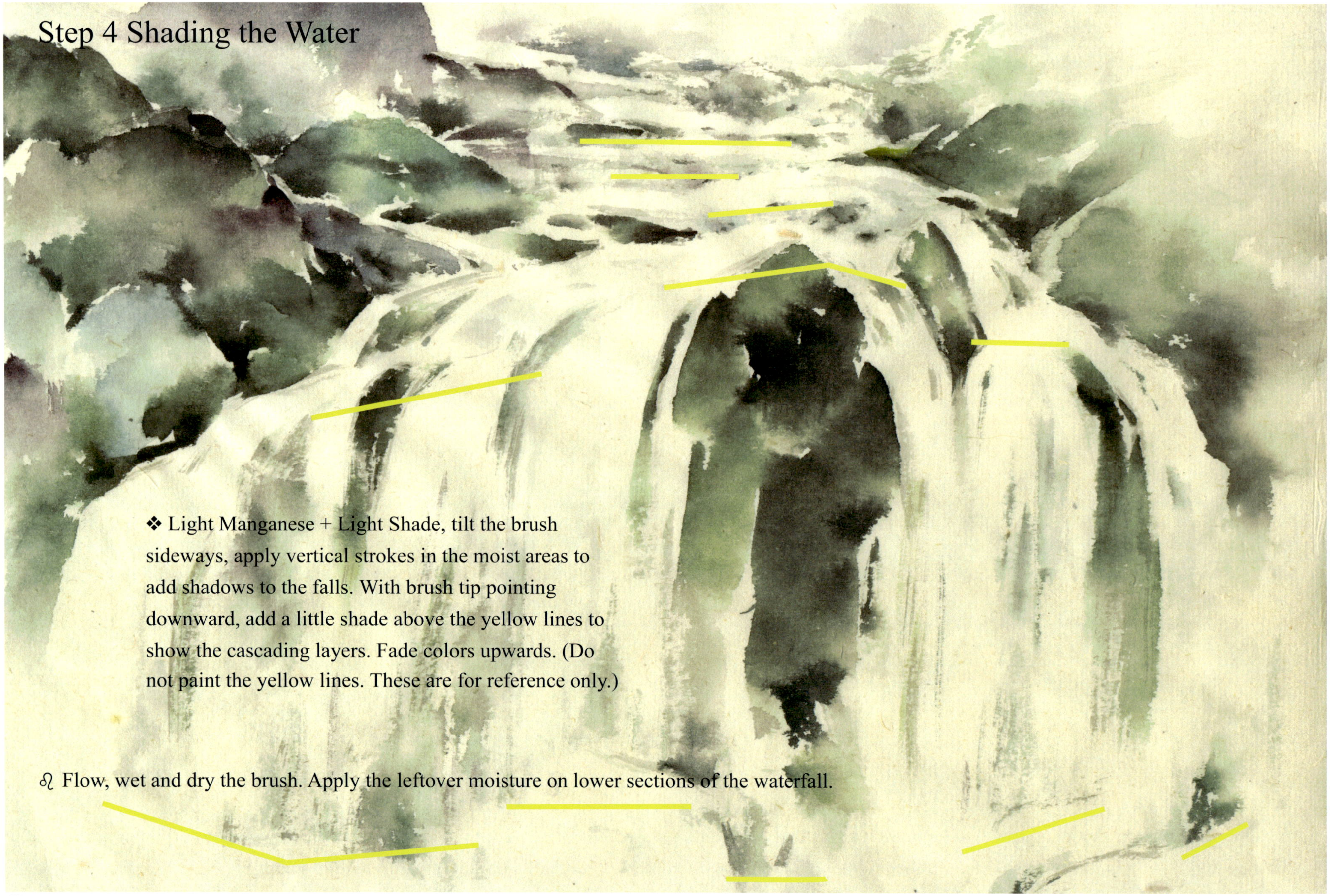

Step 4 Shading the Water

❖ Light Manganese + Light Shade, tilt the brush sideways, apply vertical strokes in the moist areas to add shadows to the falls. With brush tip pointing downward, add a little shade above the yellow lines to show the cascading layers. Fade colors upwards. (Do not paint the yellow lines. These are for reference only.)

Flow, wet and dry the brush. Apply the leftover moisture on lower sections of the waterfall.

Step 5 Mist, Dots, and Trees (notes and diagram)

Mist

Let the painting dry. Rewet the whole painting. ℓ Flow, ❖ Shade, ↓ Tilt the brush with tip pointing downwards. Intensify the shadows to define and highlight the mist below (1). Do this in other shaded areas too, to bring the brightness of water (space) out. We can also apply Shade to open spots on both sides and the top area. This way, the waterfall stands out.

ℓ Wash Brush, ❖ Shade, load on one corner of the brush, about 1" into the width. Blend. Hold the brush vertically, colored corner down. Apply Shade to the lower corners of the painting, Fade upwards (2, 3). We do this to add volume and depth to the lower mist. ❖ Purple, colored corner up, apply to the top right corner (4).

Dots and Trees

ℓ Flow, ❖ Shade + Ink, add small clusters of vertical dots to show distant trees (5). Add series of dots along lower areas of selected rocks (6). Do a few small trees (7, 8, 9).

Work foreground trees: ❖ Light Green (a), ❖ Dark Green and Shade (b), ❖ Ink (c).

❖ Brown, add branches.

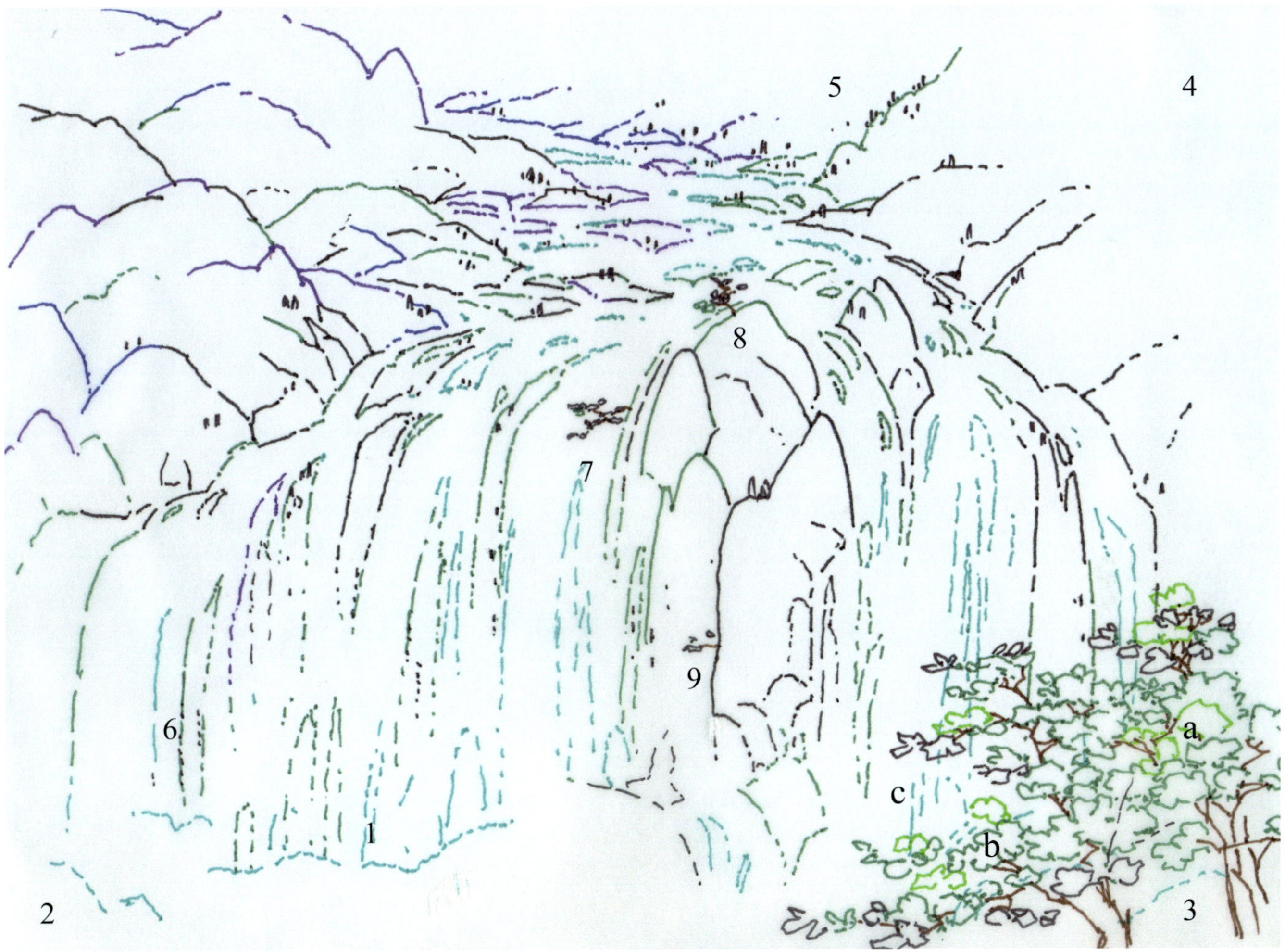

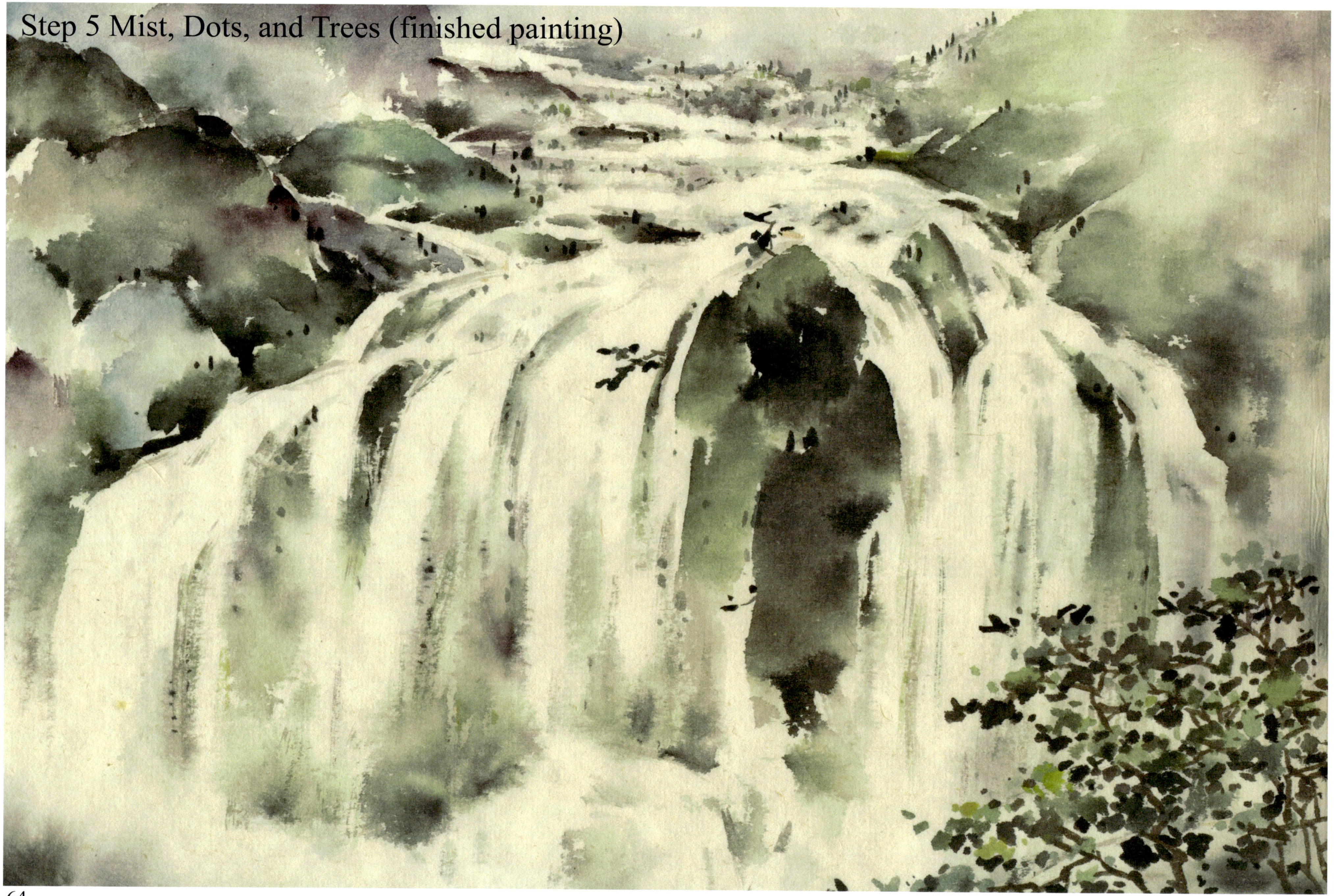

Step 5 Mist, Dots, and Trees (finished painting)

Lesson 7: West Lake Spring

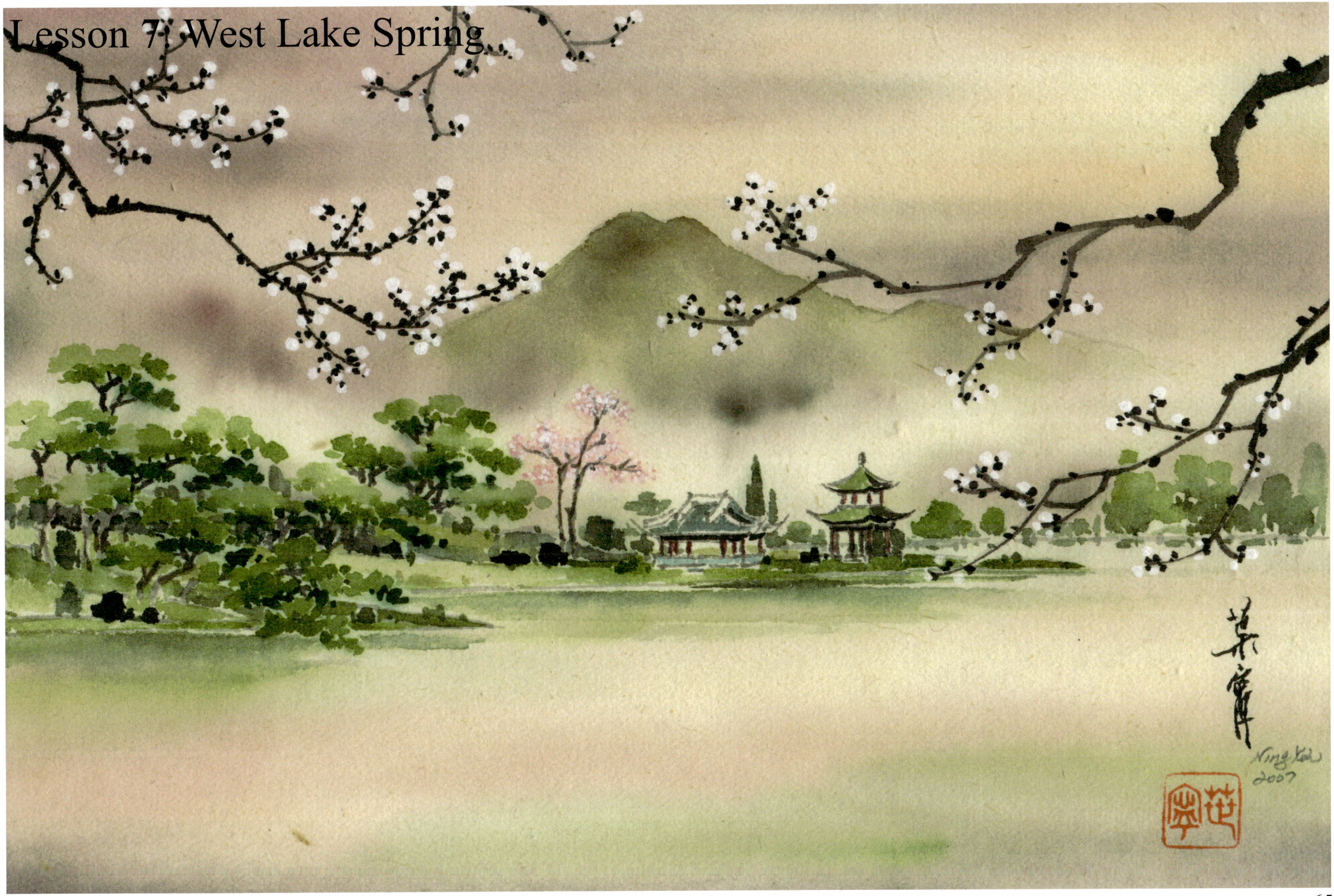

Lesson 7: West Lake Spring

I came from the lower Yangtze. It is where mountains, water, and people come to a perfect union. It is what I sense my China ought to be. This is the China where my heroes traveled and acquired inspiration for their great works. It is poetry in motion everywhere. This is my China.

Hangzhou, the capital city of my native province, was the first city I visited in 1986 since I departed China as a child. West Lake, the city's crowning feature, is the crystallization of classic Chinese beauty. It is elegantly noble, spectacularly grand, yet warmly inviting.

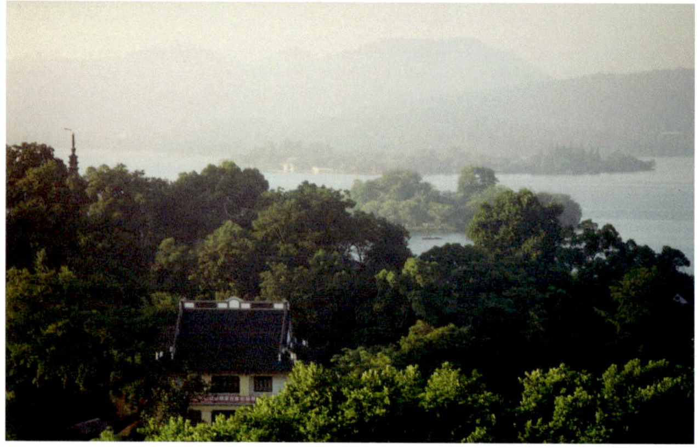

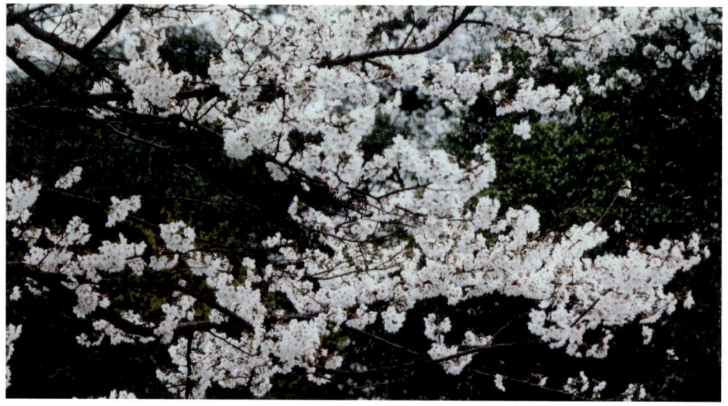

No other place in China is as romantic as West Lake. She is charming on all occasions and in all seasons. There is a princely spirit in the air. Every plant and every creature feels and shows its best. They are proud to be here. One does not want to be anywhere else but here. One feels at home. I know I do. Wherever I am, I tell myself that I came from here.

West Lake is the union of a precious gift from nature and the tasteful wisdom of brilliant men. Mother nature embraced this serene body of water with rolling emerald hills. Then came the vision of great poets like Su Tung-po and Bai Juyi. They built "a lake within a lake and an isle within an isle." They chose the perfect spot to have a pavilion to enjoy the moon. They followed the lotus pond with a winding path. They invited orioles to sing in the willows, they rang the distant temple bells in the evening. They built bridges that allow snow to only cover half of its body, and a most graceful pagoda to point the way to paradise.

Xiao (Small) Ying Zhou is the larger island with its own lake and island in the middle. The island inside Small Ying Zhou has pavilions surrounded with foliage and blossoms and can be reached by a zigzag bridge with 30 turns. Only to southern Chinese, with their leisure mentality, would a bridge like this makes sense. It attracts only those who take time to enjoy the scenery, and forsakes those who hurry through life.

Walking along the lake, there is a warm caressing glow in the morning. It is golden pink all around.

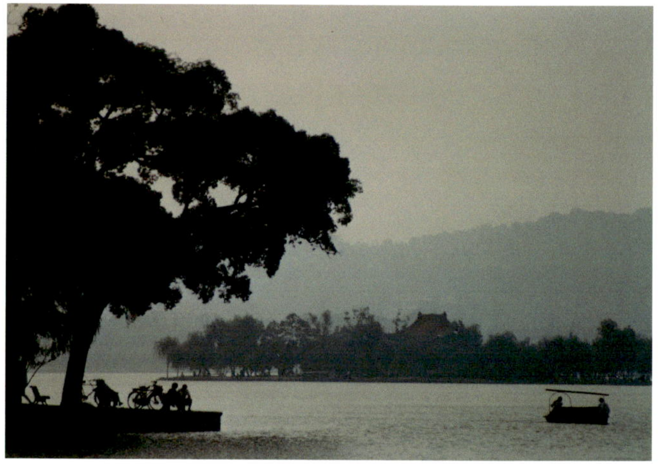

Step 1 Trees

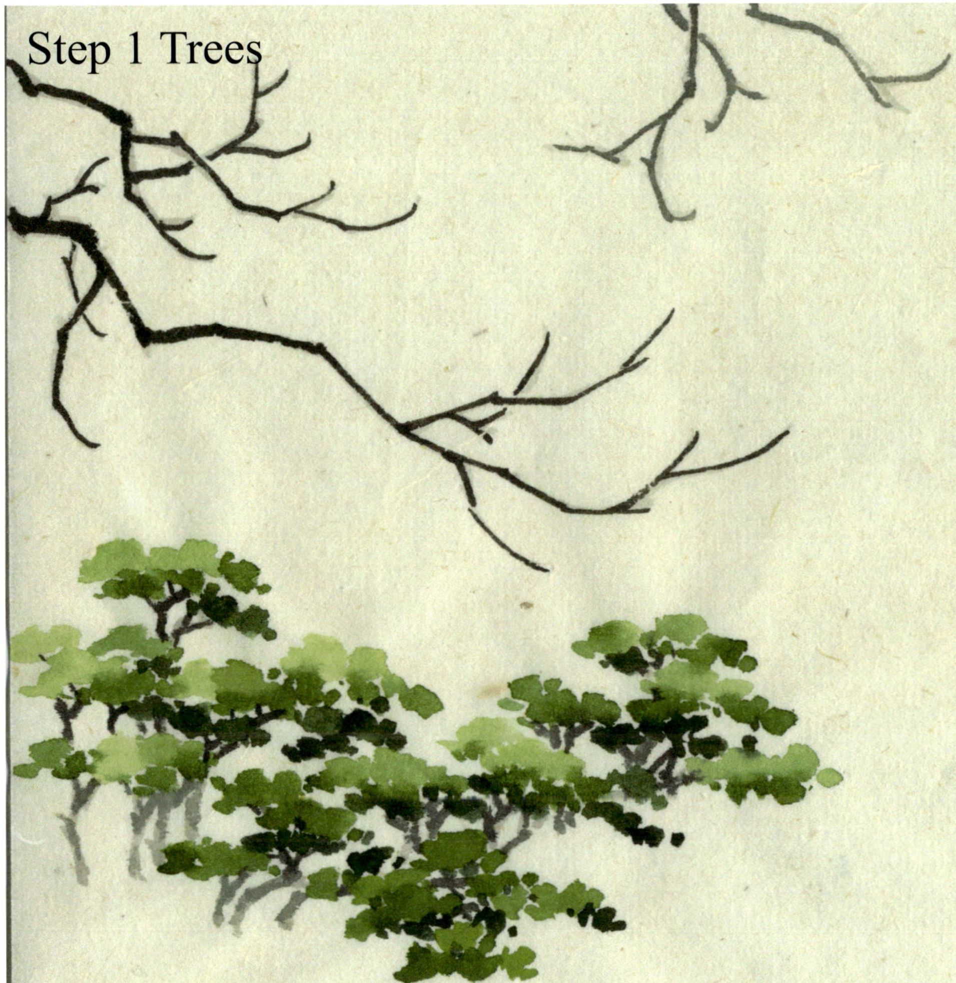

1. Foreground Branches: ♌ Flow, ❖ Light Ink, dry brush, ↓ vertical brush. Do foreground branches. ❖ Medium and Dark Ink, reinforce the lines. Branches are reaching to the center. Make the main branches heavier and twigs thinner. Think curves, not straight lines.

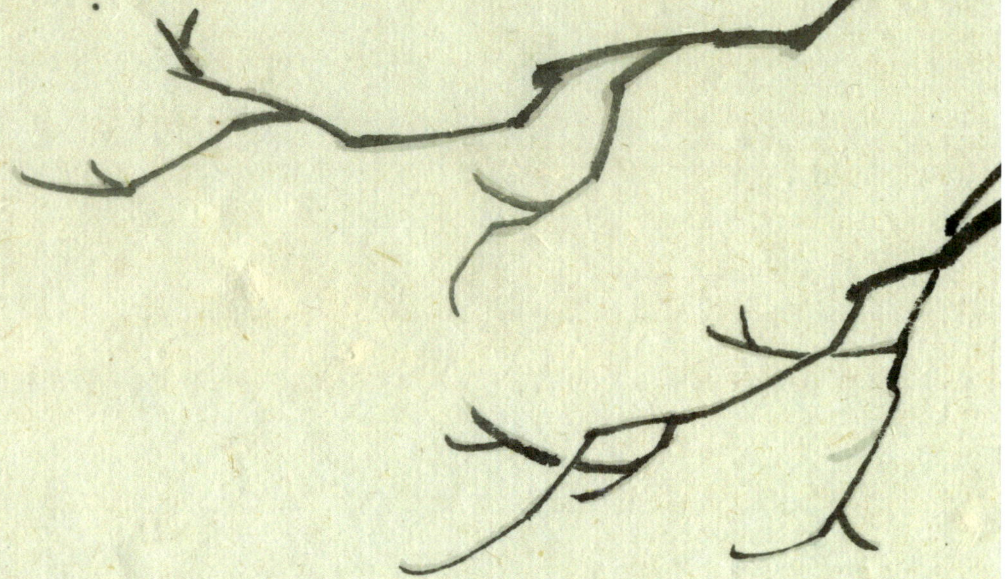

2. Foliage Clusters: ♌ Flow. ❖ Lighter clusters: White Green + Light Green. ❖ Medium clusters: Light Green + Dark Green, ❖ Dark clusters: Shade + Ink. ↖ Tilt and press the brush. Lay overlapping dots horizontally. Clusters form an uneven contour with side ones smaller. Work light clusters first. Add the medium and dark ones below and to the right of the light ones. Overlap them. Do the lower clusters first. They are closer to us.

3. Trunks and Branches: ❖ Light, Medium and Dark Ink, add branches and trunks with Light Ink. Reinforce with Medium and Dark Ink. End the base of the trunks light and at varied heights.

Step 2 Line Work

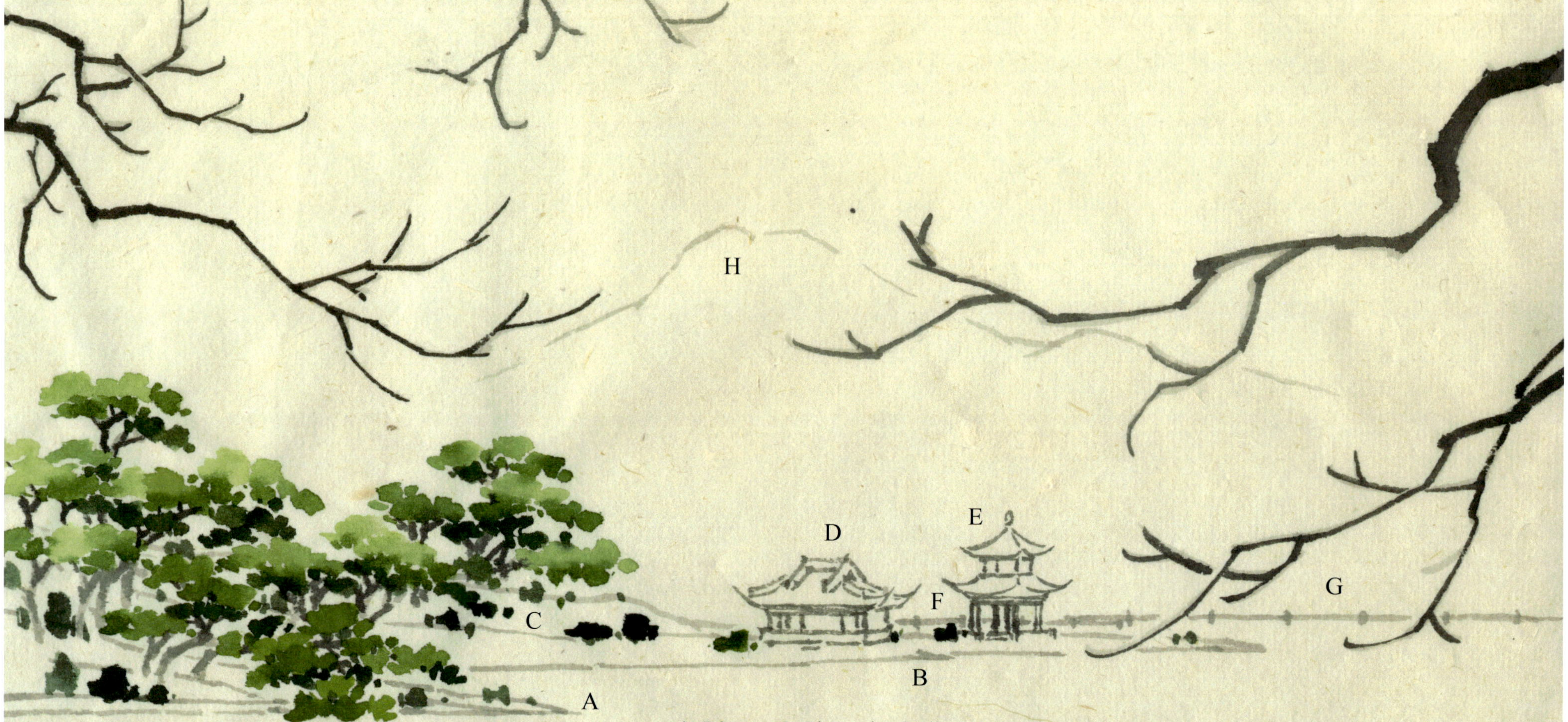

1. Lines: ♌ Flow, ❖ Medium Ink, ↓ vertical brush, add lines for the banks (A, B, C), pavilions (D, E), bridges (F, G) and distant mountains (H).

2. Bushes: ❖ Green + Shade + Ink, work dots to show bushes (I).

Step 3 More Lines and Coloring

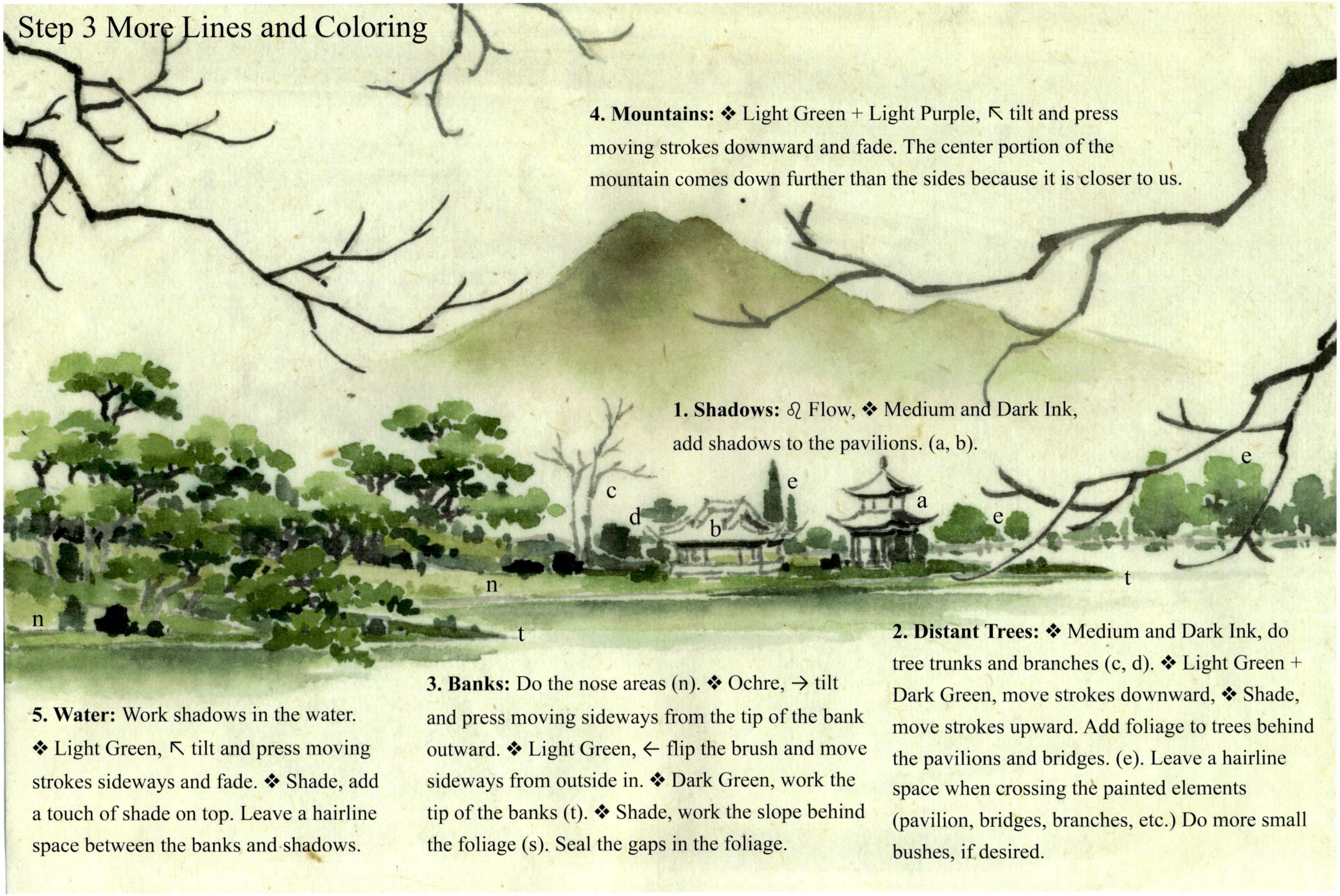

4. Mountains: ❖ Light Green + Light Purple, ↖ tilt and press moving strokes downward and fade. The center portion of the mountain comes down further than the sides because it is closer to us.

1. Shadows: Ω Flow, ❖ Medium and Dark Ink, add shadows to the pavilions. (a, b).

2. Distant Trees: ❖ Medium and Dark Ink, do tree trunks and branches (c, d). ❖ Light Green + Dark Green, move strokes downward, ❖ Shade, move strokes upward. Add foliage to trees behind the pavilions and bridges. (e). Leave a hairline space when crossing the painted elements (pavilion, bridges, branches, etc.) Do more small bushes, if desired.

3. Banks: Do the nose areas (n). ❖ Ochre, → tilt and press moving sideways from the tip of the bank outward. ❖ Light Green, ← flip the brush and move sideways from outside in. ❖ Dark Green, work the tip of the banks (t). ❖ Shade, work the slope behind the foliage (s). Seal the gaps in the foliage.

5. Water: Work shadows in the water. ❖ Light Green, ↖ tilt and press moving strokes sideways and fade. ❖ Shade, add a touch of shade on top. Leave a hairline space between the banks and shadows.

Step 4 Mist, Sky, and Water

Let the painting dry. Rewet the whole painting.

Mist

ᘯ Wash Brush, wet and dry the brush.
Keeping the body dry, load colors on one corner of the brush. ❖ Purple 2" + Shade 1", blend. Hold the brush vertically, colored corner down. Darken the base of the mountain to bring out the mist in the space below (A). Move sideways to the left then to the right. Pivot the handle (windshield wiper like) to taper the edges.

Sky and Water

ᘯ Wash Brush, ❖ Pink 2" + Purple 1" (on the same corner). Blend. Hold the brush vertically, colored corner up. Apply Pink Purple across the top and middle of the sky (B, C, D). Overlap the strokes to have a smooth coverage. Reverse the brush with the colored corner on the bottom. Work along the lower edge of the painting across (E) and above the mist (F, G).

Lower Mist Area

ᘯ Wash Brush, ❖ Pink 1/4" + Purple 1/8", colored corner down. Add colors to the lower portions of the mist area (H, I).

Wash

Prepare flat saucers. Dilute colors into a wash.

❖ Yellow with White (1, 2)
❖ Yellow with Vermillion (3, 4, 5)
❖ Light Green (6, 7, 8)

Load color on one corner of the brush, about 2" into the width. Blend. Dip the colored edge in water to soften the color. Apply strokes horizontally.

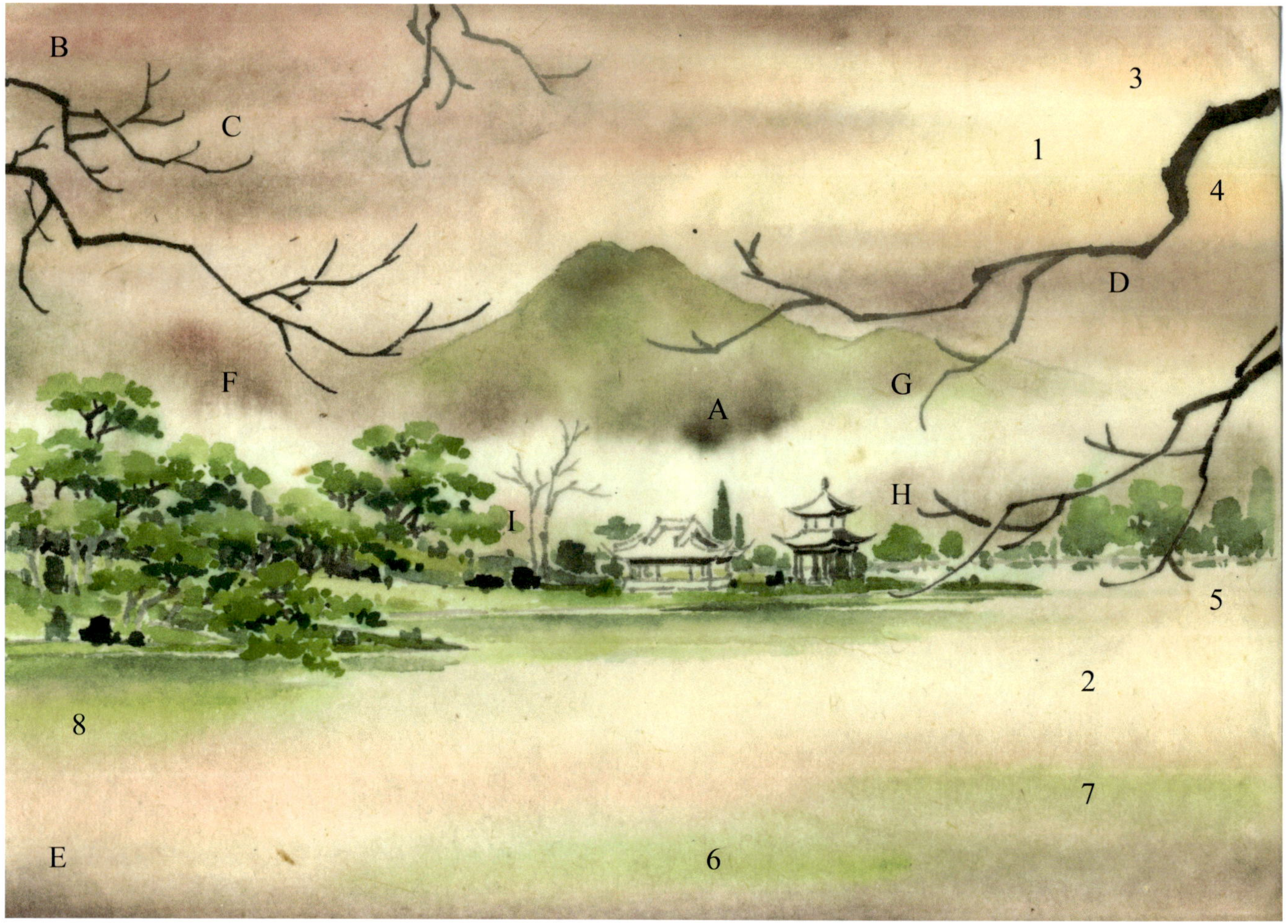

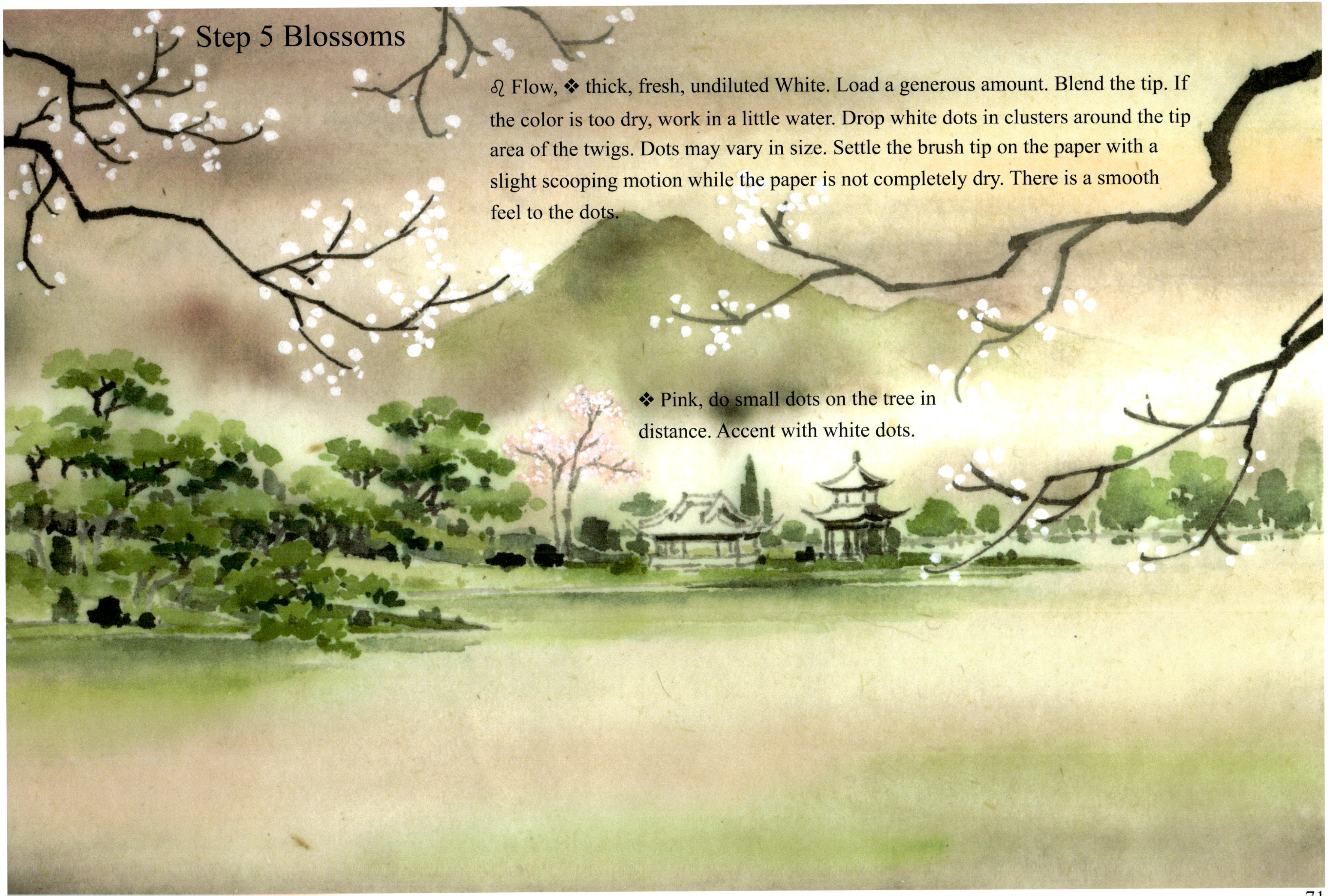

Step 5 Blossoms

♌ Flow, ❖ thick, fresh, undiluted White. Load a generous amount. Blend the tip. If the color is too dry, work in a little water. Drop white dots in clusters around the tip area of the twigs. Dots may vary in size. Settle the brush tip on the paper with a slight scooping motion while the paper is not completely dry. There is a smooth feel to the dots.

❖ Pink, do small dots on the tree in distance. Accent with white dots.

Step 6 Finishing Touches

Twigs and Dots: Wait until the painting dries. Flow, ❖ Ink, add twigs to connect the loose blossoms, if necessary. Do two or three calyx dots to attach each blossom to the twigs. Add more ink dots on the branches to show budding growth.

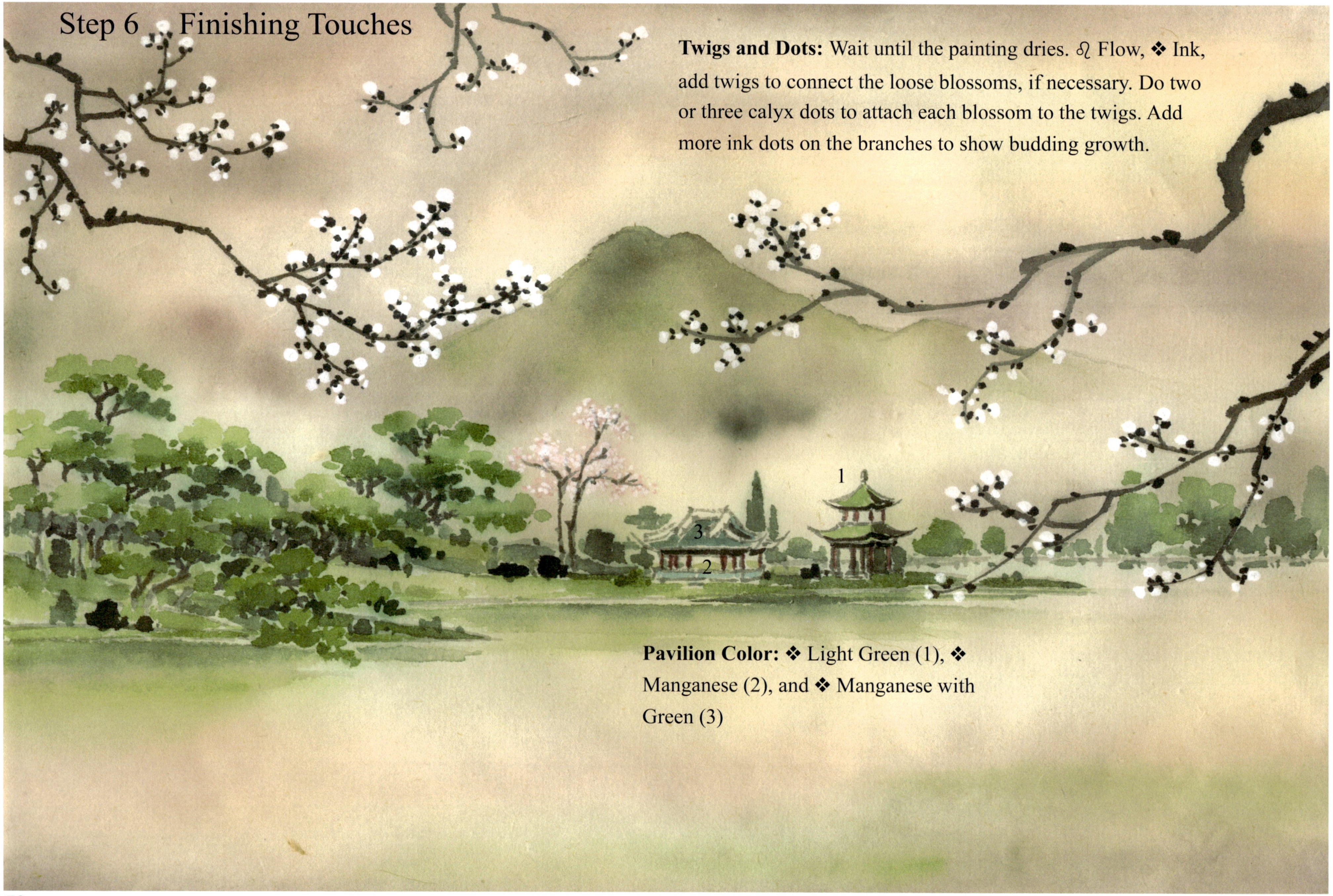

Pavilion Color: ❖ Light Green (1), ❖ Manganese (2), and ❖ Manganese with Green (3)

Lesson 8: Garden

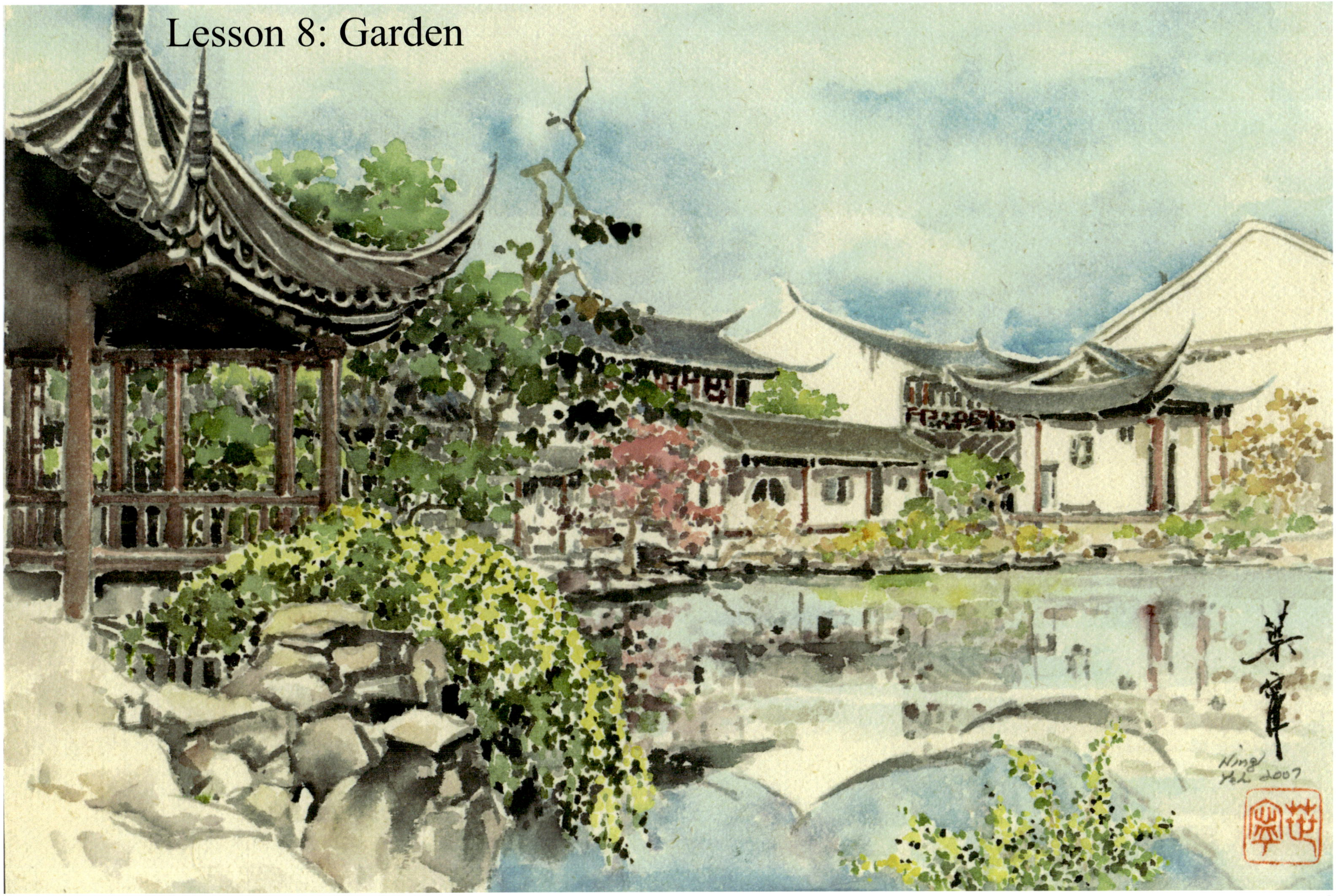

Lesson 8: Garden

Suzhou is located in east Jiangsu Province, only a short drive from Shanghai. Known as the garden city of China, it has more than 150 gardens. Most of the gardens are built around ponds. They reflect the unique taste of the ruling class in old China.

For 2,000 years, the elite culture of China was dominated by gentry-class scholars who ruled by their knowledge and skill in literary pursuits.

Their written language sets the Chinese apart from other cultures. Written characters are picture images abstracted from reality and from the association of ideas. Practicing calligraphy was a daily ritual. Within the confines of a tiny square of paper, the Chinese found their universe. The link between man and nature was immediate and direct. Through brush and ink, the beauty of composition and the rhythm of strokes were developed. Characters were expressed with spirit and vitality.

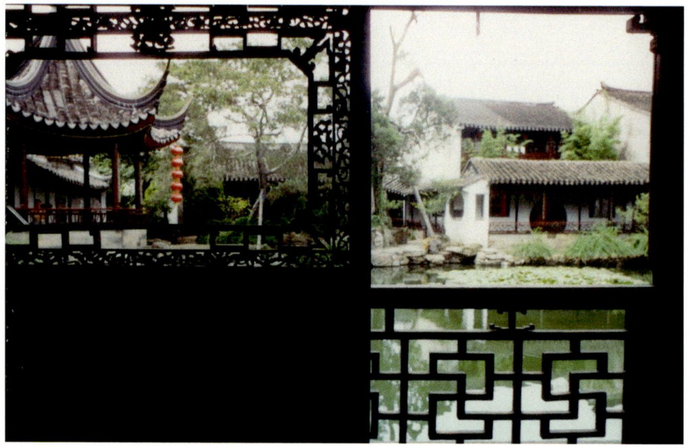

The interest in studying these characters linked the joy of calligraphy and poetry. Its natural extension was painting. Painting is an expression of calligraphy strokes with poetic ideas. Painting was done mostly with ink on white paper. A touch of red for the seals was the only color.

The Suzhou gardens were a product of these people. Upon retirement and with leisure, they injected their taste into their living quarters. In addition to painting and writing, they also developed an interest in music and chess playing. Together, these were the four literary pursuits.

The Suzhou gardens are prime examples of the clever use of space. Each garden is a miniature universe. Each corner is a subtle poem. It expresses the harmony of land and water, and man with nature. Structures are often integrated into the gardens. Plants, rockeries, and ponds represent the tangible elements of nature. They invite the intangibles—the shadows on the walls, the reflections in the ponds, the wind, the rain and the snow.

The crown jewel of gardens in Suzhou is the Master of the Nets. It is the smallest but most exquisite. Each time and season, the garden changes, yet tranquility prevails throughout.

Each step and each window frame a composition of flowers, pavilions, pools, and reflections. We can take ourselves back in time and be immersed in classical elegance.

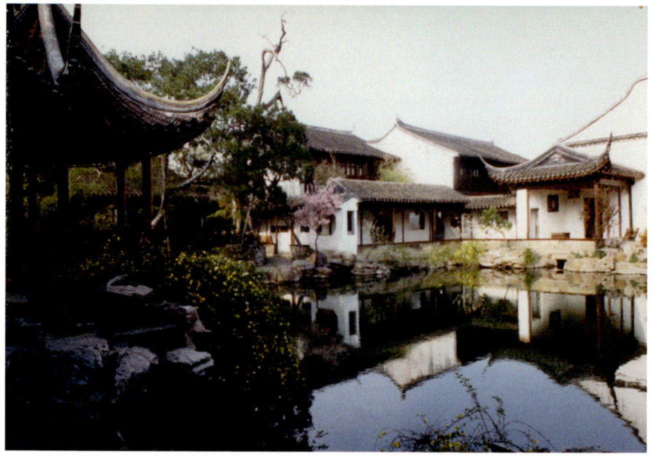

Step 1 Foreground Elements

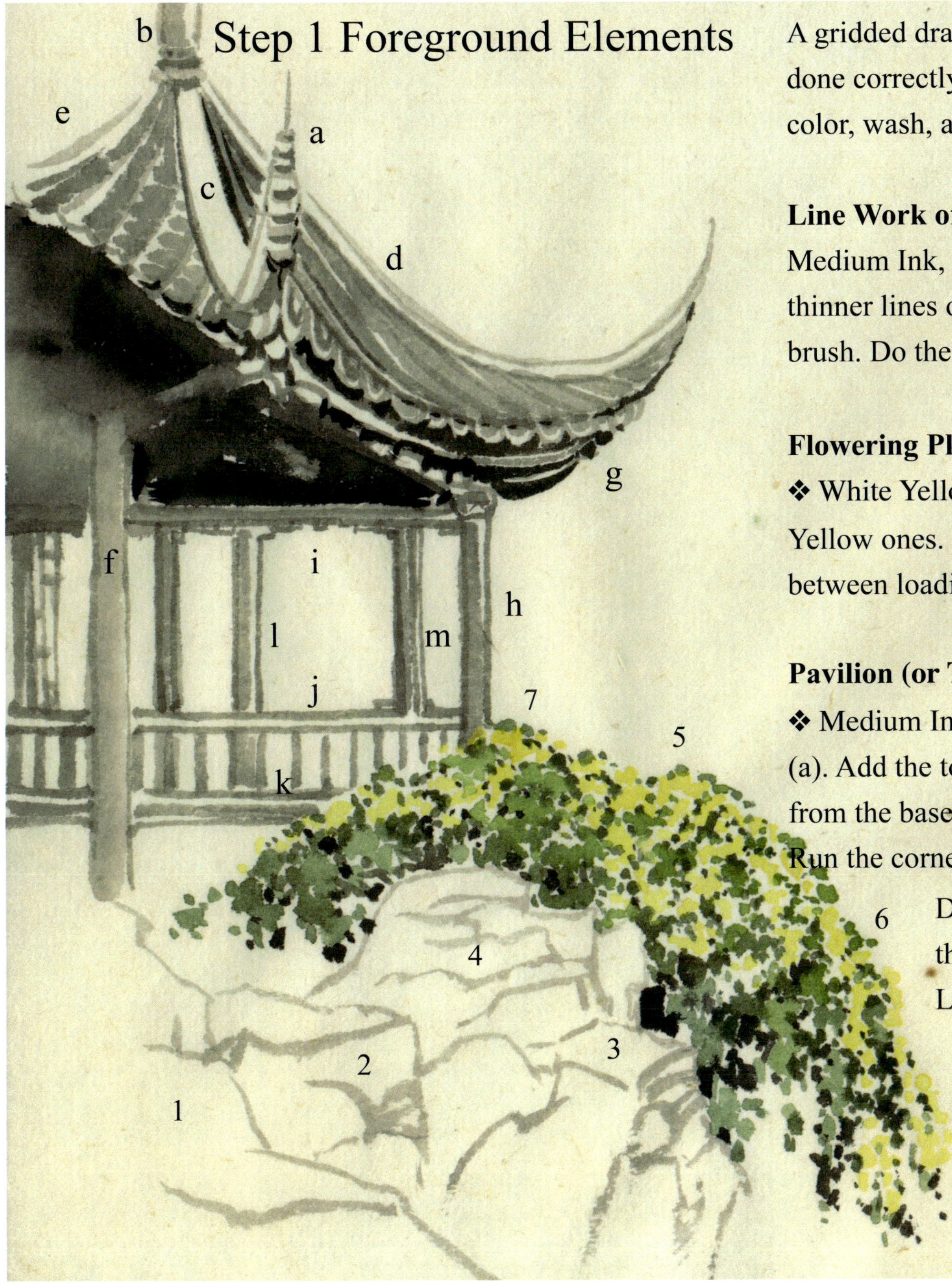

A gridded draft is strongly suggested to ensure that all vertical and horizontal elements are done correctly. The traditional approach to painting landscape uses these steps: line, ink, color, wash, and dots.

Line Work of Lower Rocks (1-4): ♌ Flow, Happy Dot, or Small Mt. Horse, ❖ Light and Medium Ink, dry the brush body so the lines show some texture. Work the rocks with thinner lines on top. Do the lower ones heavier to add dimension and shadow. Tilt the brush. Do the lines with uneven widths. Taper the ends.

Flowering Plants (5-9): ♌ Flow, ↖ tilt and press with a scooping motion. ❖ White Yellow (mix Yellow with a touch of diluted White), work flower dots. Add some Yellow ones. ❖ White Green, Light Green, and Green, do leaf dots. Do not clean the brush between loadings. Let one color carry into the other. ❖ Shade and Ink, add shadow dots.

Pavilion (or Ting in Chinese): Begin with lines. ♌ Flow, Happy Dot, or Small Mt. Horse, ❖ Medium Ink, dry body, ↓ vertical brush. Start with the roof. Do the tip coming forward (a). Add the top (b). Run roof hip c. Extend the other two roof hips (d, e). Extend a beam from the base of roof hip c and come down with a post (f). Work the base of the roof (g). Run the corner post (h), cross beam (i), top and base of railing (j, k). Add posts behind (l). Do some ornamental details to break the squares (m). Run some lines to divide the roof. Add Ink work with different tones to show shadows and dimension. Leave occasional spaces to show light.

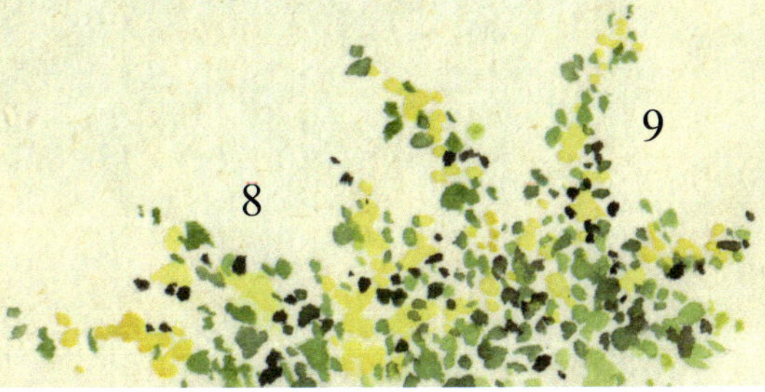

Step 2 Trees and Rock Shadows

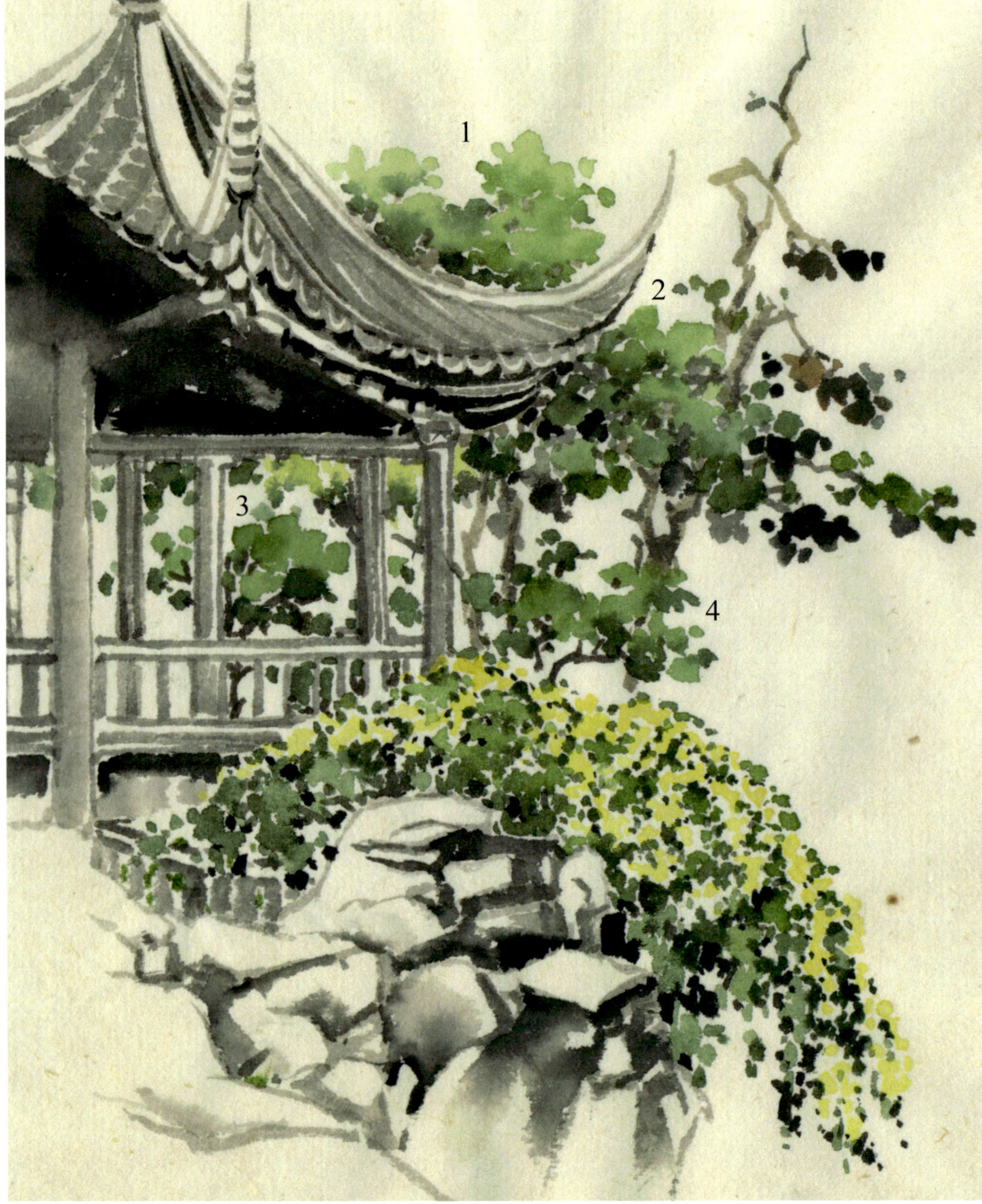

Add trees behind the Ting. Arrange the foliage to showcase the structure but leave the Ting alone. Bring some foliage between the railings to visually connect with the planting elements in the front.

Trees on the Left (1-4): ᘓ Flow, ❖ White Green, Light Green and Green, ↖ tilt the brush and do dots for the leaves. Let one color carry into the other. ❖ Shade and Ink, add shadow dots. ❖ Medium and Dark Ink, ↑ vertical brush, add trunks and branches.

Spirited Cypress on the Right: ᘓ Flow, ❖ Light Ink, ↑ vertical brush. Add trunks and branches. ❖ Accent with Medium and Dark Ink. ❖ Green, Shade, Vermillion Green, and Ink, add leaf dots.

Rock Shadows: ᘓ Flow, ❖ Medium and Dark Ink, add rock shadows.

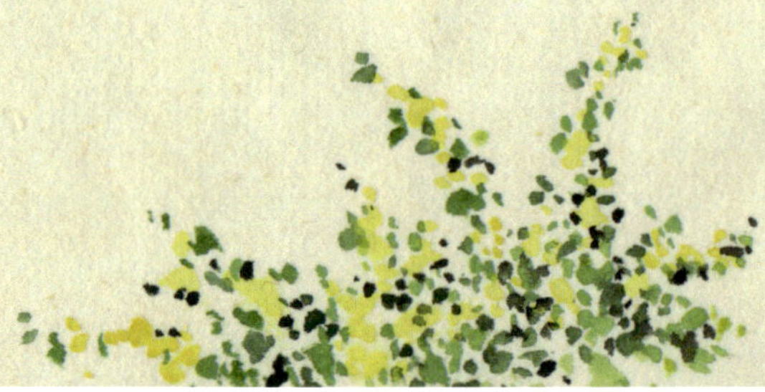

Step 3 Background Building (behind ting) and Rockeries

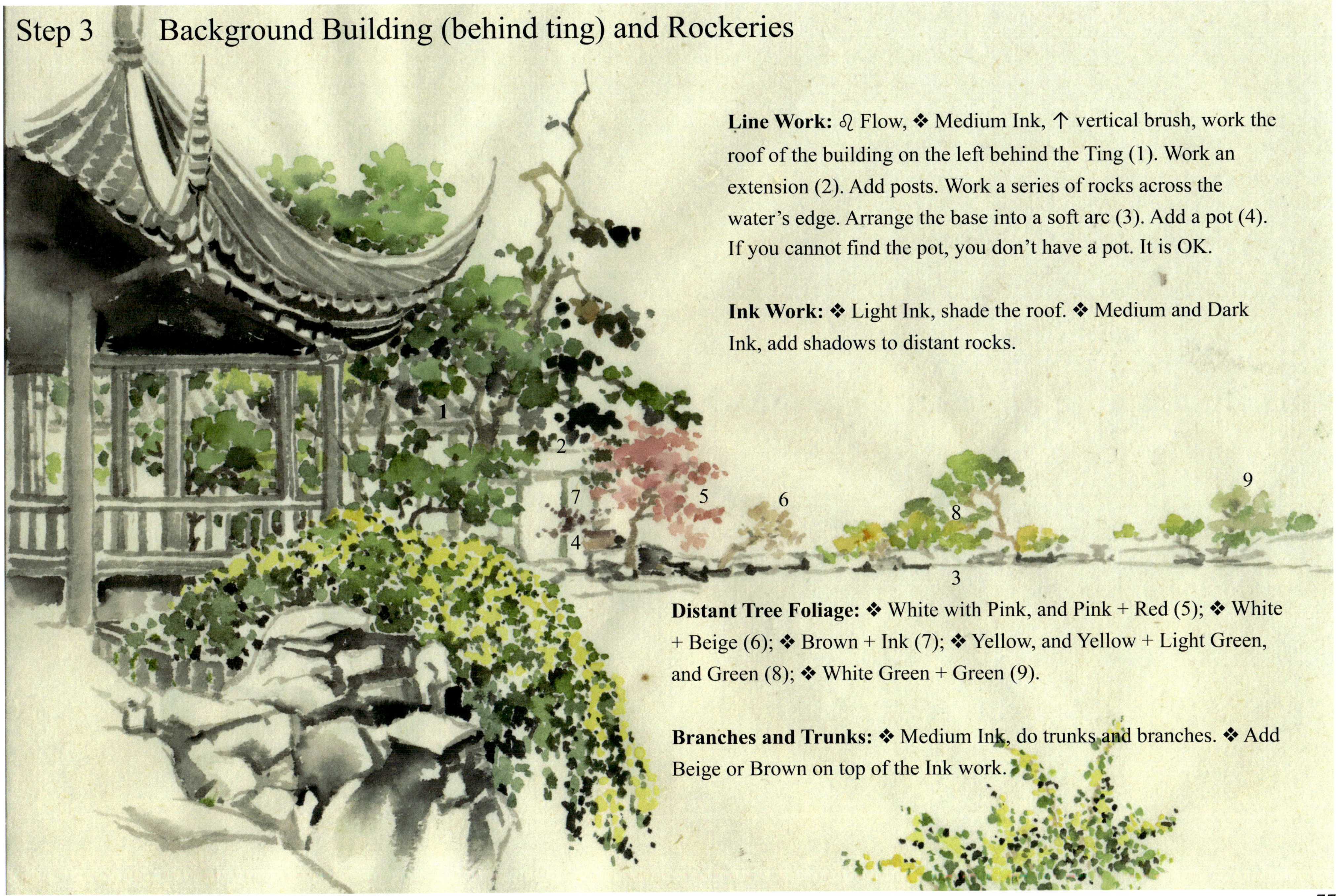

Line Work: ℓ Flow, ❖ Medium Ink, ↑ vertical brush, work the roof of the building on the left behind the Ting (1). Work an extension (2). Add posts. Work a series of rocks across the water's edge. Arrange the base into a soft arc (3). Add a pot (4). If you cannot find the pot, you don't have a pot. It is OK.

Ink Work: ❖ Light Ink, shade the roof. ❖ Medium and Dark Ink, add shadows to distant rocks.

Distant Tree Foliage: ❖ White with Pink, and Pink + Red (5); ❖ White + Beige (6); ❖ Brown + Ink (7); ❖ Yellow, and Yellow + Light Green, and Green (8); ❖ White Green + Green (9).

Branches and Trunks: ❖ Medium Ink, do trunks and branches. ❖ Add Beige or Brown on top of the Ink work.

Step 4 Main Building Quarters

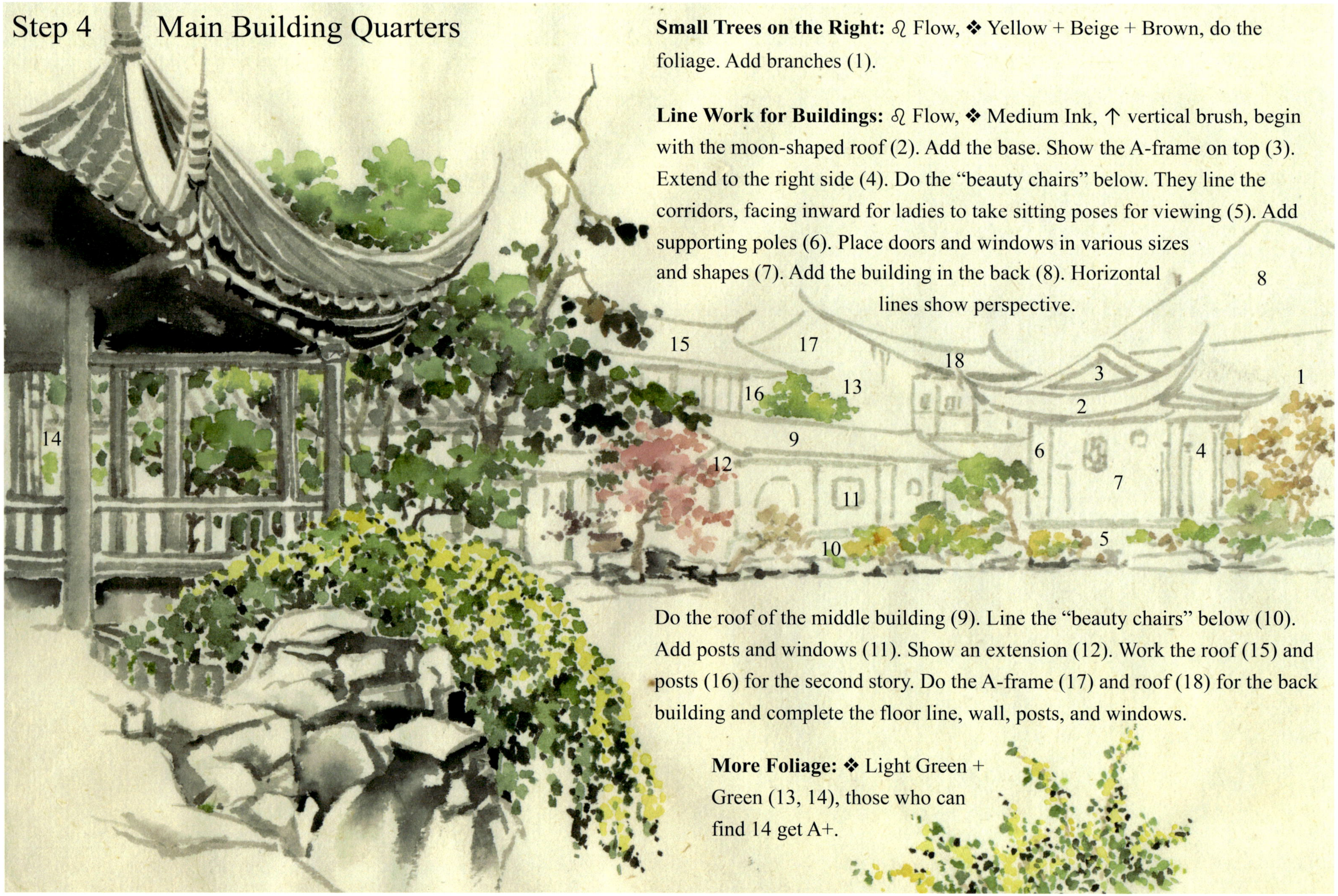

Small Trees on the Right: ♌ Flow, ❖ Yellow + Beige + Brown, do the foliage. Add branches (1).

Line Work for Buildings: ♌ Flow, ❖ Medium Ink, ↑ vertical brush, begin with the moon-shaped roof (2). Add the base. Show the A-frame on top (3). Extend to the right side (4). Do the "beauty chairs" below. They line the corridors, facing inward for ladies to take sitting poses for viewing (5). Add supporting poles (6). Place doors and windows in various sizes and shapes (7). Add the building in the back (8). Horizontal lines show perspective.

Do the roof of the middle building (9). Line the "beauty chairs" below (10). Add posts and windows (11). Show an extension (12). Work the roof (15) and posts (16) for the second story. Do the A-frame (17) and roof (18) for the back building and complete the floor line, wall, posts, and windows.

More Foliage: ❖ Light Green + Green (13, 14), those who can find 14 get A+.

Step 5 Shade and Shadows

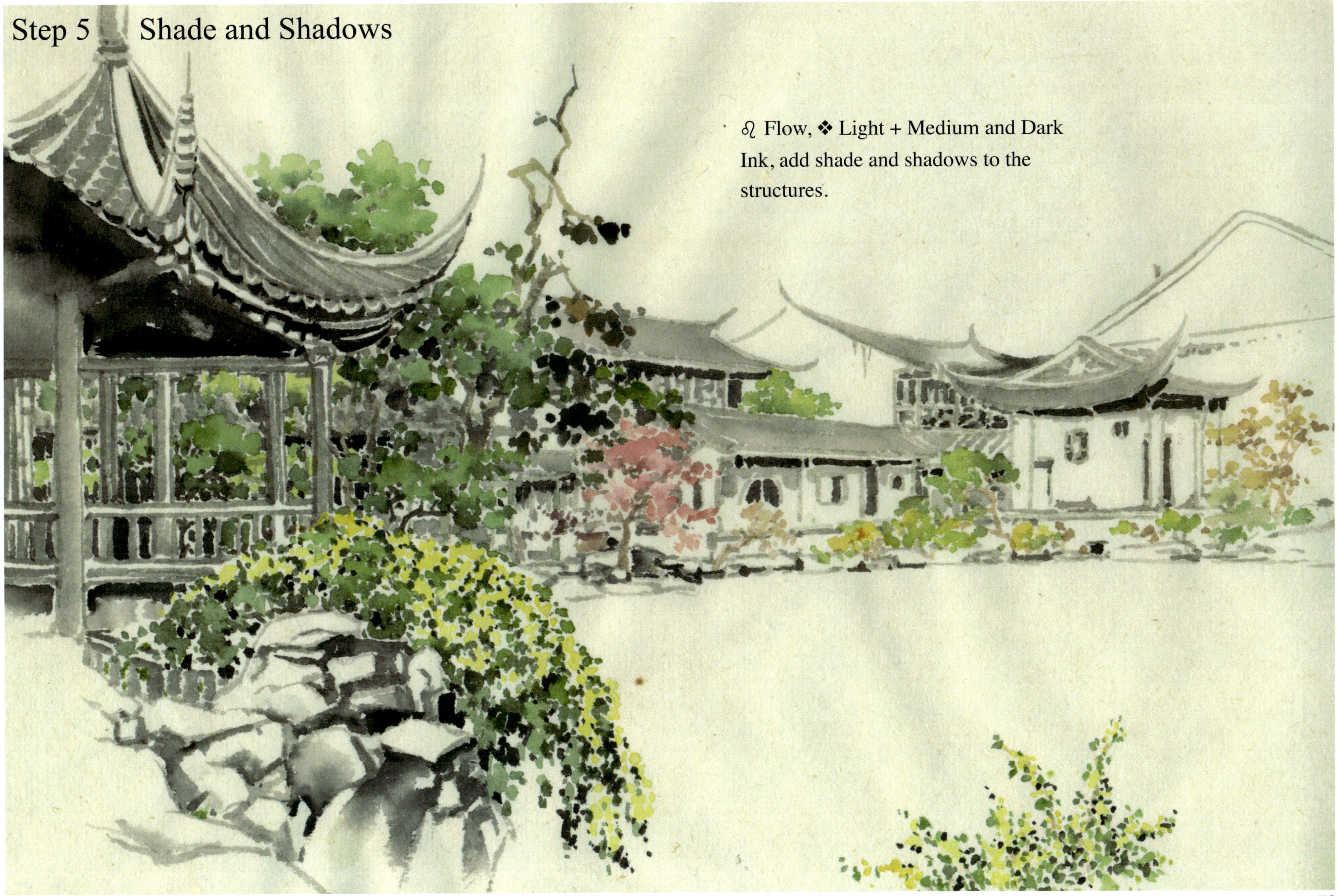

ᔓ Flow, ❖ Light + Medium and Dark Ink, add shade and shadows to the structures.

Step 6 Reflections

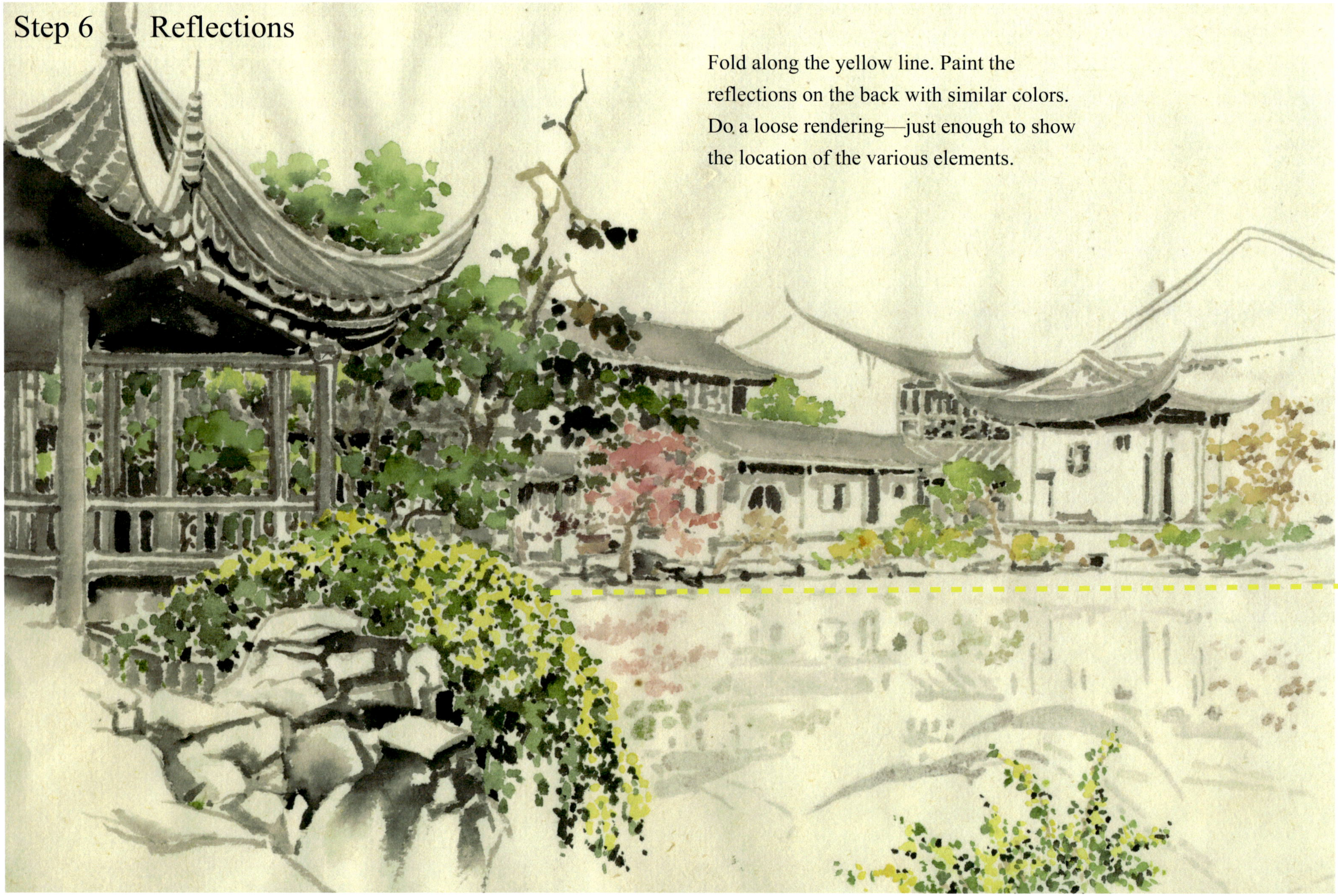

Fold along the yellow line. Paint the reflections on the back with similar colors. Do a loose rendering—just enough to show the location of the various elements.

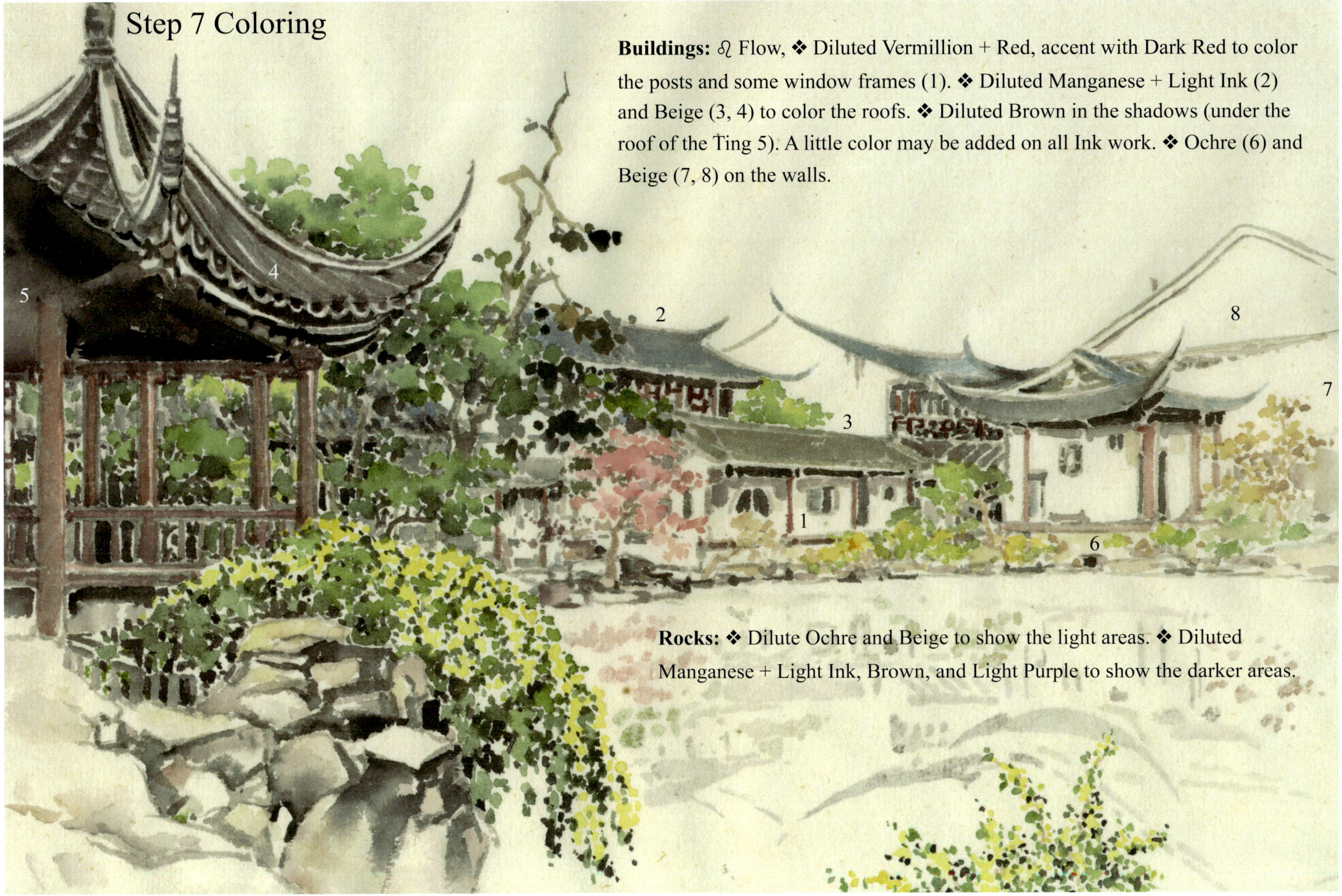

Step 7 Coloring

Buildings: ℓ Flow, ❖ Diluted Vermillion + Red, accent with Dark Red to color the posts and some window frames (1). ❖ Diluted Manganese + Light Ink (2) and Beige (3, 4) to color the roofs. ❖ Diluted Brown in the shadows (under the roof of the Ting 5). A little color may be added on all Ink work. ❖ Ochre (6) and Beige (7, 8) on the walls.

Rocks: ❖ Dilute Ochre and Beige to show the light areas. ❖ Diluted Manganese + Light Ink, Brown, and Light Purple to show the darker areas.

Step 8 Coloring Sky and Water

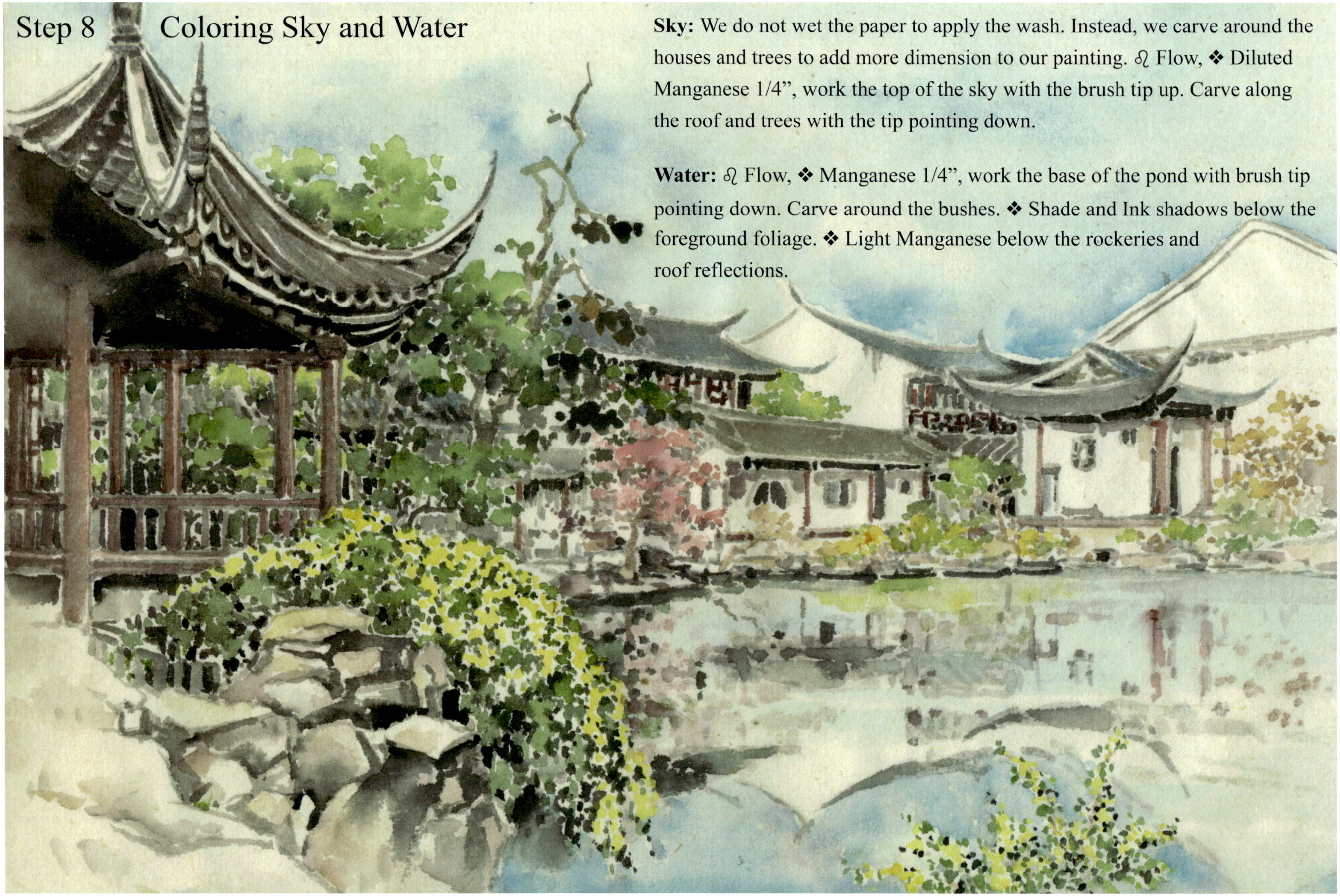

Sky: We do not wet the paper to apply the wash. Instead, we carve around the houses and trees to add more dimension to our painting. ℓ Flow, ❖ Diluted Manganese 1/4", work the top of the sky with the brush tip up. Carve along the roof and trees with the tip pointing down.

Water: ℓ Flow, ❖ Manganese 1/4", work the base of the pond with brush tip pointing down. Carve around the bushes. ❖ Shade and Ink shadows below the foreground foliage. ❖ Light Manganese below the rockeries and roof reflections.

Lesson 9: Yellow Mountain

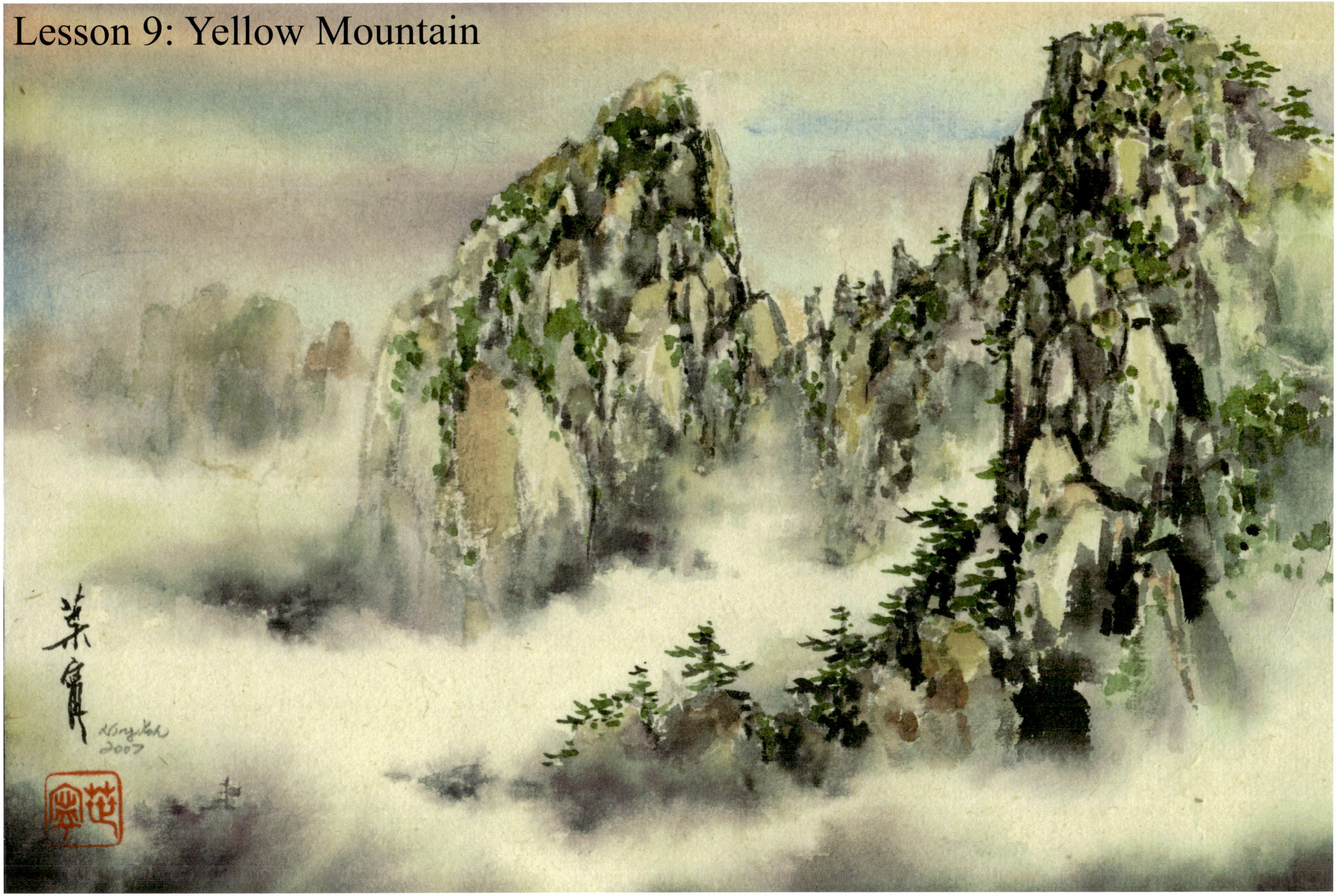

Lesson 9: Yellow Mountain

Yellow Mountain is nature's spiritual gift to the artist. Each spot on this magic mountain has an unforgettable sight that sets the stage for constant drama. An all-star cast created by the Almighty.

There is an area on the mountain called "Now I Believe." The term refers to people who initially do not believe such a mountain could exist. Upon seeing this spot, the non-believer could not help but exclaim "Now I believe!"

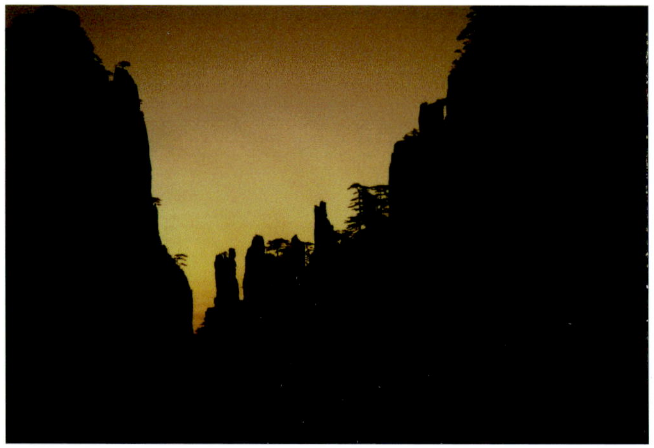

One of nature's theaters in "Now I Believe" is "The Prime Minister Viewing the Chess Players." This is a group of four rock figures between two peaks: a Prime Minister with two chess players, and a lady bearing a gift basket.

The Prime Minister is most prominent. He wears a first-ranking official's hat and leans over to watch two seated chess players from one side. The chessboard is covered with a little pine umbrella. The lady bearing gifts is climbing up to them from the other side.

Let us enjoy this magic moment when the playful mist comes to visit the Prime Minister at dawn. This painting follows the traditional steps: line, ink, dots, coloring, and wash. Enjoy!

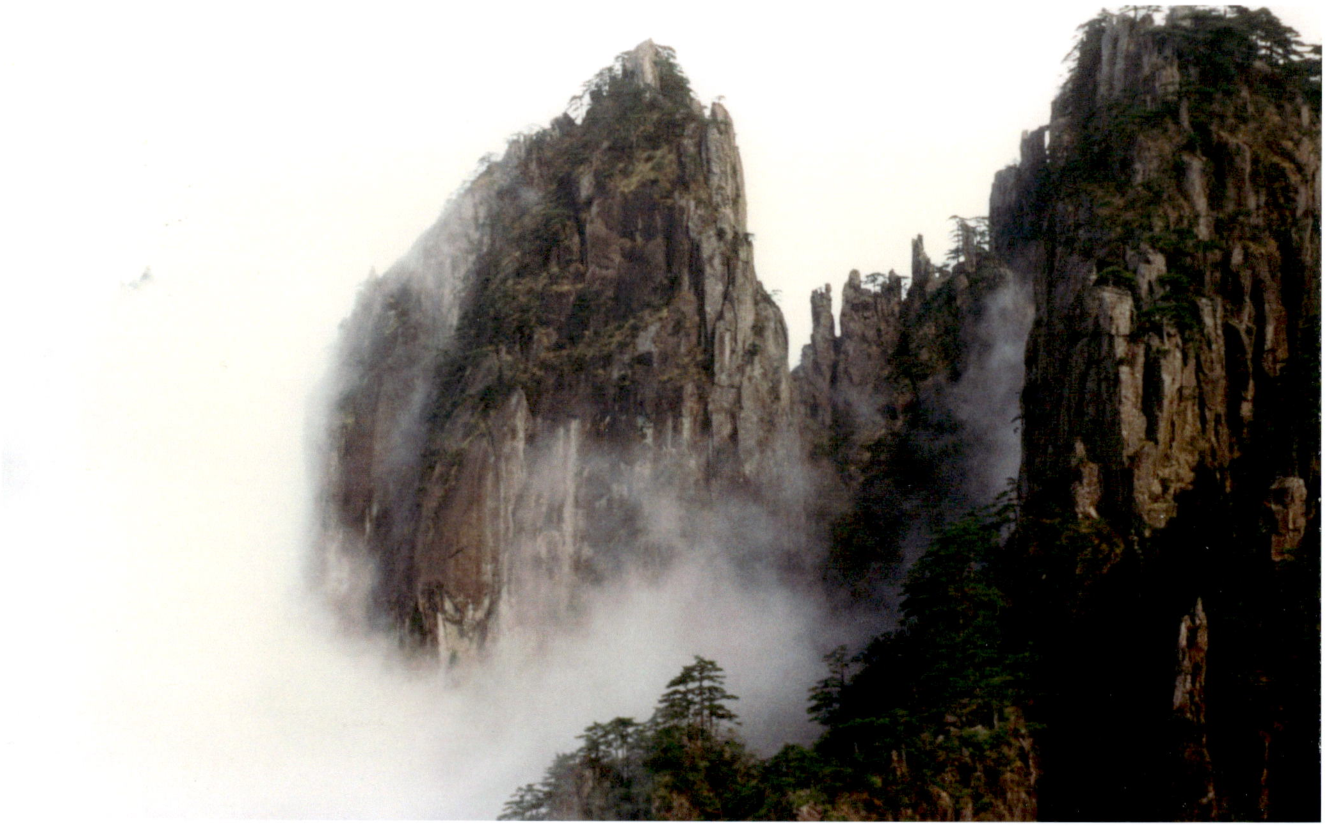

Step 1 Draft

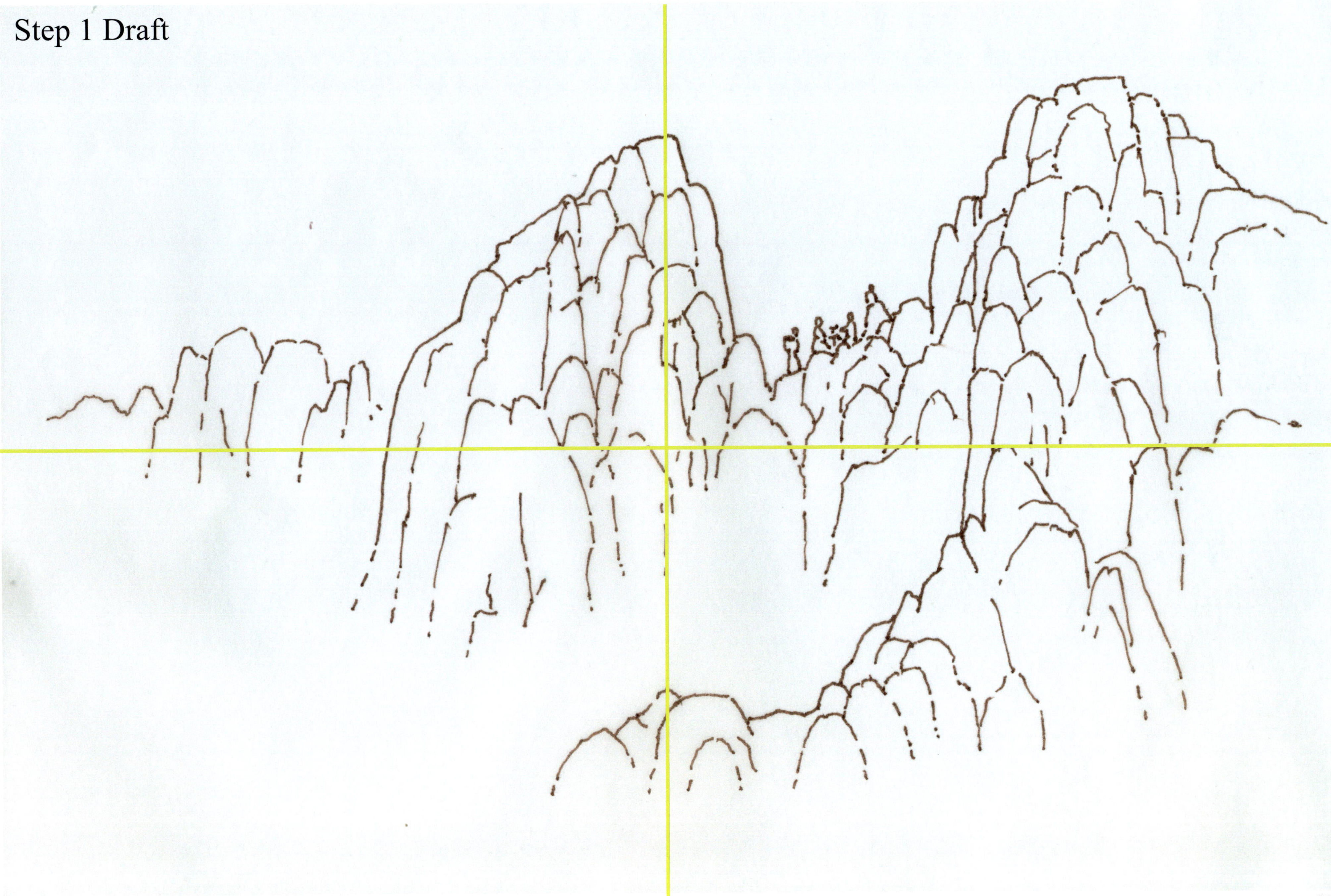

Step 2 Line and Ink Work

♌ Small Mt. Horse, ❖ Light Ink, dry the brush body, so the lines show texture. Develop the lines for the mountains and trees. ❖ Medium and Dark Ink, do lines for the rocks in the shadows.

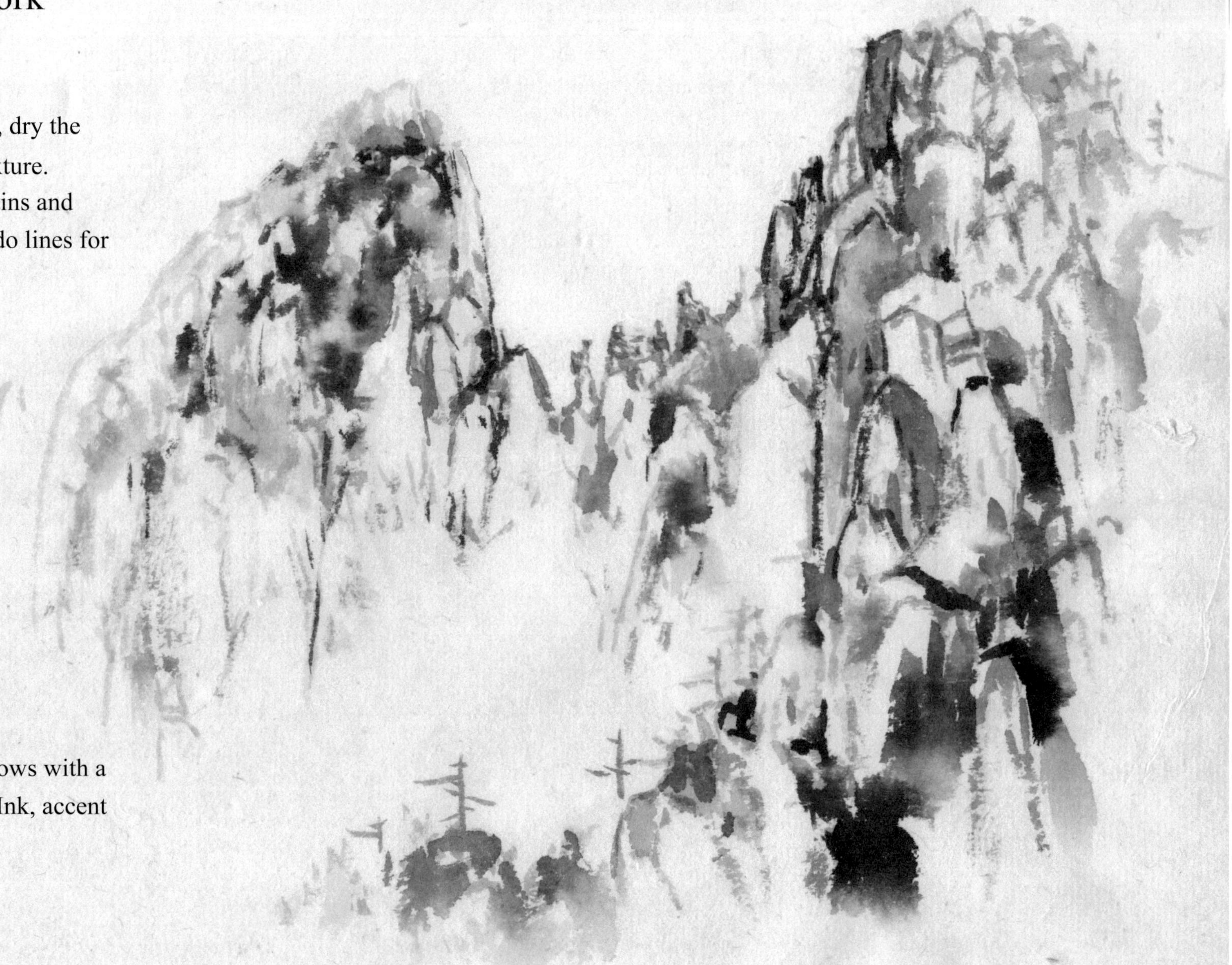

♌ Flow, ❖ Light Ink, work shadows with a dry brush. ❖ Medium and Dark Ink, accent shadow areas with darker tones.

Step 3 Foliage

♌ Flow, ❖ Light Green and Green, add foliage dots on the mountain. ❖ Accent with Shade and Ink.

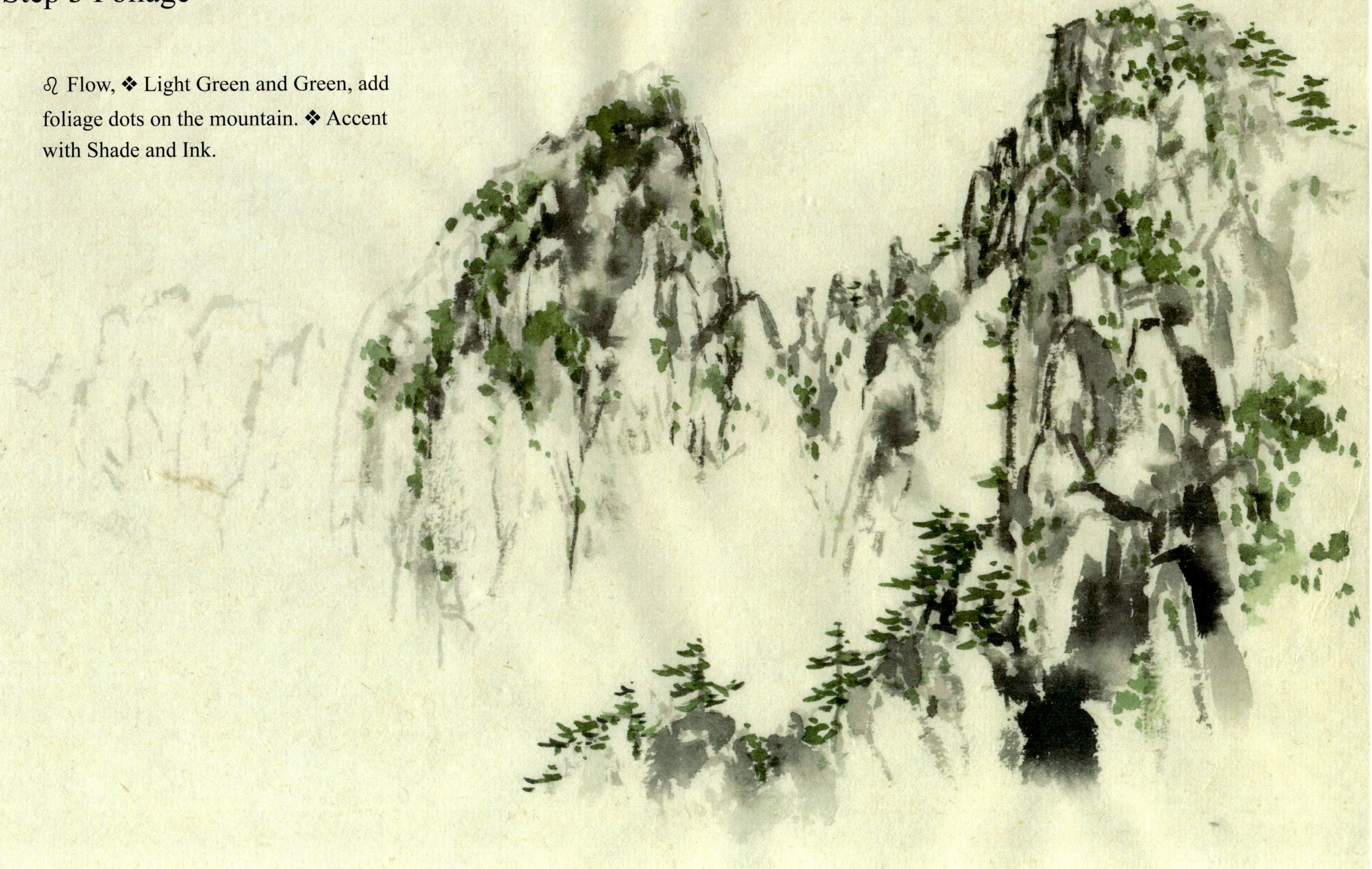

Step 4 Coloring

ℓ Flow, ❖ Diluted Ochre and Beige, show lighter areas. ❖ Diluted Vermillion, Light Purple + Purple, do the darker areas. Fade all colors at the base of the mountains.

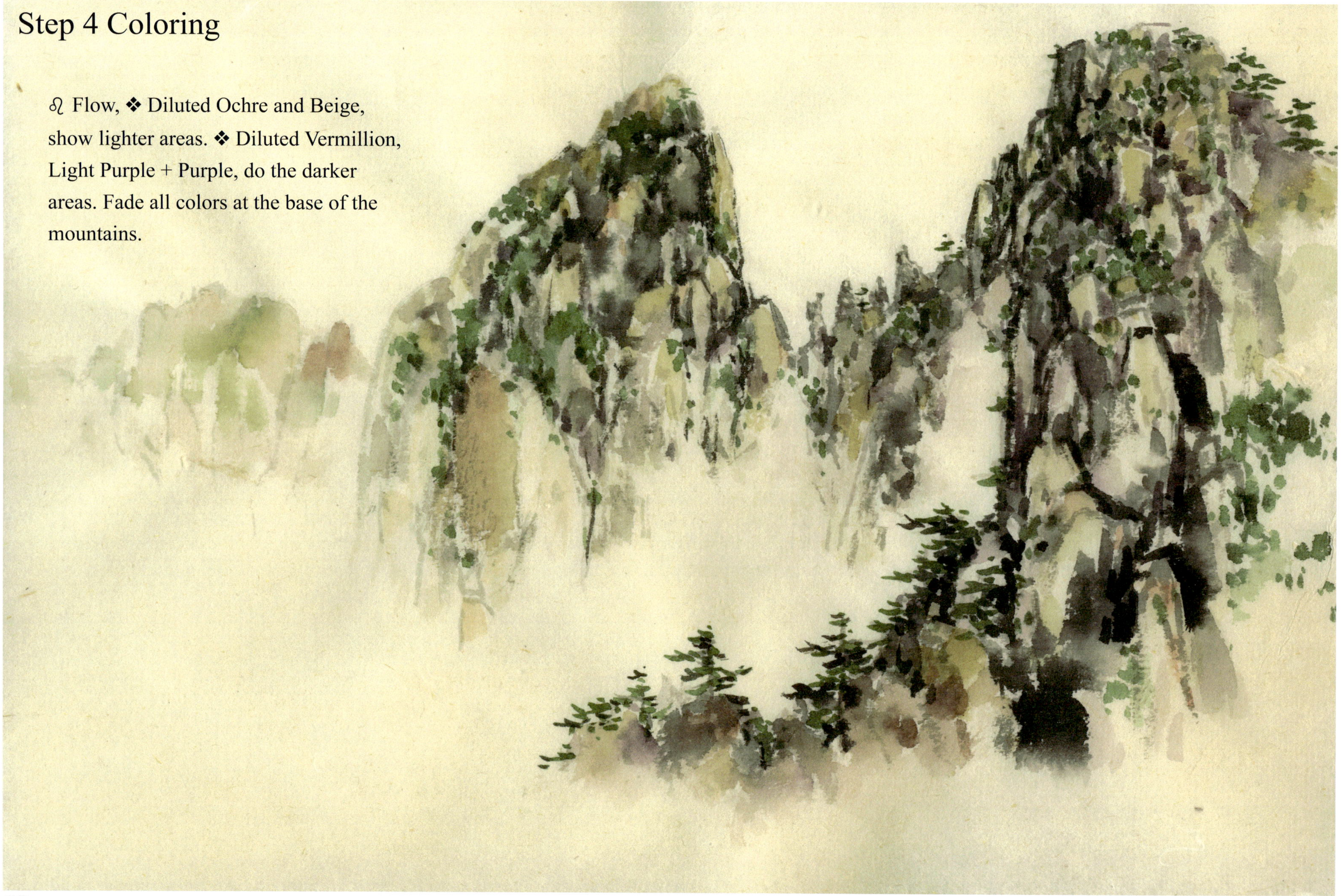

Step 5 Mist

Let the painting dry then rewet the whole painting. ℓ Wash Brush, dry the brush body.

❖ Purple 2" + Shade 1", load colors on one corner of the brush only then blend. Hold the brush vertically, colored corner down.

Shade the base of the painting (1) and darken the base of the mountain (2, 3, 4) to bring out the mist in the space below. Move sideways, left then right. Pivot the handle (like a windshield wiper) to taper the edges. Apply what's left on the brush to other areas of the mountain base.

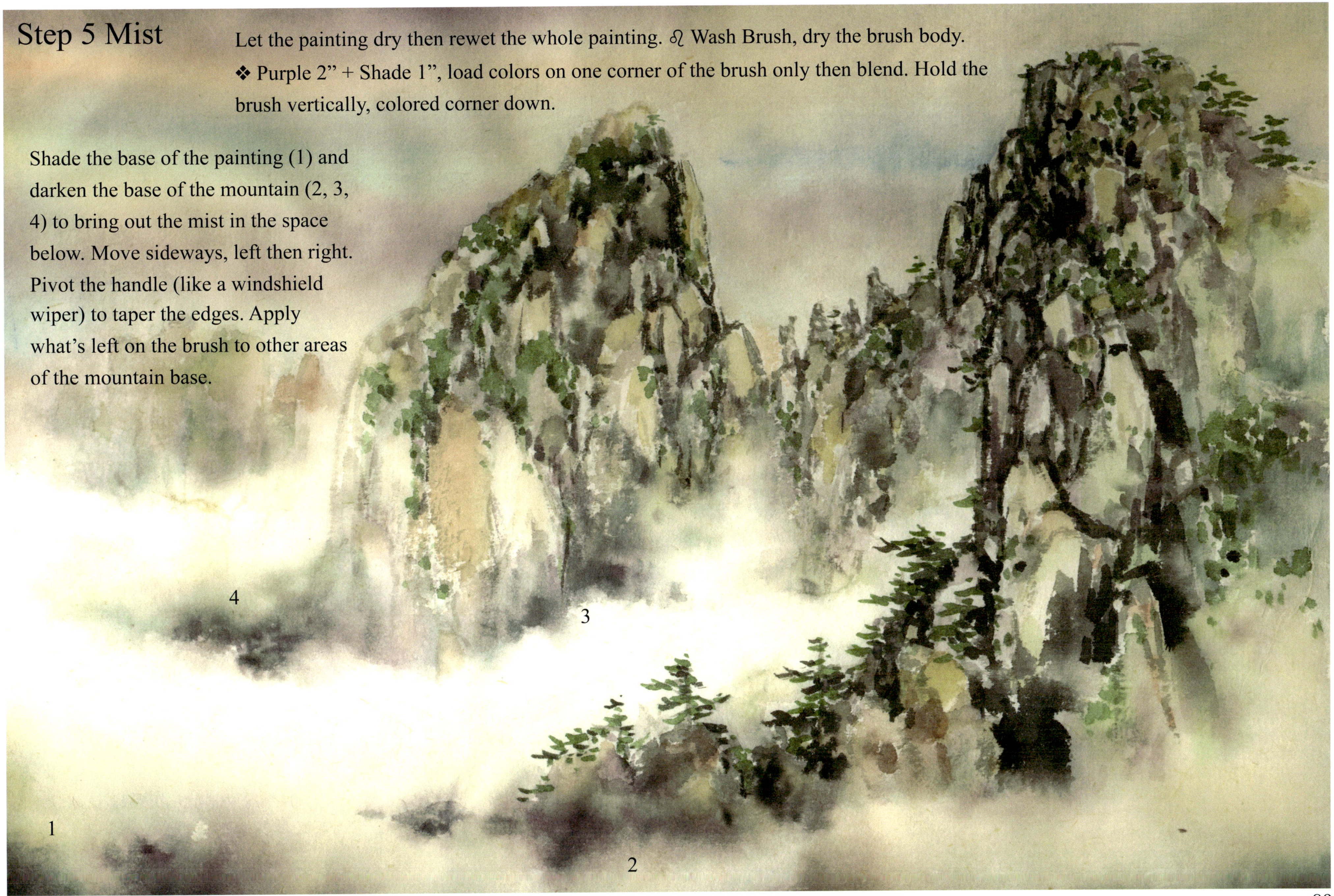

Step 6 Wash

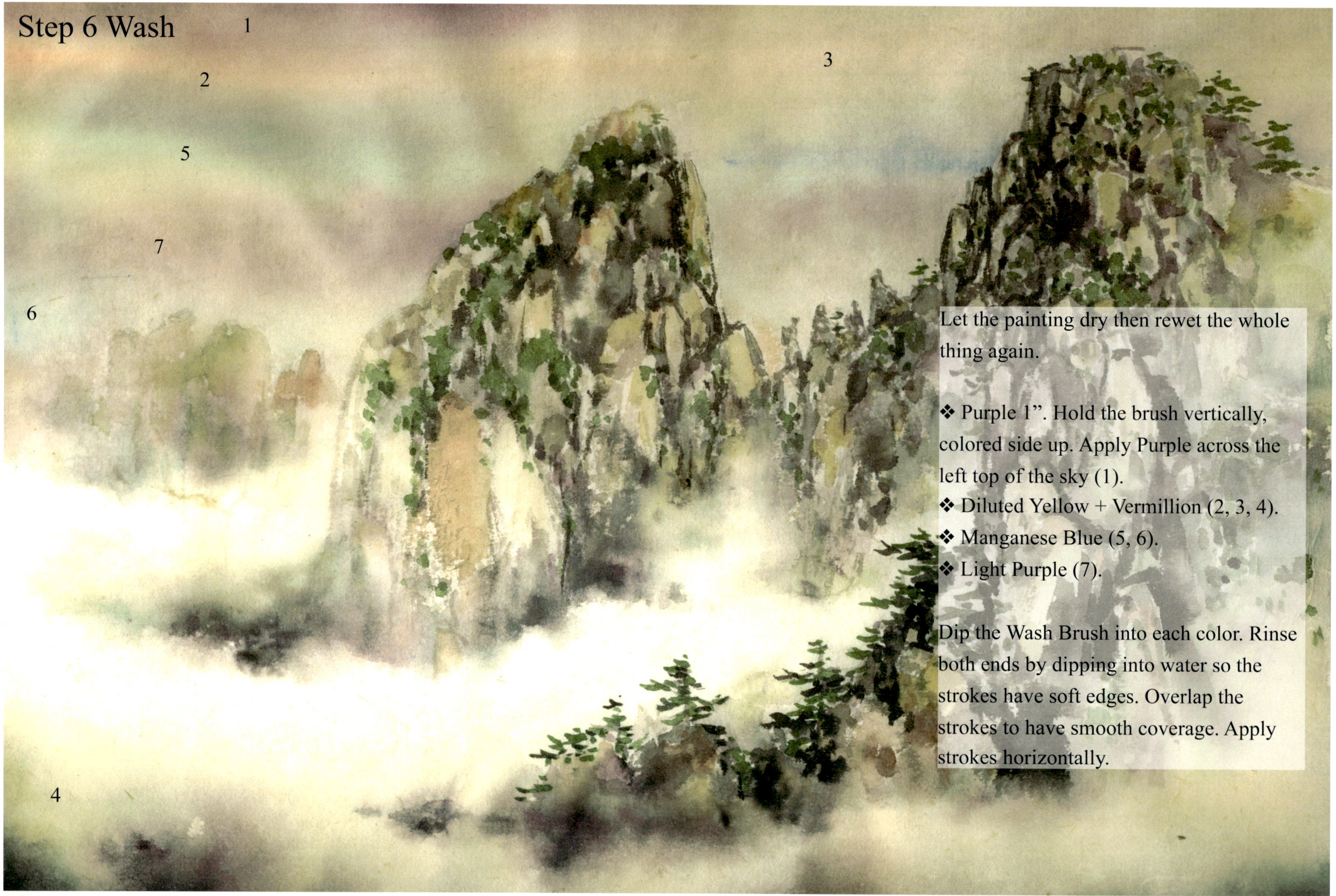

Let the painting dry then rewet the whole thing again.

❖ Purple 1". Hold the brush vertically, colored side up. Apply Purple across the left top of the sky (1).
❖ Diluted Yellow + Vermillion (2, 3, 4).
❖ Manganese Blue (5, 6).
❖ Light Purple (7).

Dip the Wash Brush into each color. Rinse both ends by dipping into water so the strokes have soft edges. Overlap the strokes to have smooth coverage. Apply strokes horizontally.

Lesson 10: Silk Road

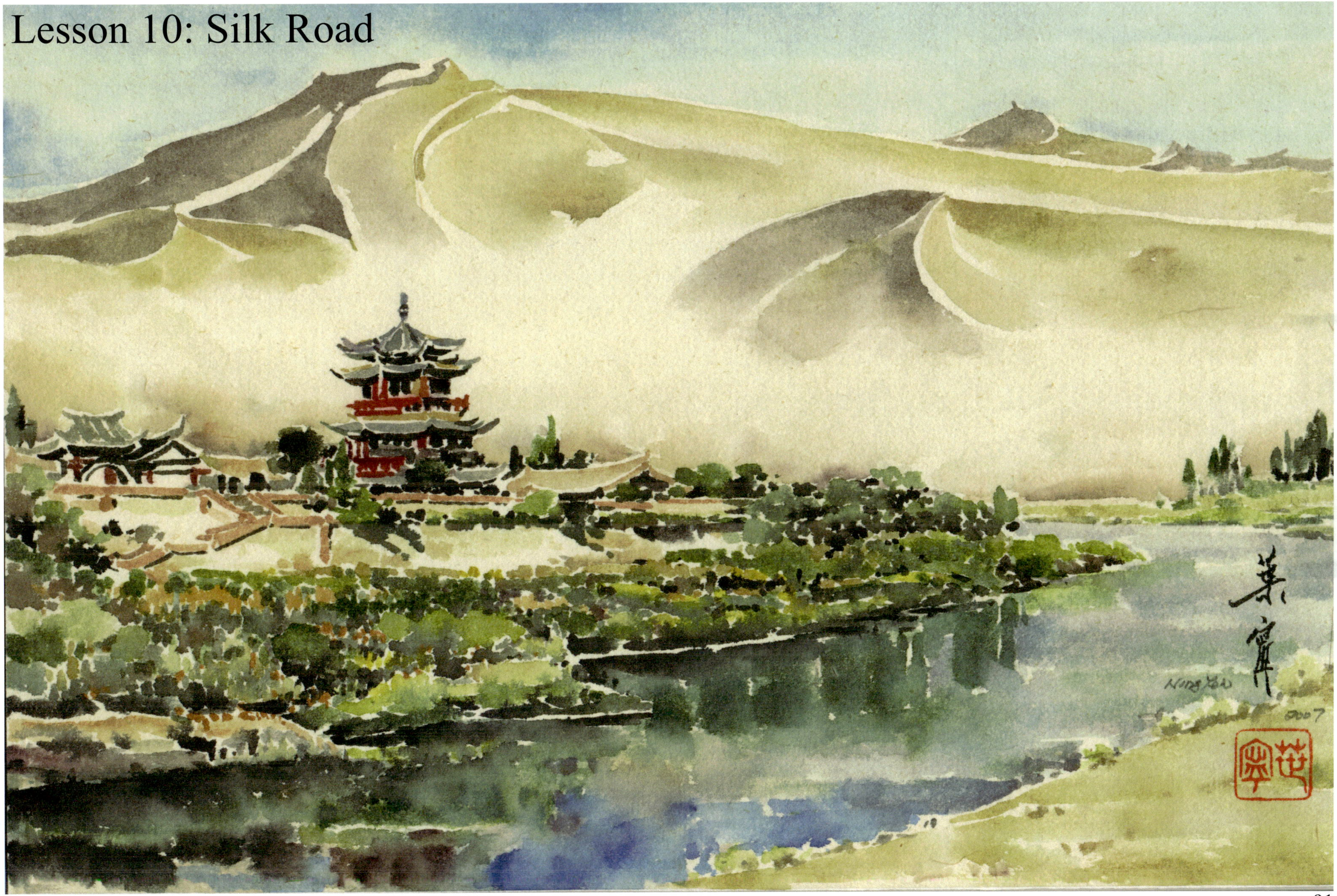

Lesson 10: Silk Road

The "Silk Road"— what an enchanting, splendid, and exquisite name, filled with mystic romanticism. This glorious road linked ancient China with India and Rome. Since the Han Dynasty (206 BC to 221 AD), Chinese traders exchanged silk for gold with the Romans.

I traveled along this ancient road twice. The journeys took place in 1999 and 2000. We flew to the eastern end of the Silk Road, Dunhuang, the most important oasis along the corridor west of the Yellow River.

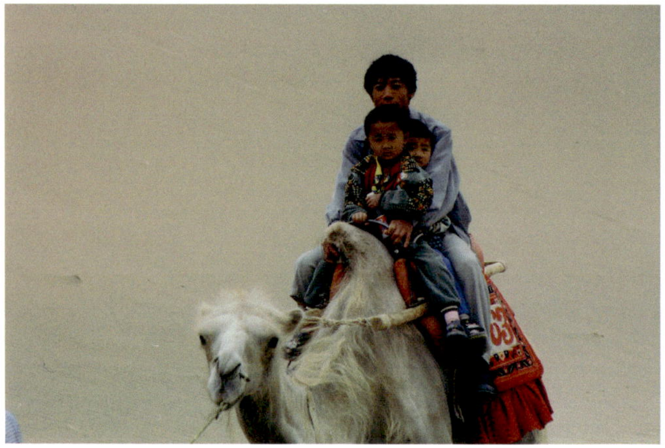

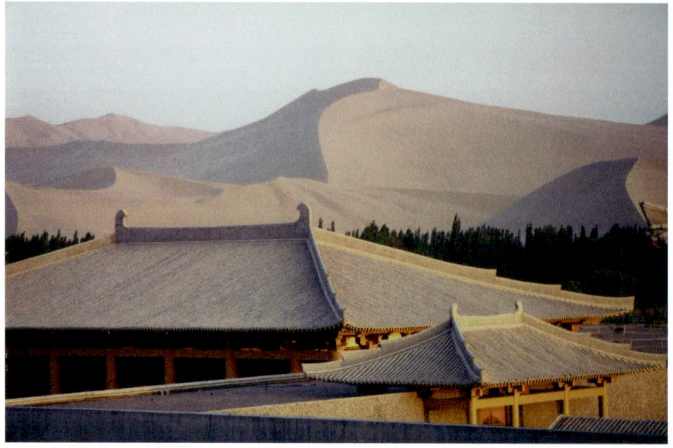

Dunhuang is much more than the name of a city. For Chinese, it symbolizes a treasure of past glory and the vitality of "East meets West." Dunhuang offers a complete record of Chinese art.

We visited the Mogao Grottoes. It was here that Chinese traders commissioned artists to paint or carve the temple caves from steep cliffs to bless their journey or to celebrate their successful return. It is the most fabulous artistic oasis preserving world-renowned treasures dating back 1,500 years.

Nowhere could one study art in its full 1,500 year glory at one location as completely as here. One could go into a cave then go to the next one housing works done 1,000 years earlier. And this is not a museum where things are brought for display. This is where the artists lived and worked on site.

We stayed at the Silk Road Dunhuang Hotel, a grand castle-styled palace by the Whispering Sand Dune (Mingsha Hill). The Creator did a masterful job in carving the shape of this cluster of sand dunes. We rode a camel caravan up the Whispering Sand. We reached the pagoda by Crescent Moon Lake.

Can you imagine what joy it was for those ancient travelers to see this beautiful lake in the middle of the desert?

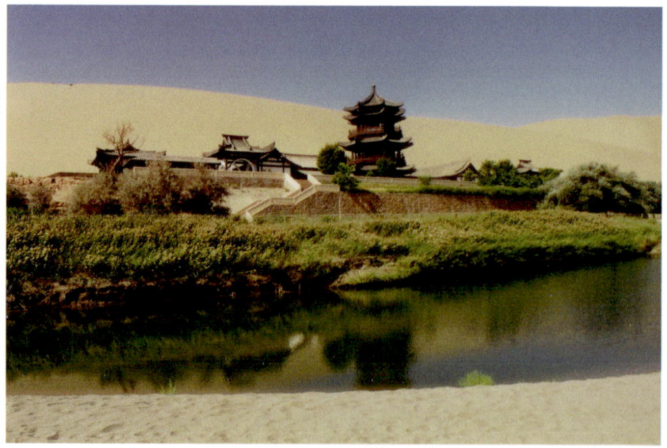

Step 1 Draft

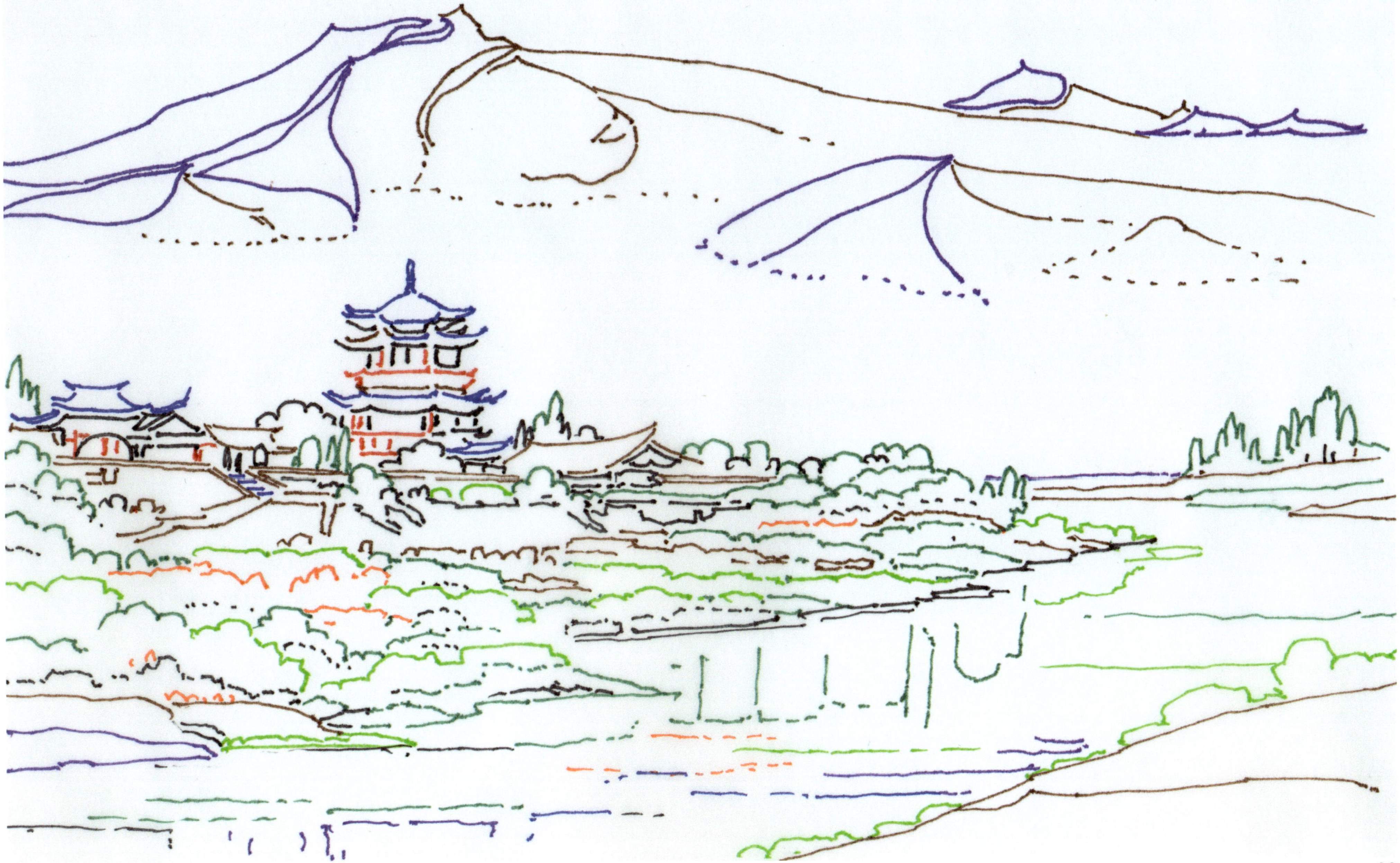

Step 2 Sand Dunes

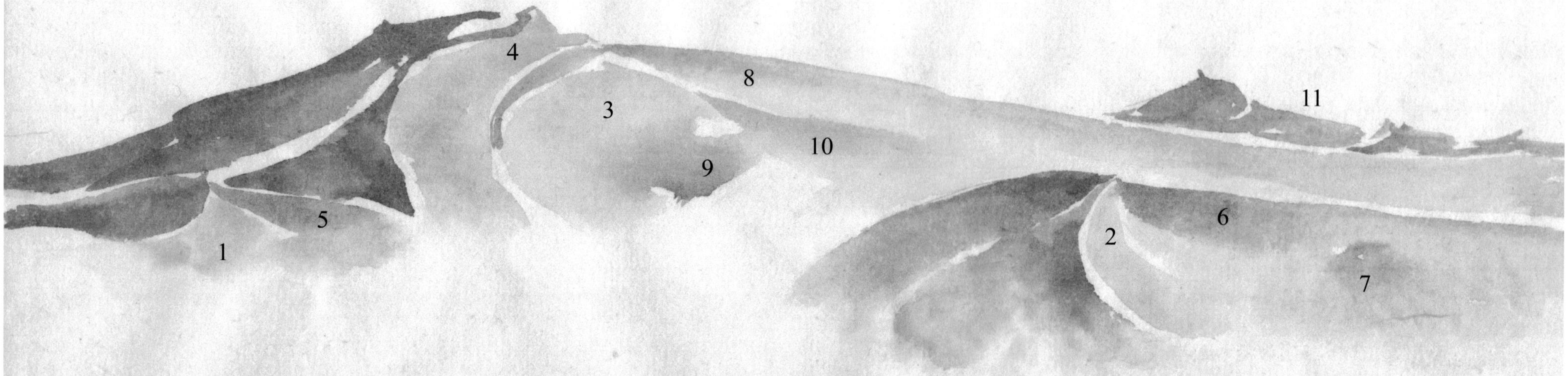

♌ Flow, ↖ tilt and press, fading colors at the base of the hills.

❖ Ochre, do the light areas in the center of the hills (1-4).

❖ Ochre + Beige, do the medium colored areas (5-11) on the right side of the hills.

❖ Ochre + Beige + Light Purple, do the shadow side. Accent some areas with Purple.

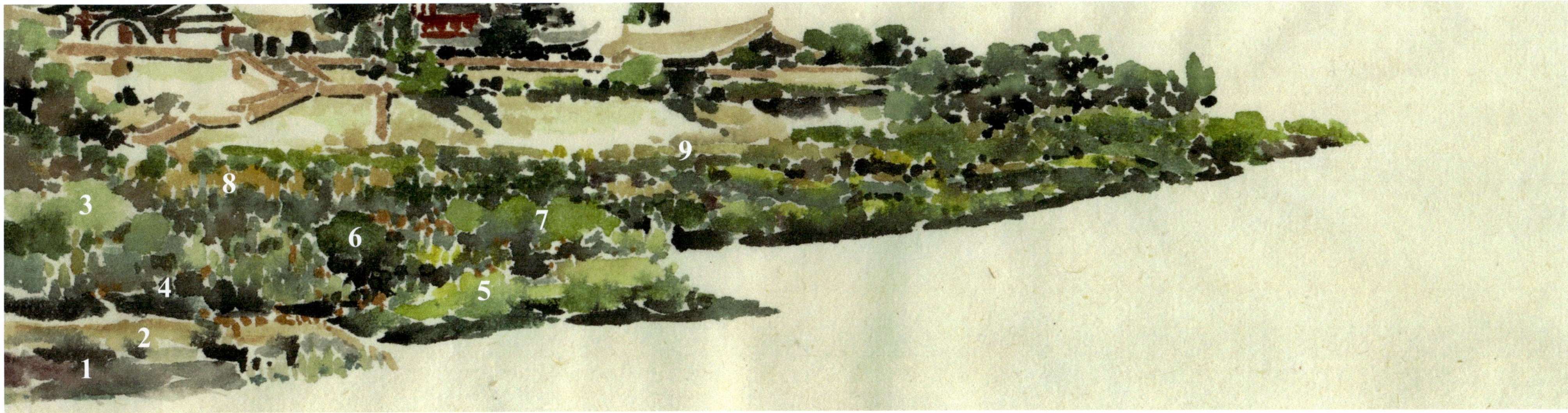

Step 3 Banks

ᔕ Flow, ↖ tilt and press to do the lower banks first with foliage dots on top. Use the following colors: ❖ Light Purple + diluted Shade (1); ❖ Diluted Ochre + Beige (2); ❖ White Green (3); ❖ Shade (4); ❖ Yellow mixed with Light Green (5); ❖ Green (6); ❖ Light Green (7); ❖ Ochre + Vermillion (8); ❖ Ochre + Light Green (9). ❖ Shade + Ink, work shadows with the brush tip pointing down, moving sideways. Occasionally, leave hairline spaces between the horizontal layers of foliage. Continue this technique to complete the bank areas tapering to a point on the right. The diagram below identifies some of the color locations.

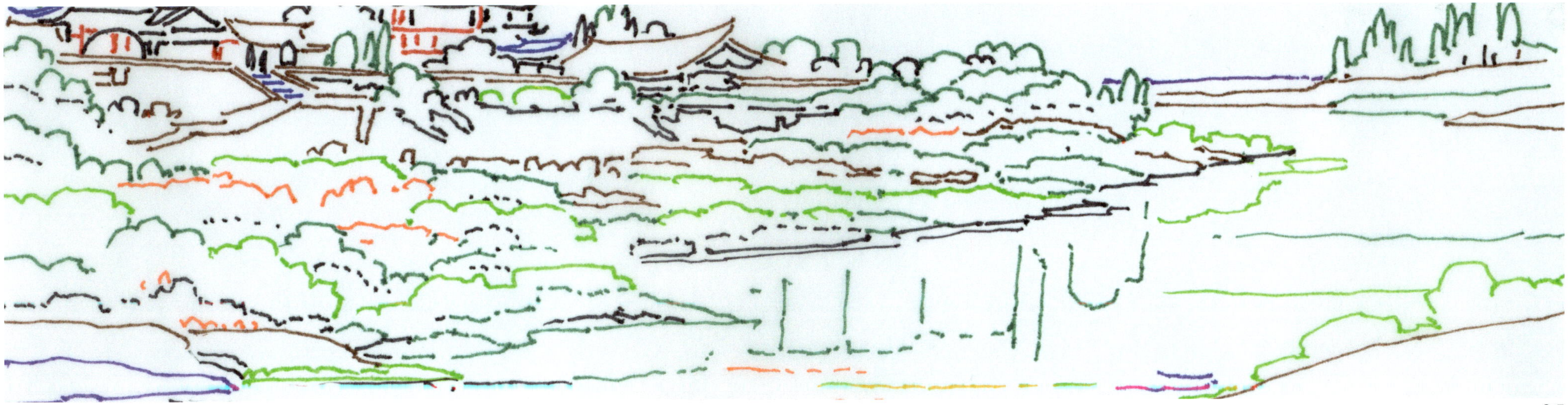

Step 4 Buildings

ꩭ Flow. **Foreground Elements (A-D):** ❖ Vermilion, do the wall railings (A). ❖ Ink, add shadows below the railings. ❖ Light Green, Green, Shade, and Ink, place foliage between the layers of walls (B). ❖ Ochre, color the walls (C). ❖ Light Green, Green, Shade and Ink, add trees above the walls (D). **Main Structures (E, F):** ❖ Diluted Manganese mixed with Light Ink, do the roofs (m). ❖ Vermillion, Red, Dark Red, and Ink, do the railings and poles (r). ❖ Ink, do the shadow areas (i). ❖ Ochre, Beige, show bright spots. **Supporting Structures (G, H, I):** ❖ Ochre, do the roofs (o). ❖ Ink, add shadows (i). ❖ Light Green, Green, Shade, and Ink, add trees.

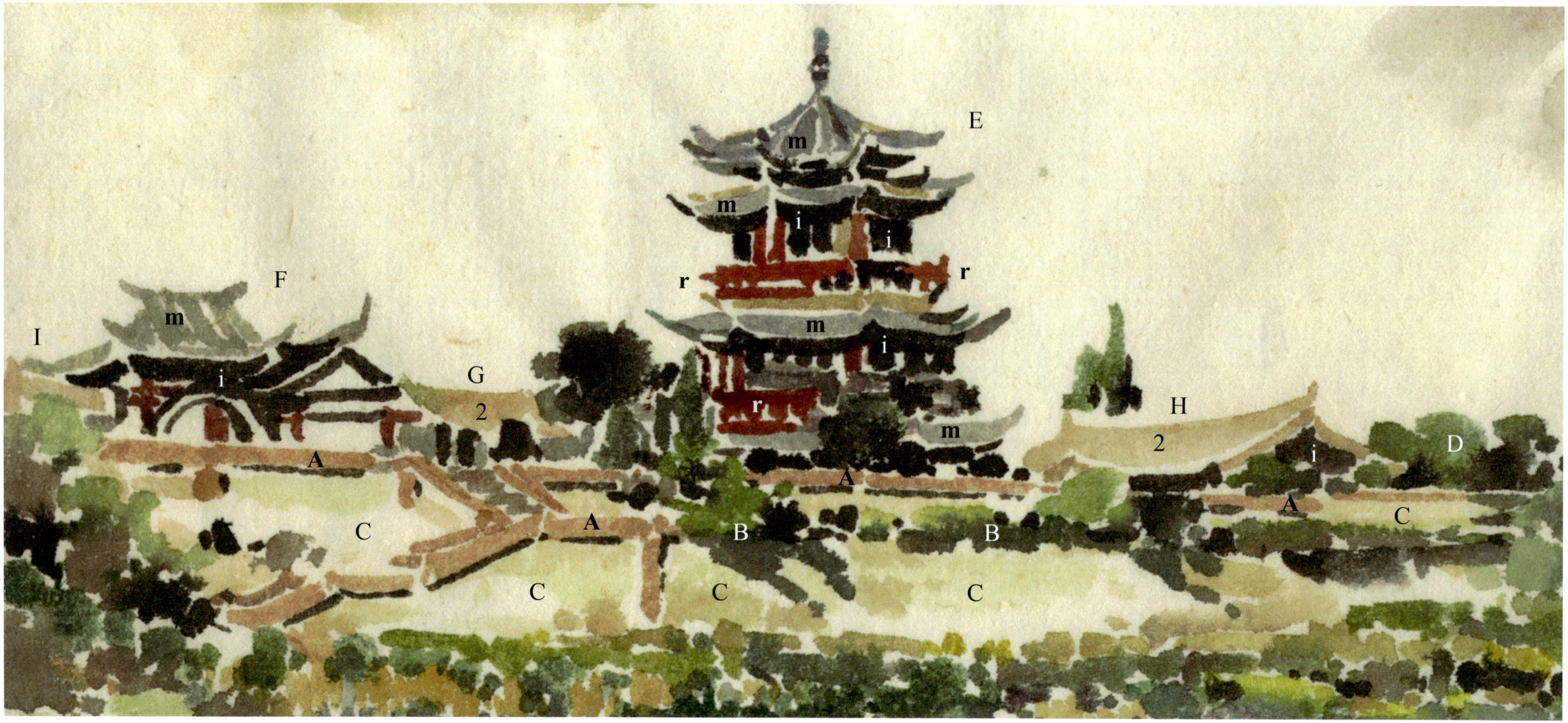

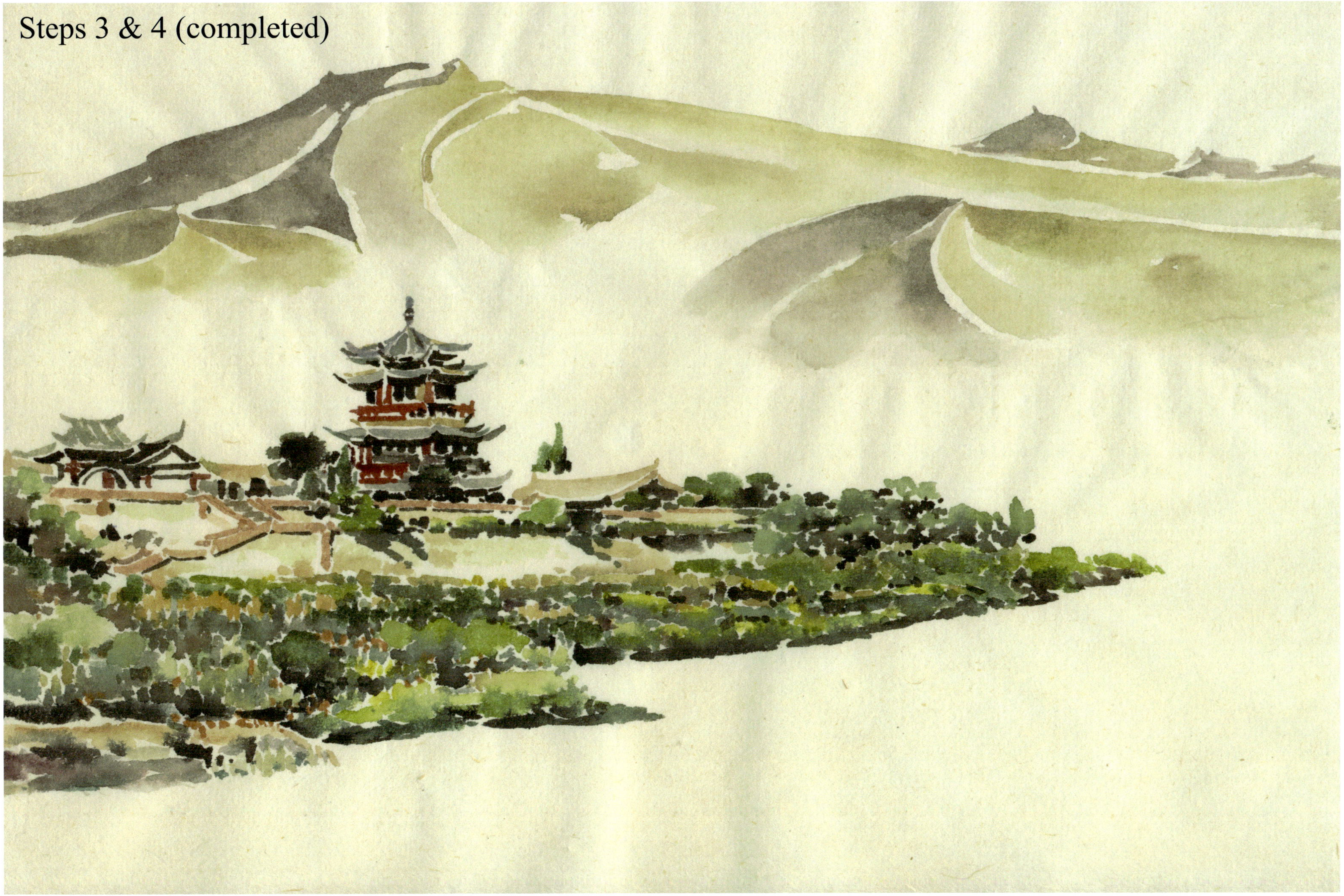

Steps 3 & 4 (completed)

Step 5 Lake

Banks (1-6): ♌ Flow, ❖ Ochre, work the bank in the front (1,2). ❖ Tip Beige, add shadows to show layers. ❖ Yellow + Light Green, do small bushes on top (3). ❖ Dark Green + Shade, add shade below (3). ❖ Ochre, work the bank in the distance (4), ❖ Tip Light Green, work the distant bank on the right (5). ❖ Shade, use along the base (6). ❖ Green + Shade, add trees. ❖ Ink, show shadows.

Lake (7-17): ❖ Shade, apply below the left bank (7). ❖ Mix Sky Blue and Shade to create a Jade Green, apply across the lower left area of the lake (8), and work vertical blocks (9). ❖ Shade, apply at the lower left corner (10). ❖ Purple, show the reflection in line with the tall structure (11). ❖ Mix Manganese with Sky Blue into a Bright Blue, apply to the lower right side of the lake (12). ❖ Dilute the Bright Blue and add Light Purple, apply to the adjacent area (13). ❖ Add White Green, work the remaining areas (14-17). We have a beautiful lake with multiple bright colors and shadows. Keep hairline spaces between the lake and the shores. Leave some space between horizontal strokes in the lake. Work fast to allow everything to blend together.

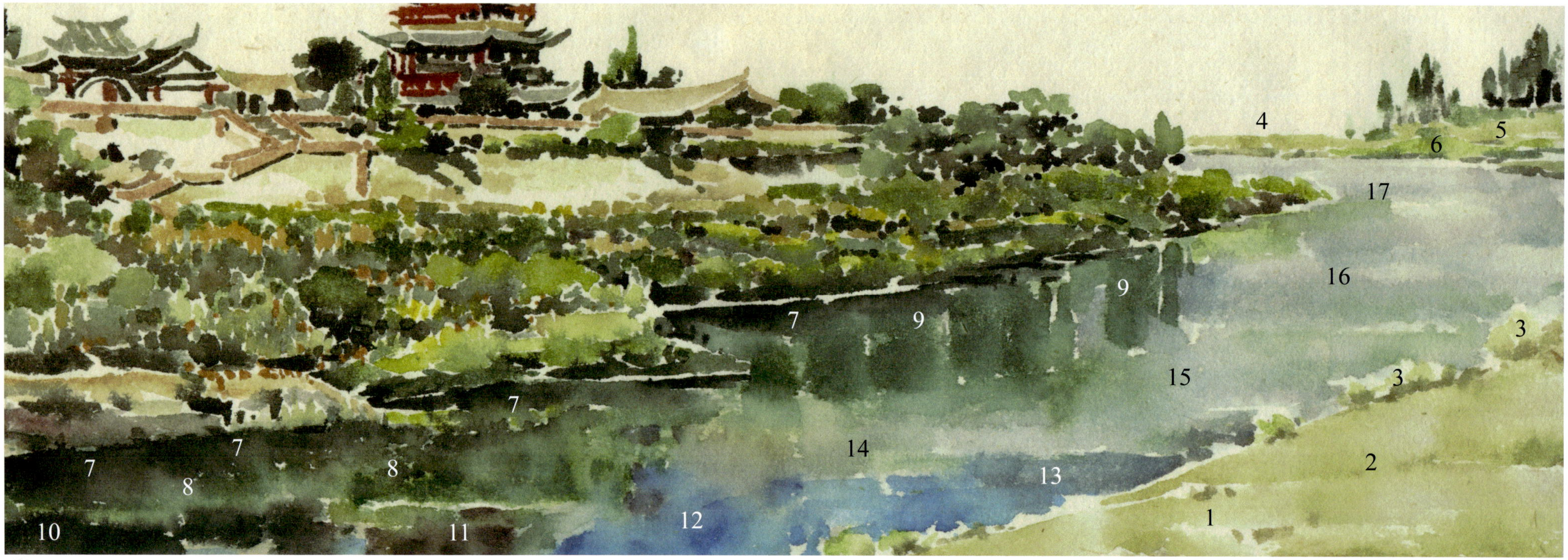

Step 6 Sky

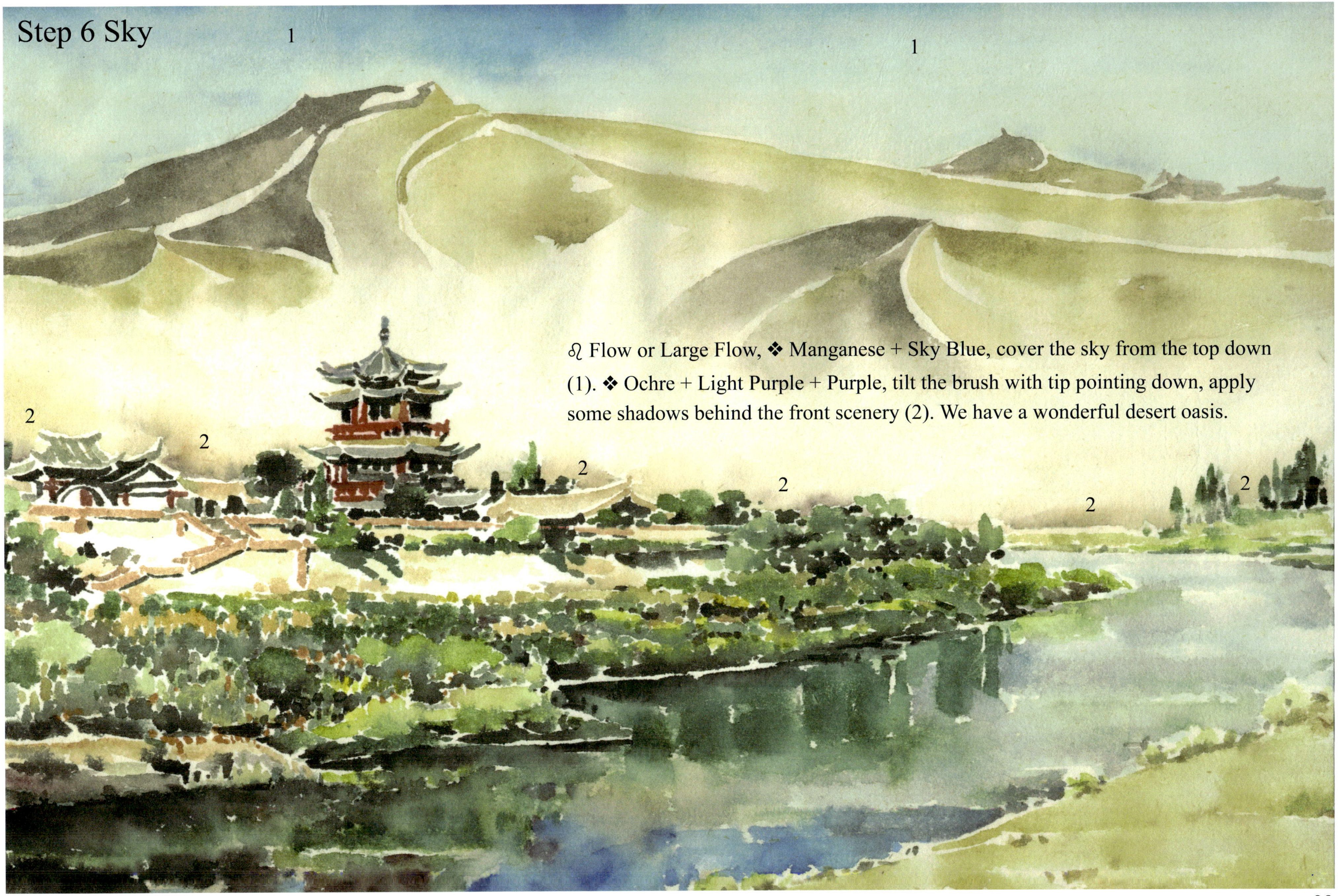

ℓ Flow or Large Flow, ❖ Manganese + Sky Blue, cover the sky from the top down (1). ❖ Ochre + Light Purple + Purple, tilt the brush with tip pointing down, apply some shadows behind the front scenery (2). We have a wonderful desert oasis.

Lesson 11: Cypress and Waterfalls

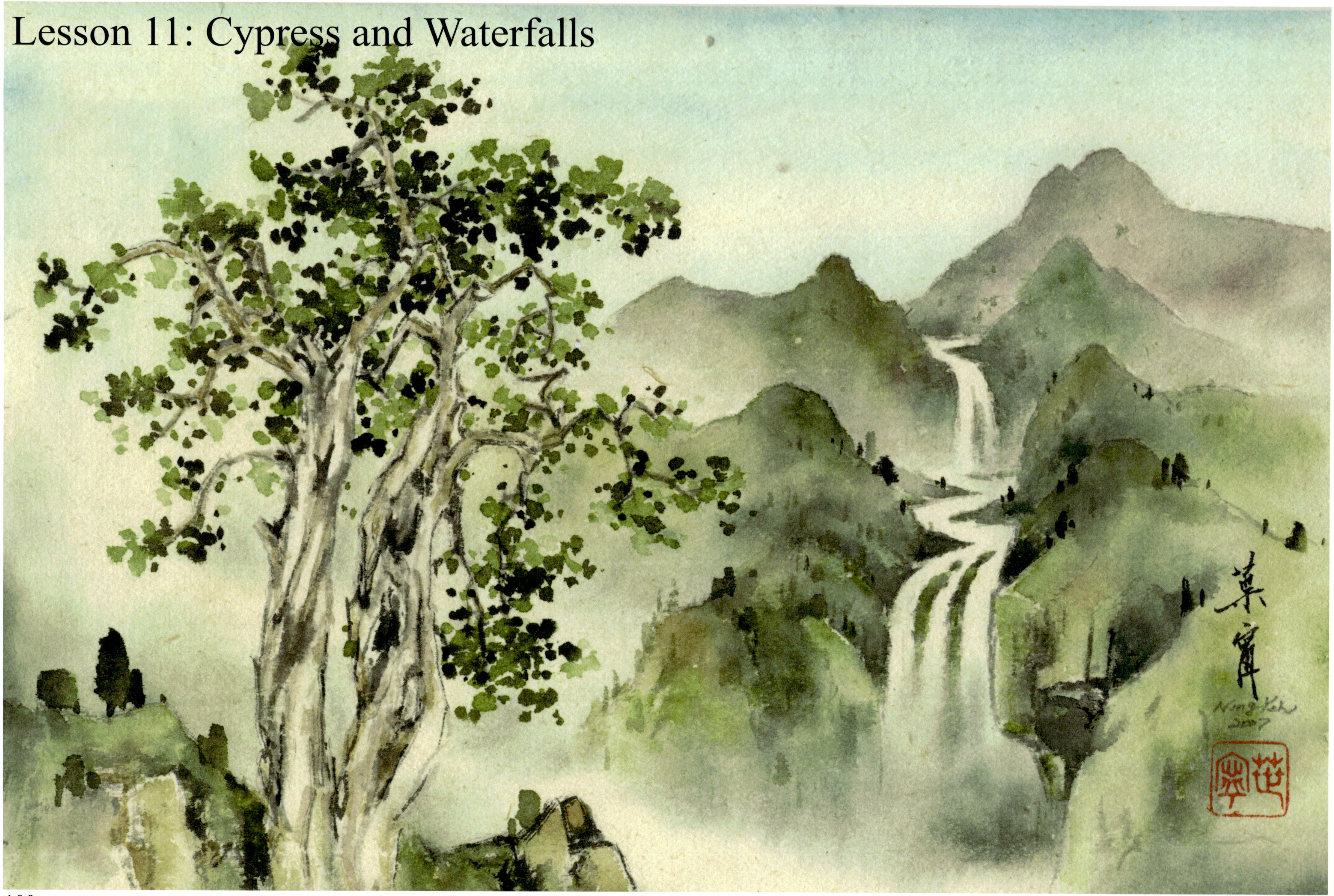

Lesson 11: Cypress and Waterfalls

Pine and cypress are the most honored trees in China. They represent the spirit of Dragon with their twisted bodies and their dancing branches waving like claws. They are symbols of nobility and longevity.

Many temples in north China house cypress trees dating back thousands of years. These trees were originally planted on holy sites. Remarkably, people have maintained these temples and trees for generations.

In a private academy in Shanxi, a giant cypress has a big hole that can allow five people inside. According to historical accounts, the hole occurred during the Han Dynasty.

The second Han emperor visited the academy. He was greatly impressed by the first cypress that he saw. He gave the tree the title of "Top General." As he turned the corner, he noticed another cypress that was even taller and fuller. Being the emperor, he could not go back on his word. He could only give the second tree the title of "Lieutenant General." The taller tree could not swallow such injustice. He was so angry that he broke open his trunk.

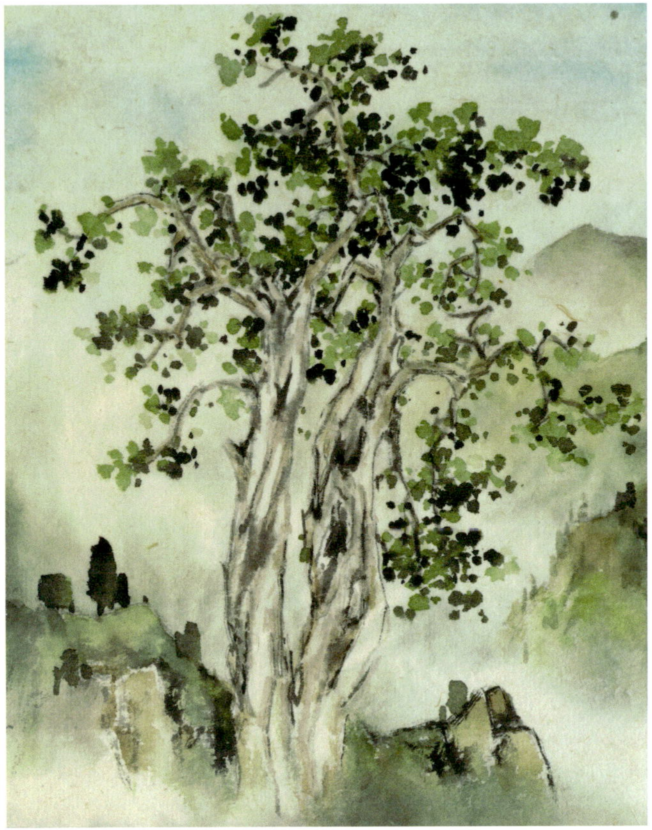

This lesson was done before my first trip to Shanxi. I will visit the tall cypress and do a portrait of him to show the world.

This lesson really consists of two paintings: the trees and the waterfalls. Chinese love two-for-one bargains. Here they are. Enjoy!

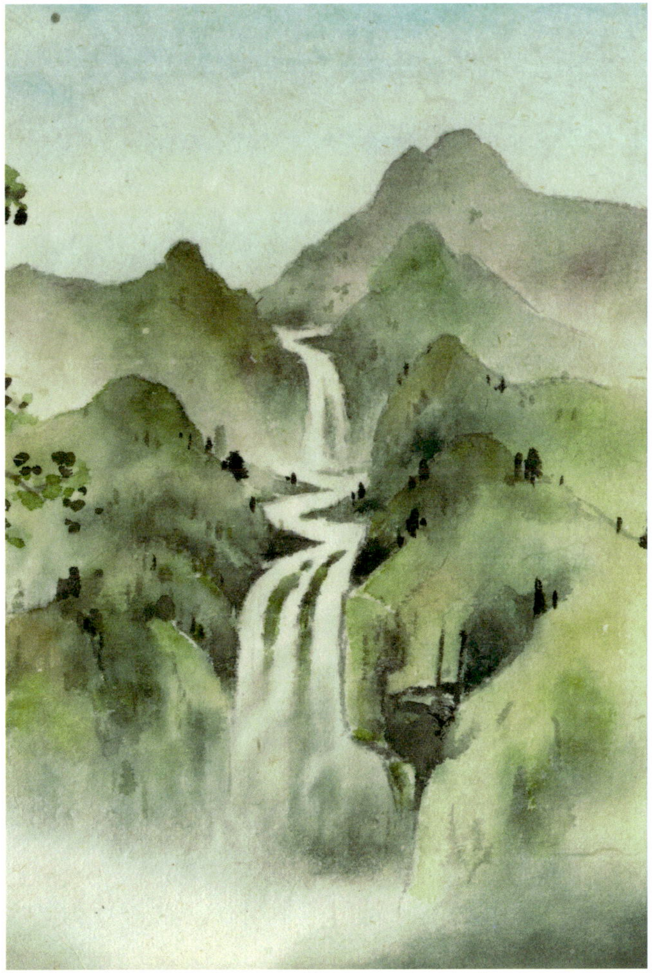

Step 1 Tree Trunks

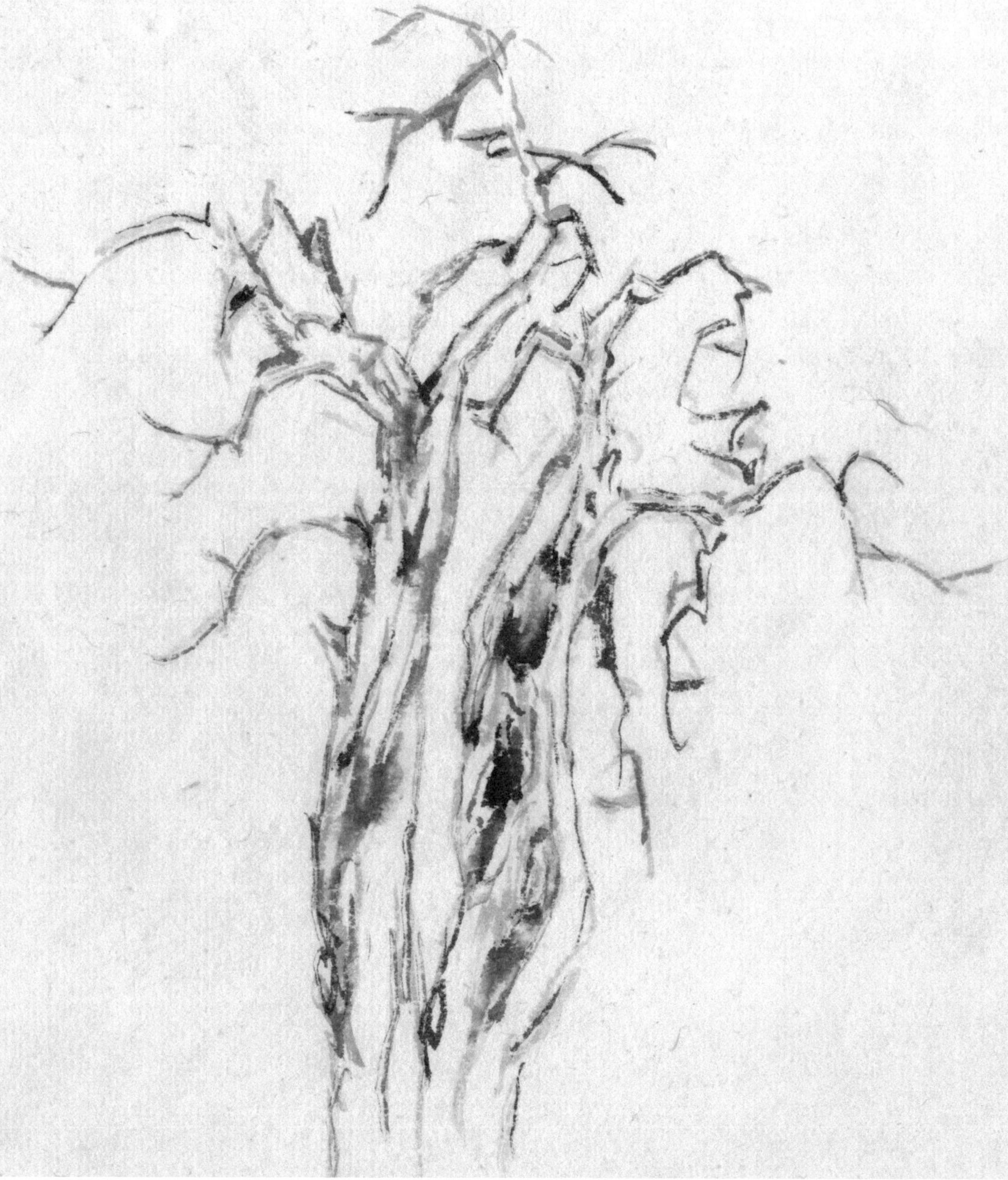

Line and Ink Work:

ᘓ Flow or Mt. Horse, ❖ Light Ink, dry the body of the brush so the lines show texture. Work the trunks first. Start with texture in the middle, then expand out. Add branches.

Cypress trunks have magnificent postures and interesting patterns to show movement. Pay attention to the space between the textures. Picture streams of flowing water, or think of a bodybuilder displaying muscles.

Also, pay attention to the space between the two trunks and among the branches. Make them into interesting shapes. The two trunks are a loving couple. They are rooted together, sharing the same experiences, caring for each other for thousands of years. They are seasoned, yet ageless.

❖ Add Medium and Dark Ink (dry body) to accent the shadow areas while the light ink is still wet.

Step 2 Foliage

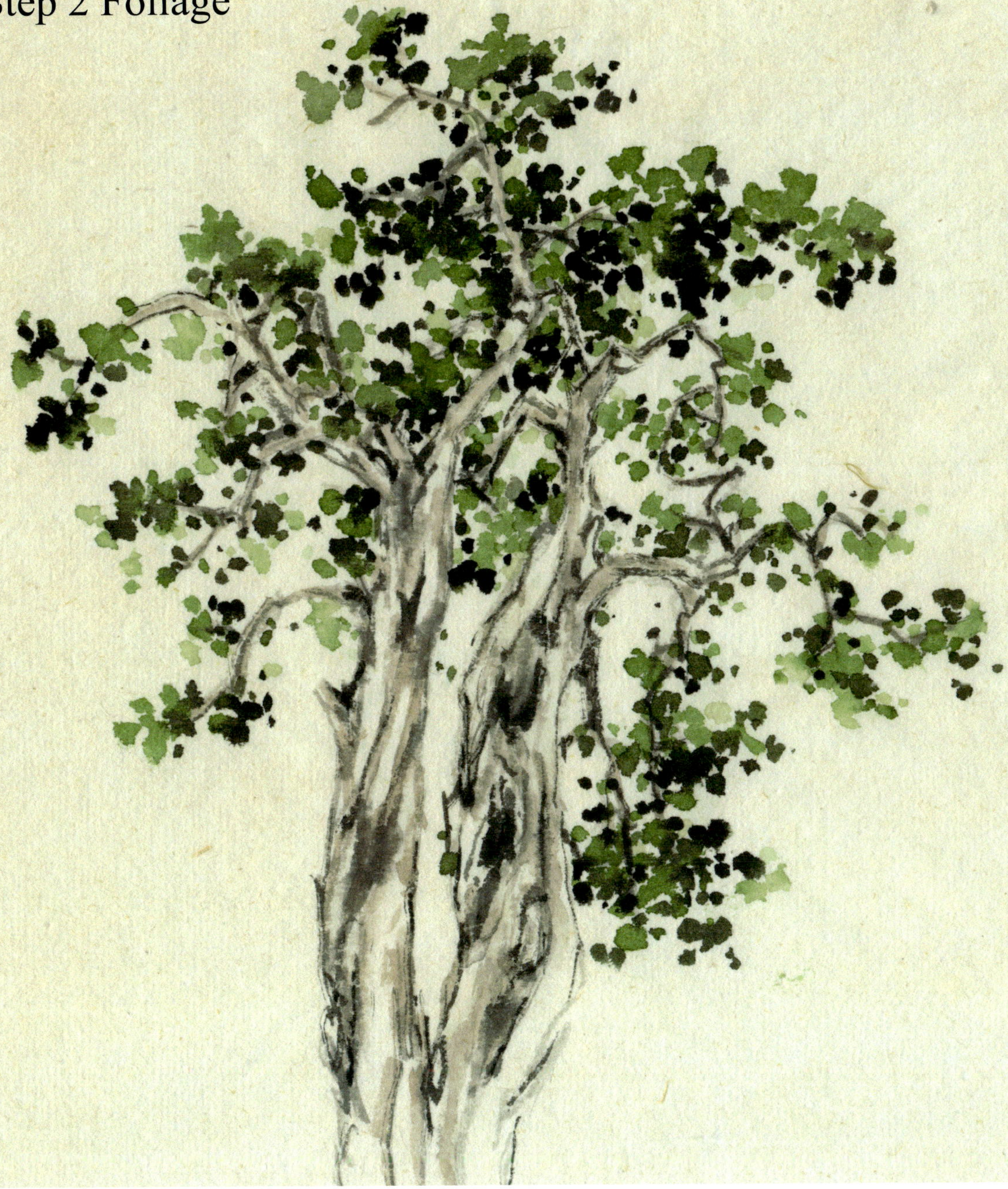

ᘐ Flow, wet tip.

❖ Light Green + Dark Green, do the foliage with overlapping dots.

❖ Shade + Ink, add shadow dots. Apply shadows in the lower areas of the foliage clusters and near the trunks.

❖ White Green + Light Green, show foliage dots in the back and outreaching points in each direction.

Make the overall contour of the foliage go in and out. Do not stuff the middle. Show host and guest, continents and islands.

Step 3 Waterfall Line Work

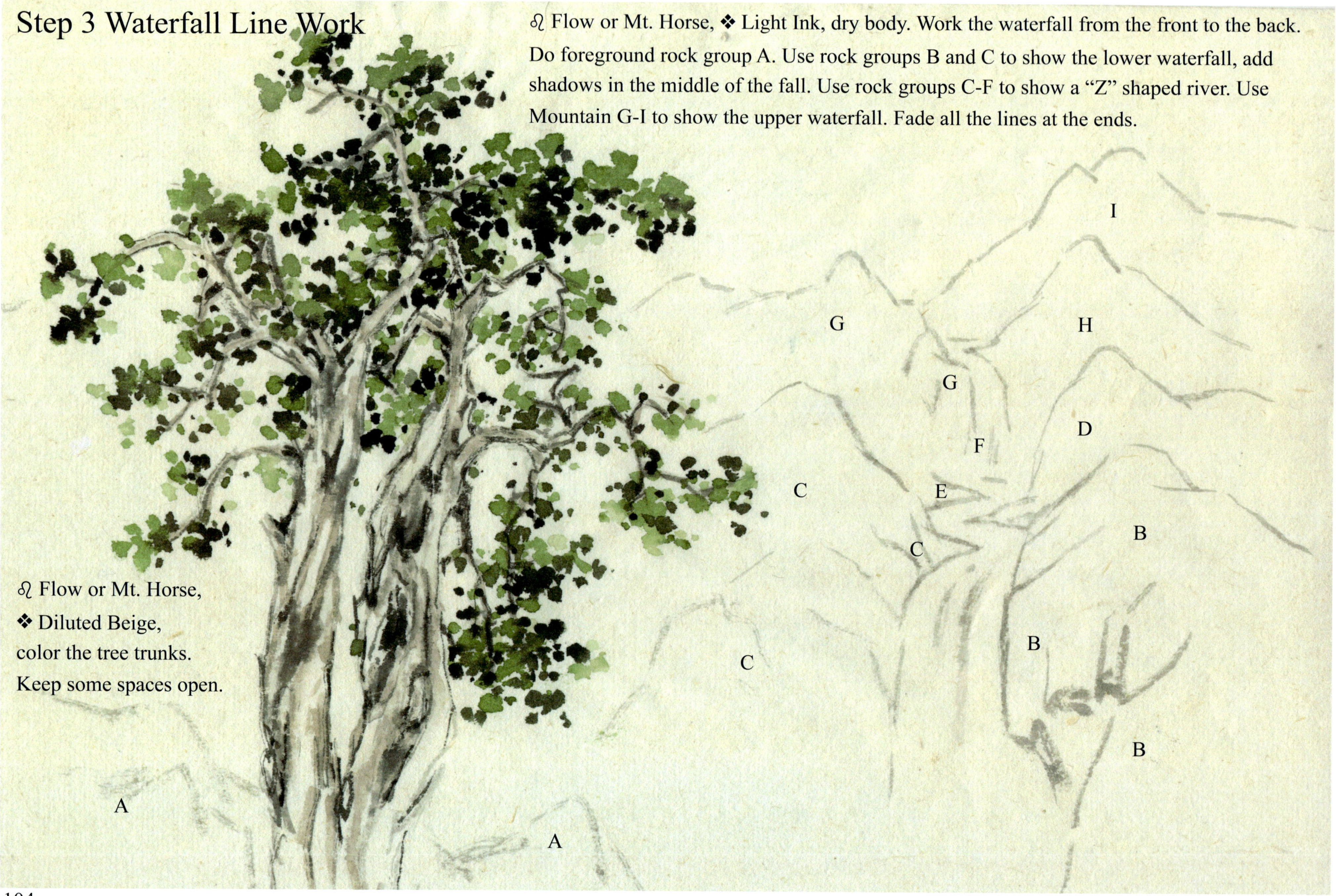

ꝭ Flow or Mt. Horse, ❖ Light Ink, dry body. Work the waterfall from the front to the back. Do foreground rock group A. Use rock groups B and C to show the lower waterfall, add shadows in the middle of the fall. Use rock groups C-F to show a "Z" shaped river. Use Mountain G-I to show the upper waterfall. Fade all the lines at the ends.

ꝭ Flow or Mt. Horse, ❖ Diluted Beige, color the tree trunks. Keep some spaces open.

Step 4 Waterfall Ink Work and Dots

ᘐ Flow or Mt. Horse, ❖ Medium or Dark Ink, dry brush. Darken the lines on the foreground and front rocks of the waterfall, leave the outer ends light.

ᘐ Flow, dry body. ❖ Light Ink, shade the rocks and mountains.

❖ Tip Medium + Dark Ink, accent the shadow areas.

Front areas show more contrast.

Back areas are more integrated.

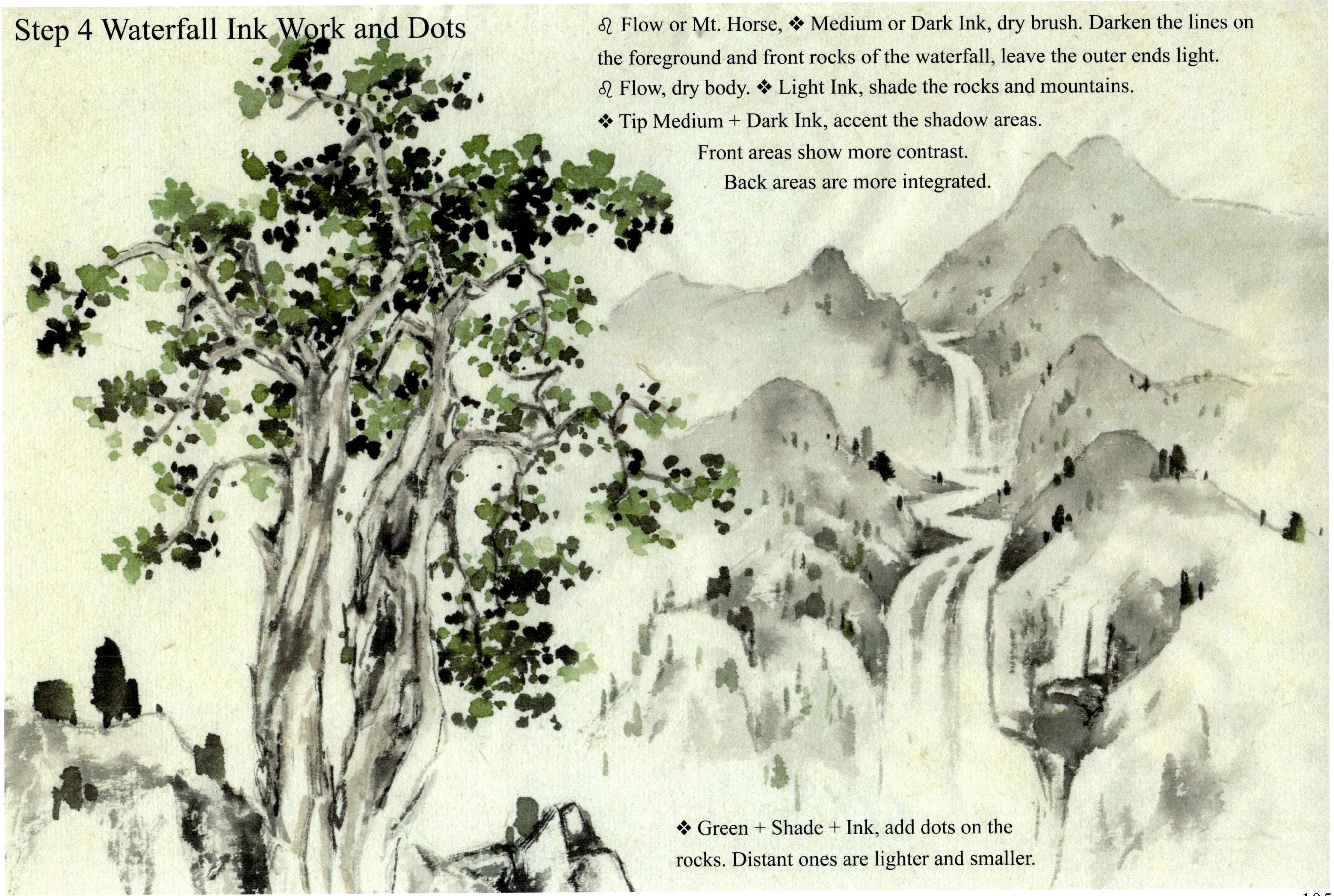

❖ Green + Shade + Ink, add dots on the rocks. Distant ones are lighter and smaller.

Step 5 Coloring

Color code:

O	Ochre
B	Beige
WG	White Green
LG	Light Green
DG	Dark Green
LP	Light Purple
S	Shade

The front scenery has warmer colors (Ochre, Green). The distant scenery has cooler colors (Purple, Blue). Integrate the various colors. Use the principles of "host and guest" and "triangles" to distribute colors. Keep hairline spaces between color areas and borderlines to prevent bleeding. Fade colors and leave room for other colors or mist. Load multiple colors on the brush rather than layering them on the paper.

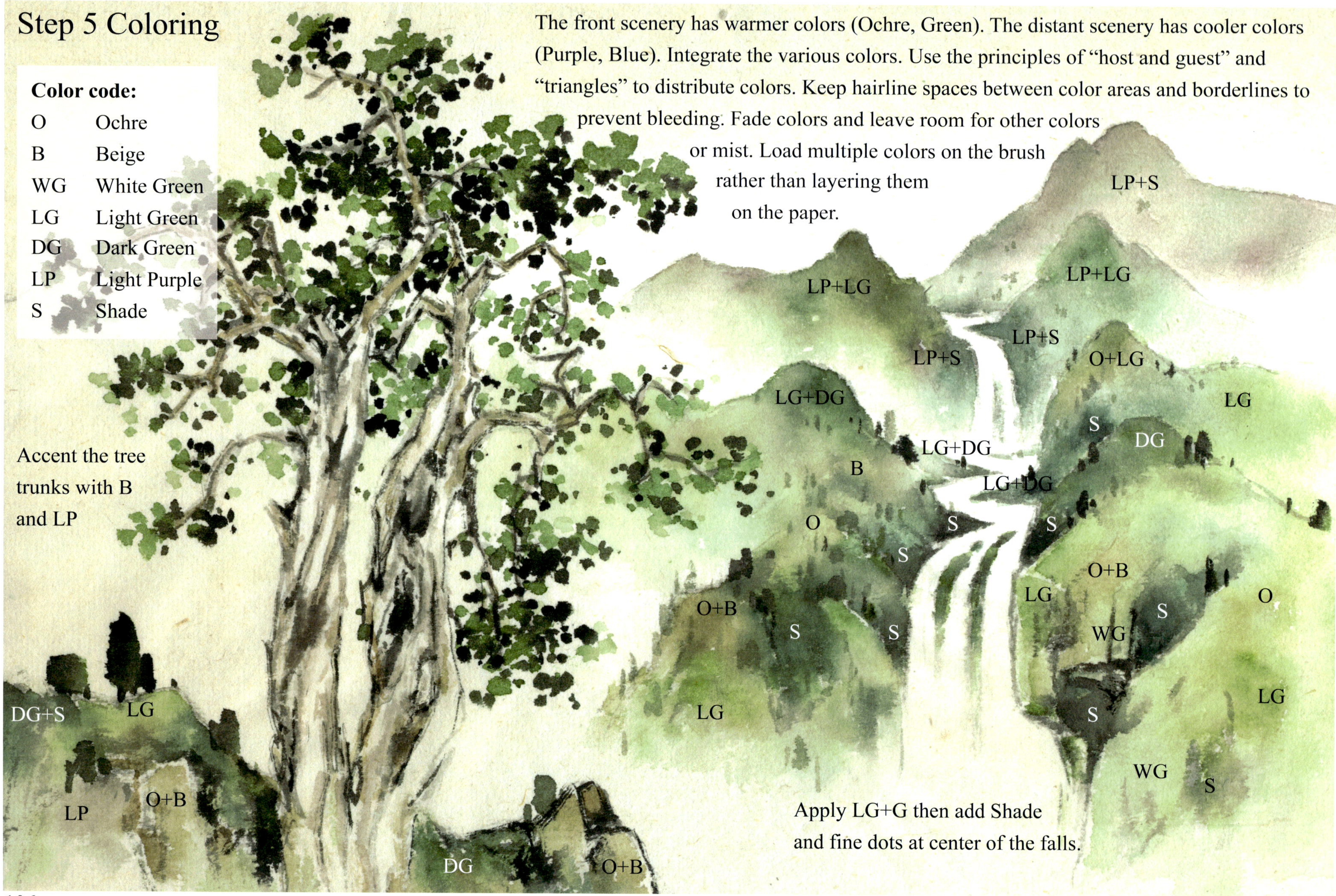

Accent the tree trunks with B and LP

Apply LG+G then add Shade and fine dots at center of the falls.

Step 6 Sky and Mist

When the colors dry, lightly spray/wet the whole painting with water. ♌ Wash Brush, keep the brush body dry. ❖ Load Shade 1/2" on one corner of the brush, blend. Hold the brush vertically, colored corner down. Shade selected areas along the base of the painting (1, 2). Apply shade above the foreground rocks (3).

❖ Manganese Blue 1" on one corner, vertical brush, colored corner up. Apply color across the sky (4).

♌ Flow, ❖ Shade, blend. Tilt the brush with tip pointing down, shade the base of waterfalls, fading upwards (5, 6). Apply light Shade along the base of the mountain to show mist below (7, 8).

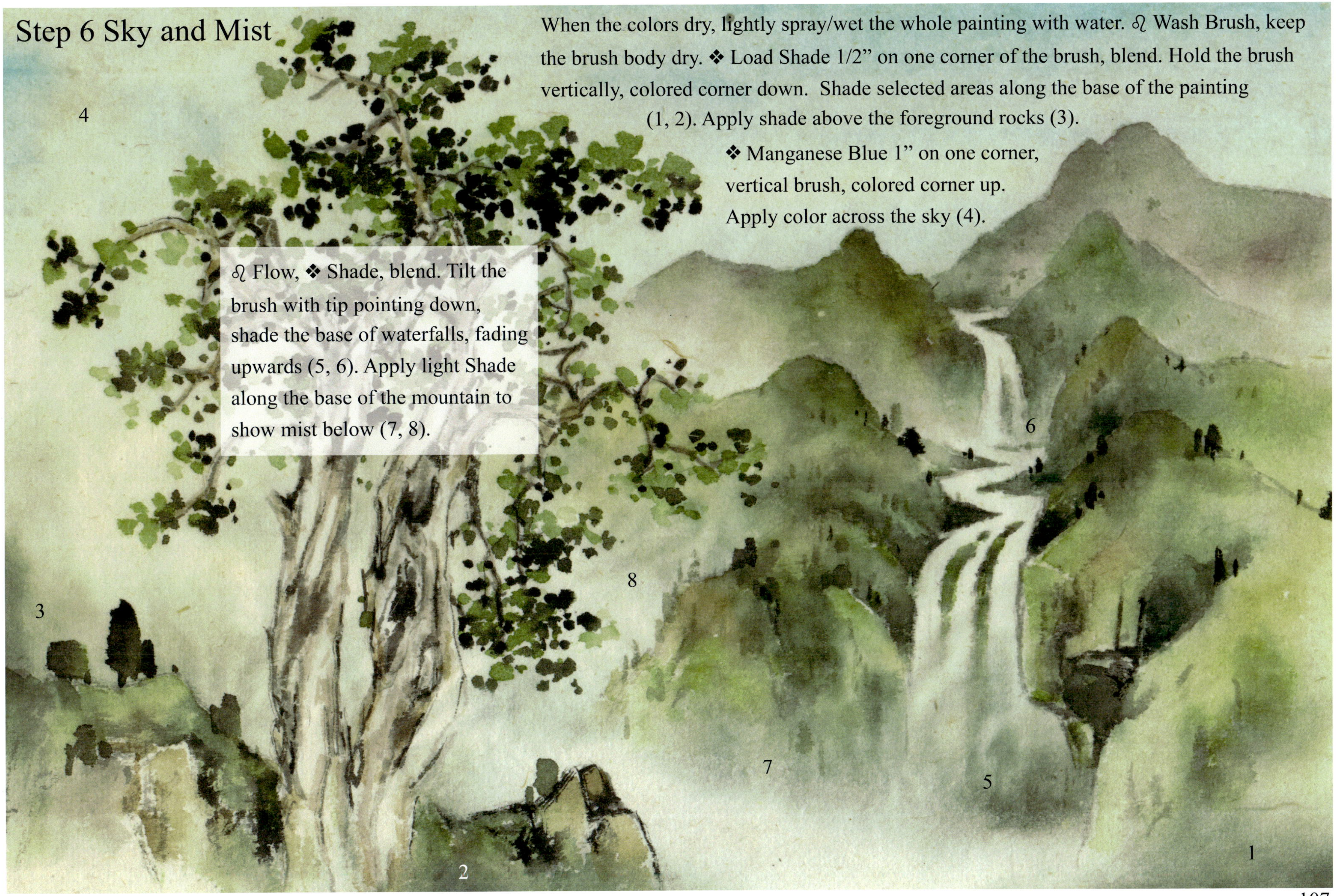

Lesson 12: Sunrise

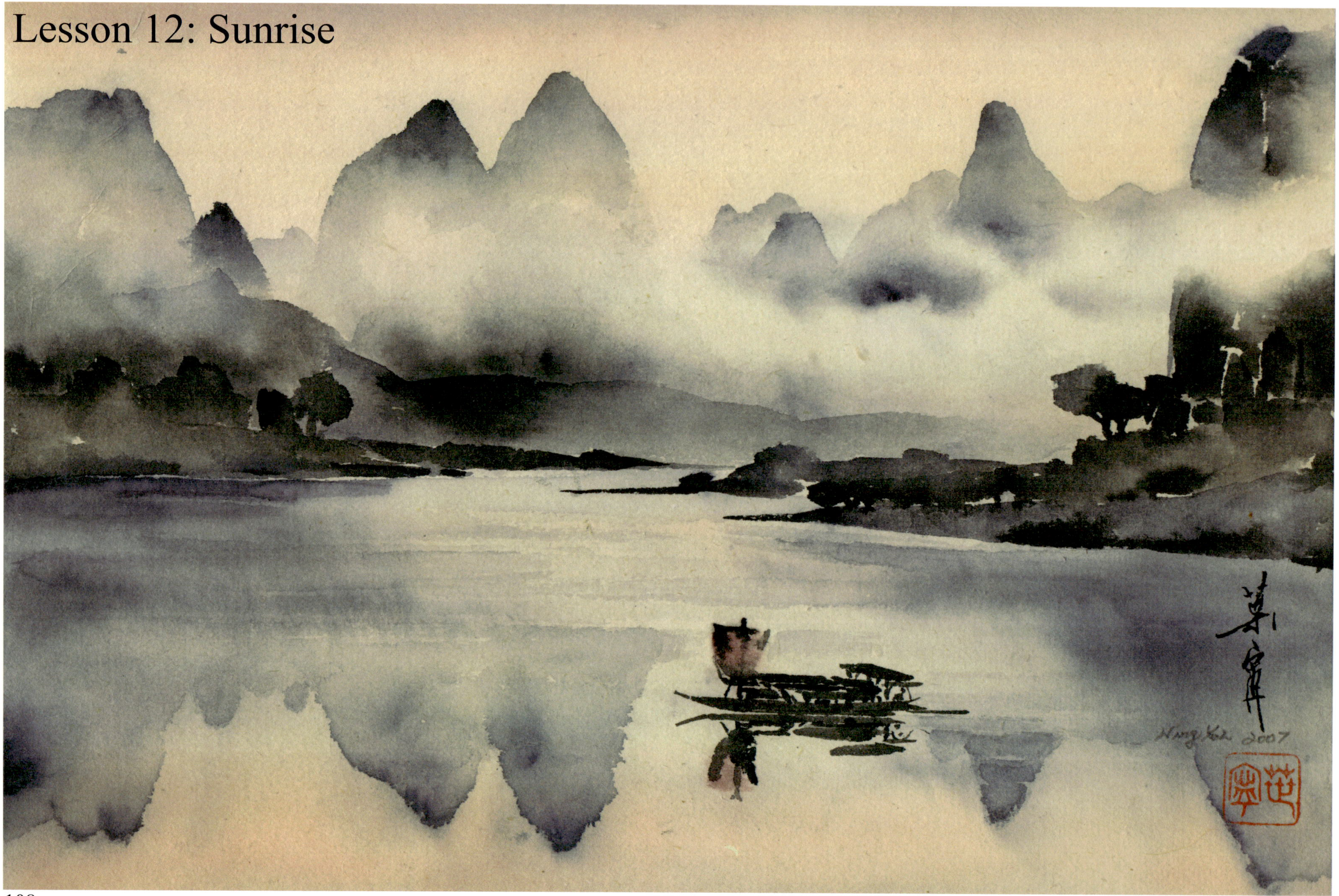

Lesson 12: Sunrise

How is it possible to enjoy the scenery before our eyes knowing full well that magnificent scenery also exists behind us? Indeed, there are two occasions in China where one wishes to have more than one pair of eyes. The first is on Yellow Mountain when the mist is rising. The second is on board the Li River Cruise.

The four hour Li River Cruise runs from Guilin to Yangshuo. I do not know of any other place where one could enjoy such panoramic views of spectacular peaks embracing calm, jade-like water. Every turn brings a beautiful composition. There is plenty of activity along the river: folks pulling their little boats, ladies washing clothes in

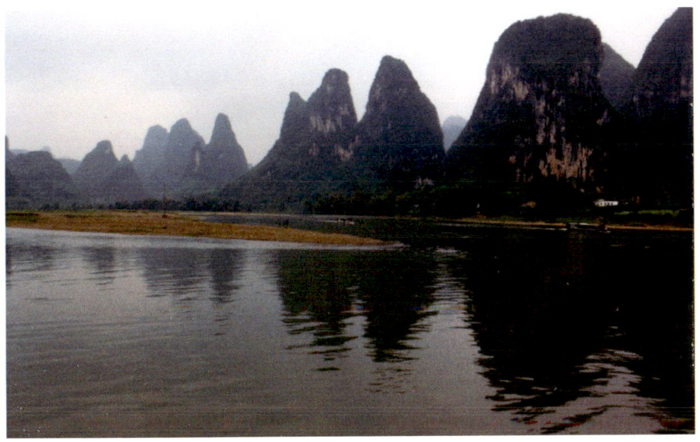

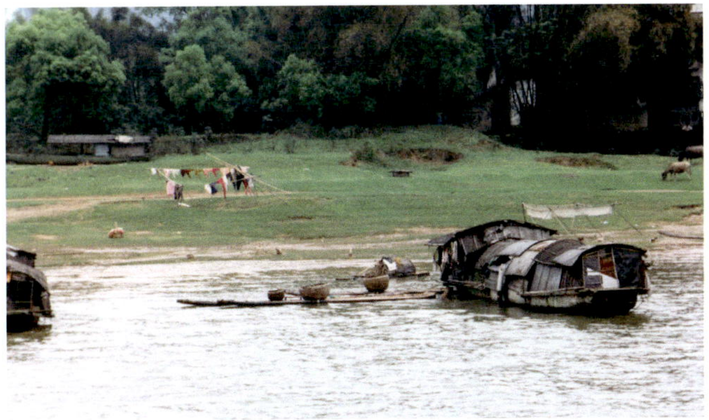

front of their villages, cormorants on their fishing watch, ducks paddling along the riverbanks, playful water buffaloes in huge groups, children waving on their boats to school, luxurious green rice fields by the Phoenix-tail bamboo groves…

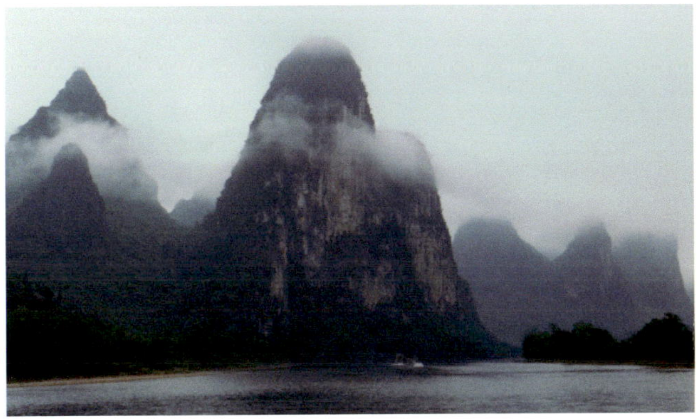

It is a story of living. There is a close kinship between the scenery and people. There is a sense that generations are the children of these mountains and waters.

Any number of scenes can be masterpieces along the river. There is no need to be accurate either. A slight change of angle can alter the composition entirely. We paint our own Guilin mountains.

To watch the sunrise, one needs to get up at 4:00 a.m. The best location is near Xingping, around the mid-point of the river cruise. So far, I have been unable to get my tour members to do this. Years later, they still remember my door pounding.

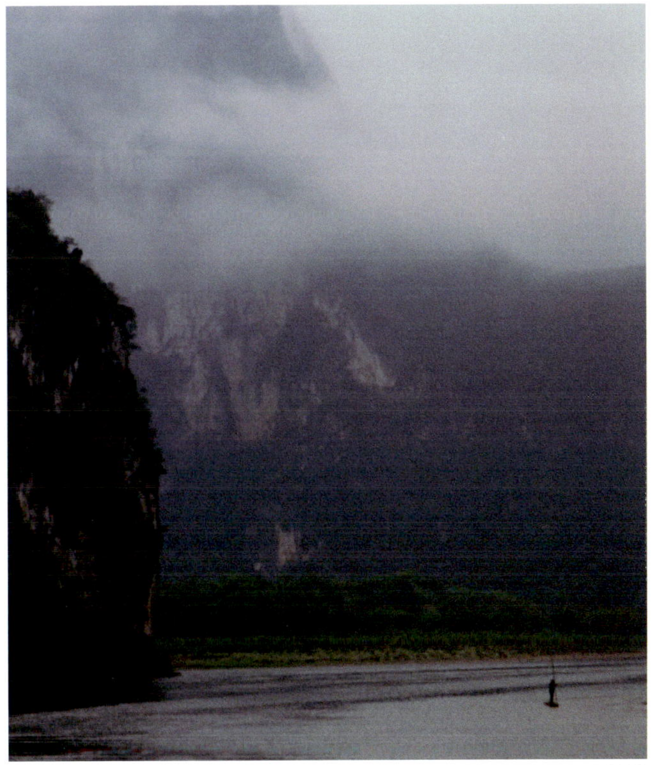

Step 1 Banks and Boat

Prepare Blue Purple by mixing Purple with Indigo and Ink. Alternatively, use Winsor & Newton Neutral Tint.

River Banks: ♌ Flow, ❖ Blue Purple (or Neutral Tint) + Ink, work banks from the tips moving outward. Do bank A. Add foliage dots (a). Accent with Ink. Do bank B. Add foliage dots (b). Accent selected area near the base with Ink. It is desirable to allow elements to bleed into one another to enhance a misty feel. Do bank C. Add foliage dots (c). Accent with Ink. Do bank D.

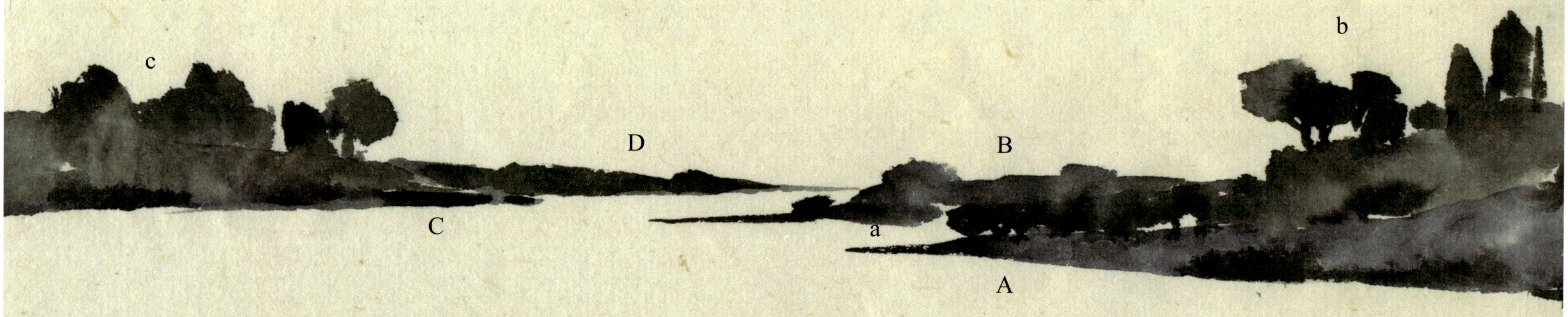

Boat: ♌ Flow, ❖ Blue Purple (or Neutral Tint) + Ink. Use this combination throughout much of the painting. Accenting with Ink. Do the body of the boat (1). Keep the base flat. Add a lady (2). She is preparing breakfast. ❖ Ink, work the cabin roofs, add poles and interior elements (3). ❖ Diluted Vermillion + Dark Red, do the sail. ❖ Ink, accent the sail and show the mast (4). Add the reflections of the boat (5). Leave occasional horizontal spaces.

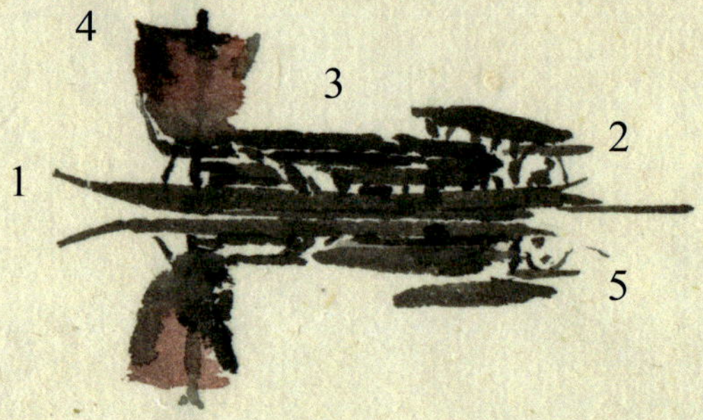

Step 2 Front Mountains

♌ Flow, ❖ Blue Purple (or Neutral Tint), work the top of mountain A. Do the nose area, move downward and fade (a). ❖ Blue Purple (or Neutral Tint) + Ink, work the left side downward and fade (b). Do the top upward off the paper (c). Work the base of the mountain from the bottom and fade upward (d, e).

Work mountain B from the middle, move right and fade, then move left (f). Add the shoulder (g) and tip (h). Move left and fade. ❖ Tip Ink, add shadow from base up (i). Do mountain C and D from the top, fade downward.

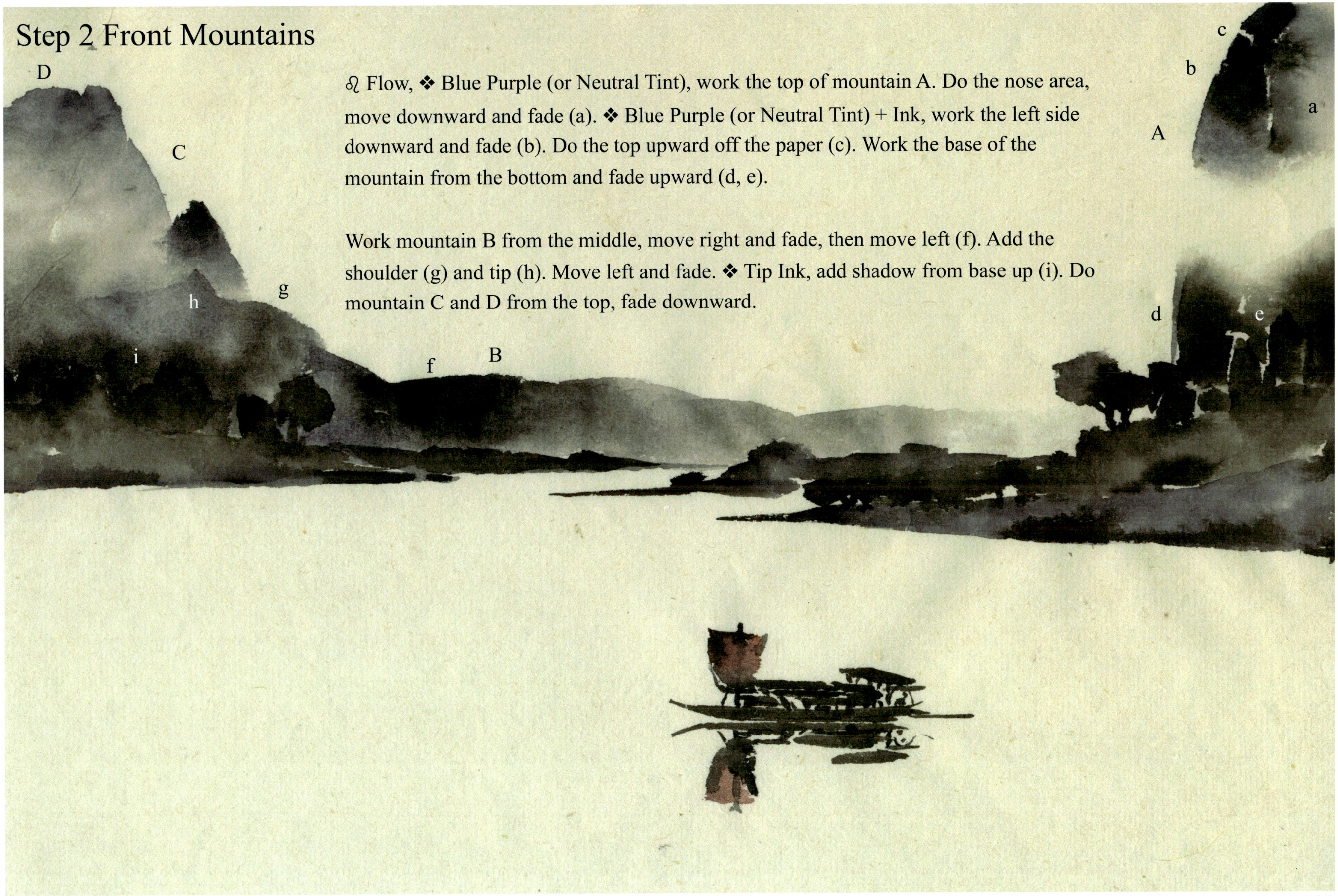

Step 3 Distant Mountains

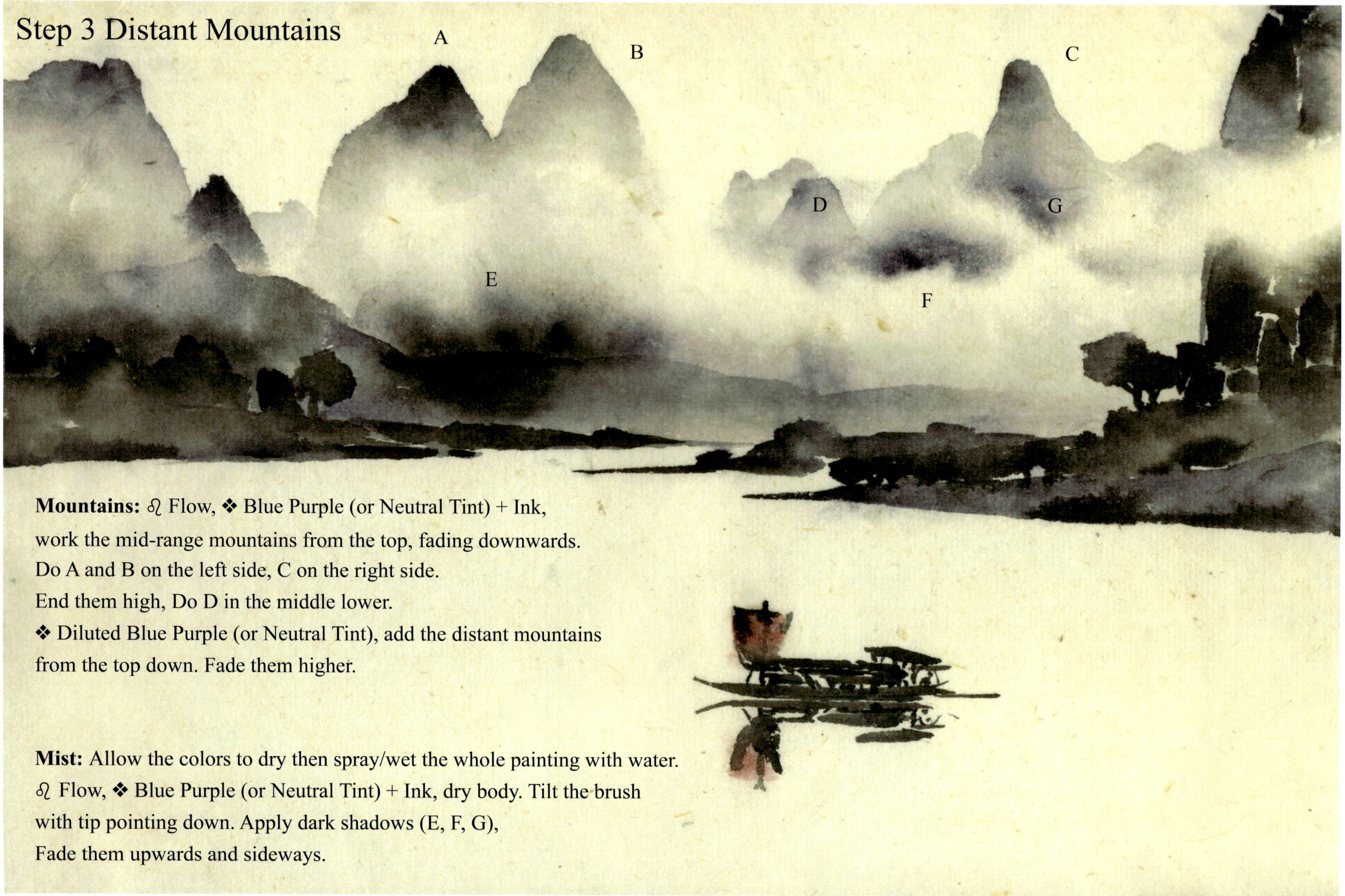

Mountains: ♌ Flow, ❖ Blue Purple (or Neutral Tint) + Ink,
work the mid-range mountains from the top, fading downwards.
Do A and B on the left side, C on the right side.
End them high, Do D in the middle lower.
❖ Diluted Blue Purple (or Neutral Tint), add the distant mountains from the top down. Fade them higher.

Mist: Allow the colors to dry then spray/wet the whole painting with water.
♌ Flow, ❖ Blue Purple (or Neutral Tint) + Ink, dry body. Tilt the brush with tip pointing down. Apply dark shadows (E, F, G),
Fade them upwards and sideways.

Step 4 Reflections

When the painting dries, fold along the base of the distant bank (a). ❖ Light Blue Purple, mark the mountains on the back of the paper. ❖ Medium Blue Purple, work the reflections of the mountains from bottom of the painting upwards. The reflection of the mountain on the right needs to follow another fold along its own baseline (b).

Do the reflections with horizontal strokes. Leave streaks of space occasionally (c, d).

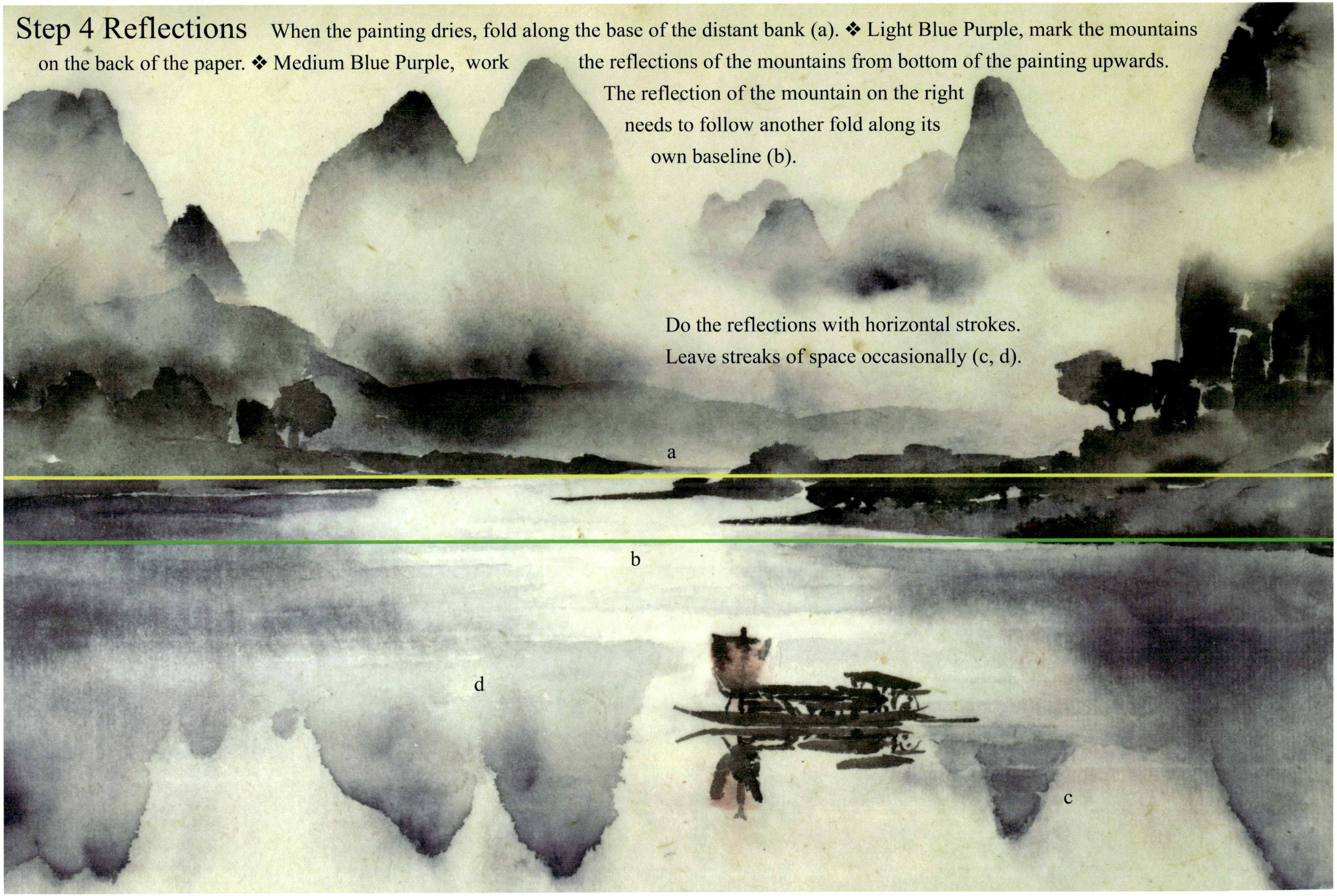

Step 5 Reflections Continued

Show darker shadows near the closer banks (e, f). Leave hairline spaces (g, h). The boat area does not need mountain reflections. Wet the whole paper before reflections dry to allow for natural bleeding and to integrate the water into one body. Use a paper towel to blot any excessive bleeding. Leave the center area open (i).

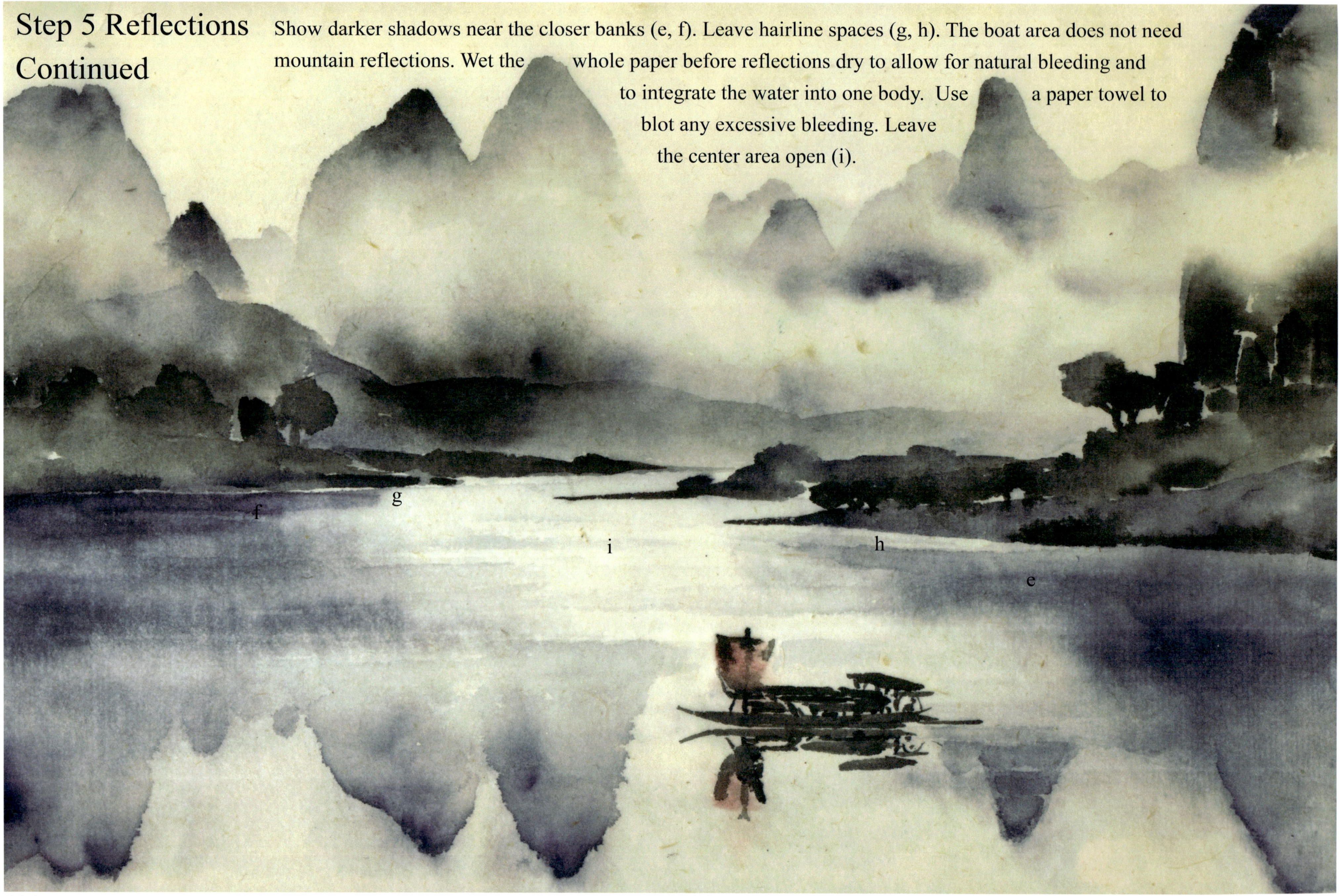

Step 6 Sky and Water

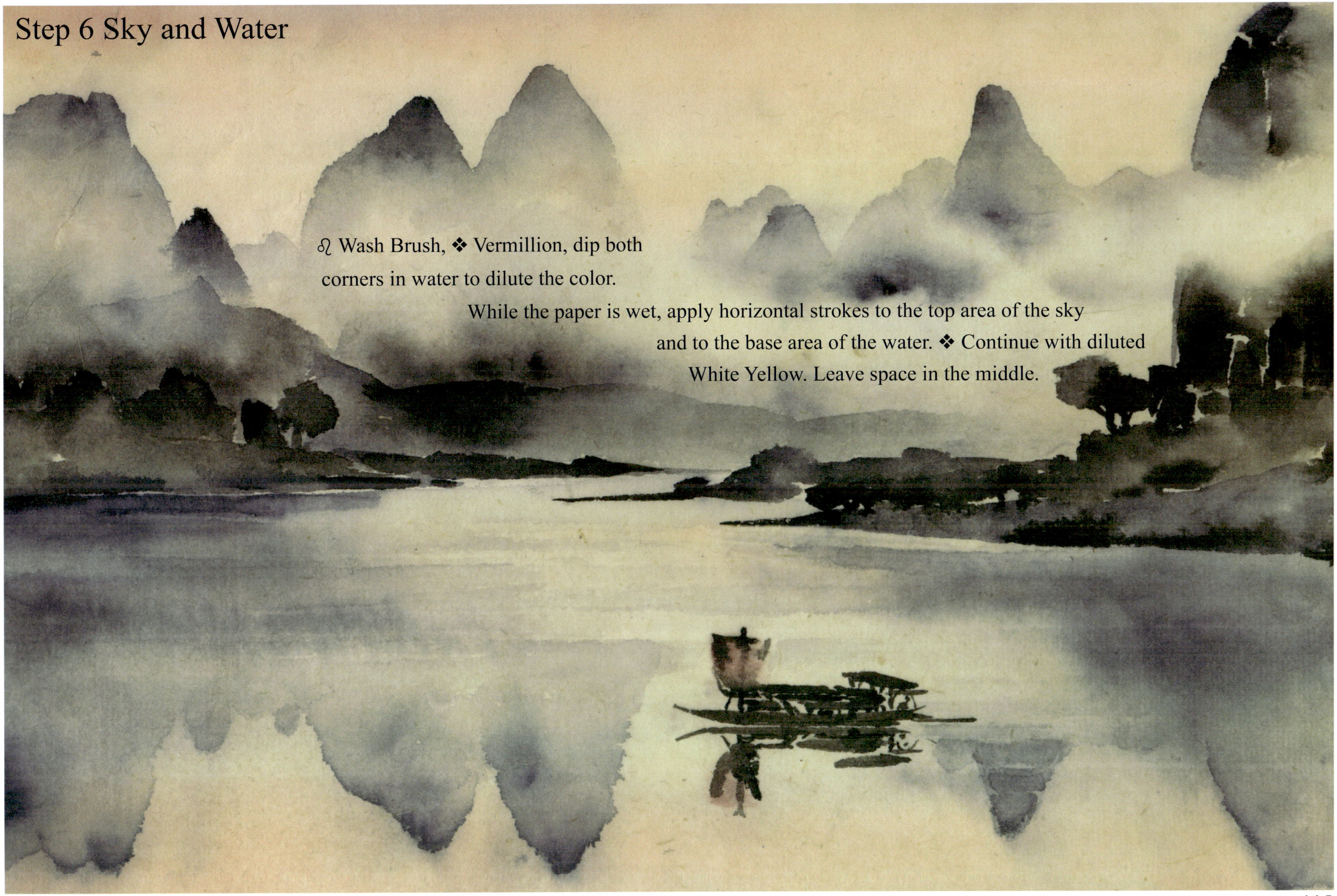

♌ Wash Brush, ❖ Vermillion, dip both corners in water to dilute the color.

While the paper is wet, apply horizontal strokes to the top area of the sky and to the base area of the water. ❖ Continue with diluted White Yellow. Leave space in the middle.

Lesson 13: Valley

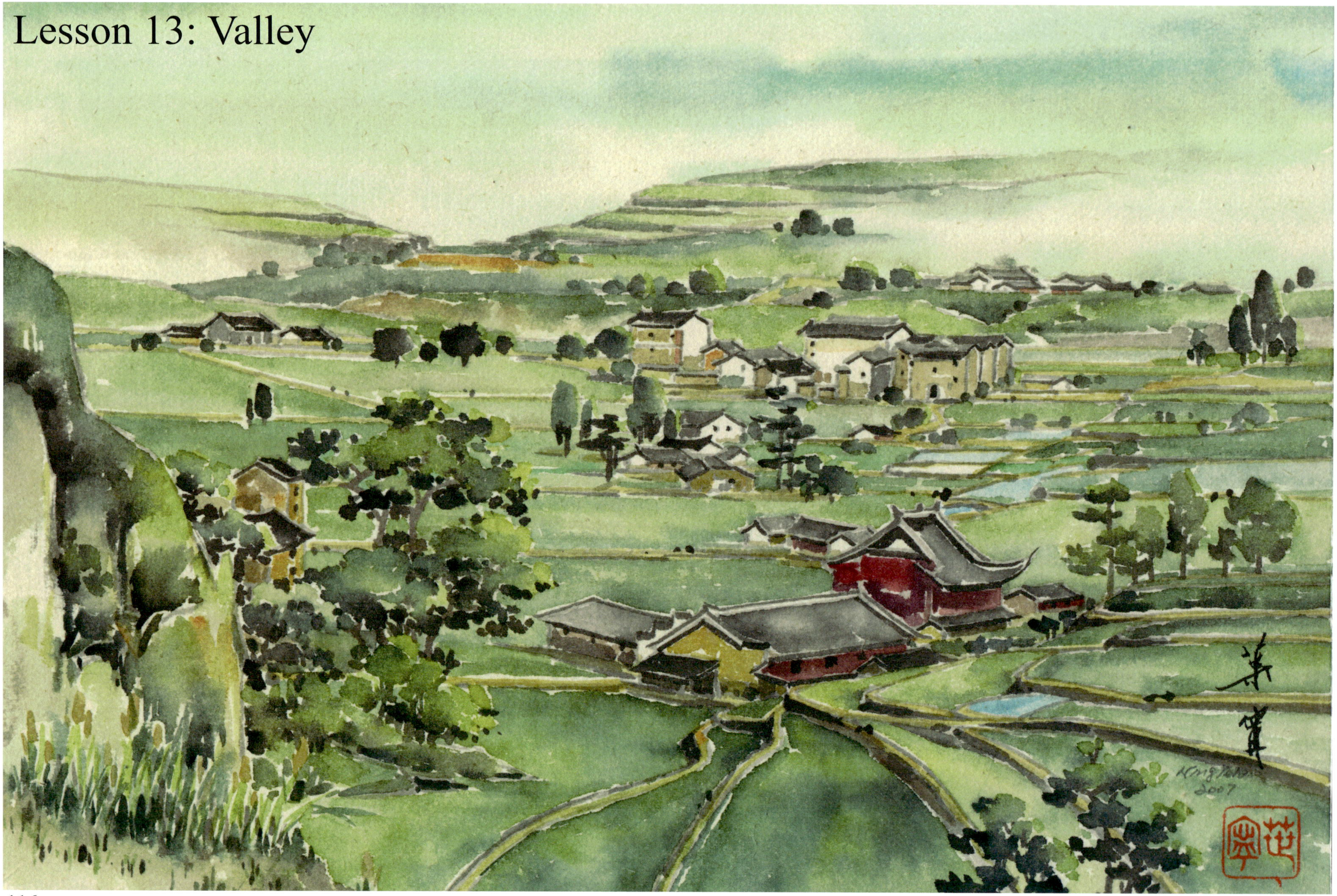

Lesson 13: Valley

The Yellow Mountain region is a huge area in south Anhui province. Many places are named "Keng" (hole), isolated from the world outside.

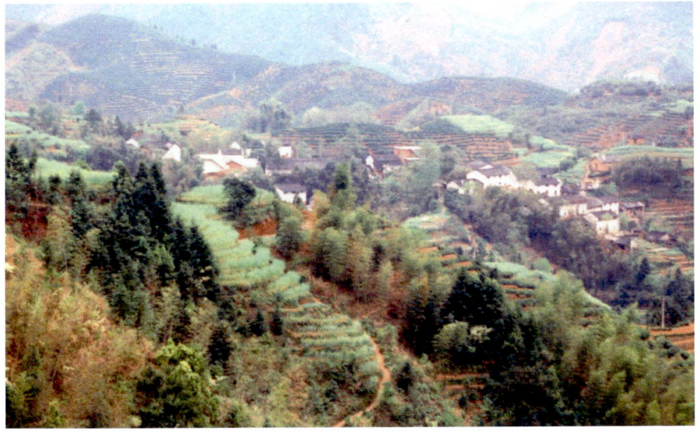

No other place in China has villages as elegant as here, each a living museum. Many are listed as the world's most treasured cultural relics by the United Nations.

One should never underestimate the cultural heritage of the common folk in this part of the world. In every hole, ditch, and crevice, there lies a crouching tiger and hidden dragon. There is no shortcut to culture. It takes time and the collective wisdom of generations.

The Four Treasures of Literary Pursuit—brush, paper, ink stick, and ink stone—were all developed in and around this area. My whole existence evolved with these wonderful tools.

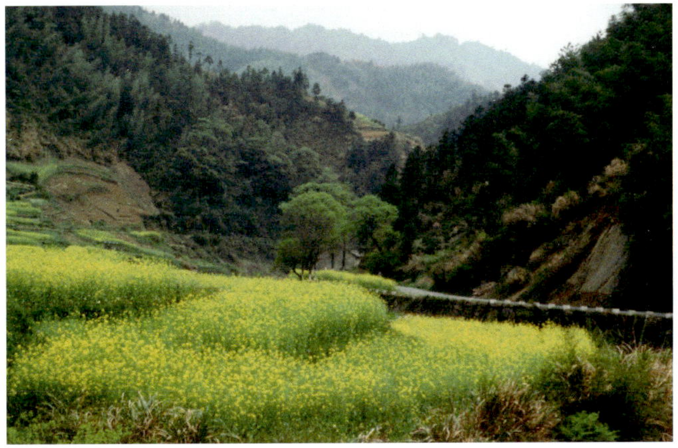

Poet Tao Yuanming (Tao Chien, 365-427AD) refused to bow to his superior and retired here. He spent the rest of his life as a gentleman farmer growing mums, drinking wine, and writing

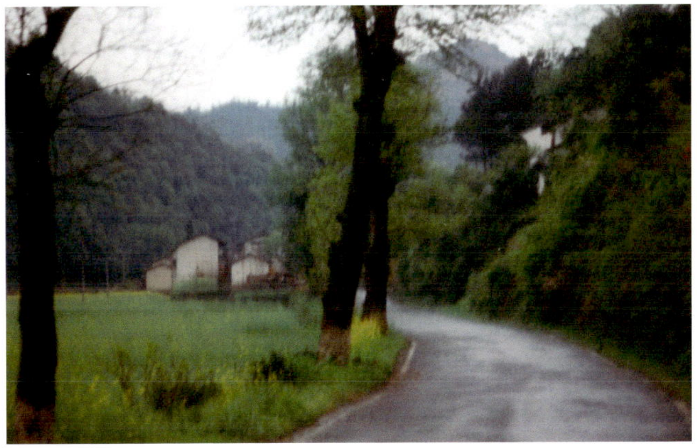

poetry. The scenery and people inspired him to write the first essay in China about Utopia.

Tao wrote *The Journey to the Source of Peach Blossom River* some 1,400 years ago. It described a fisherman who got lost following a narrow canyon at the source of the Peach Blossom river. He entered a wonderland. The folks there were descendants of refugees escaping the tyranny of the First Emperor. They had lost contact with the outside world. They worked and enjoyed life together with no fear and worry. There was no government, no crime, no tax, no war.

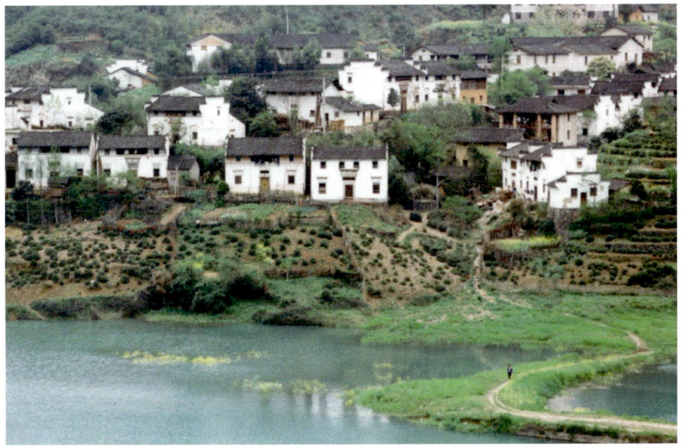

If one wishes to find a traditional Chinese village, look no further. It is all here, completely intact.

Composition Looking down from a hill on a lovely afternoon, the light is shining from our right. On our left, there is some grass below. The nose of our hill extends down (A). There are groves with tall trees and a couple of tall houses behind (B). The terraced fields come down from our right (C). All paths lead to the temple group in the lower middle, like fish looking for the same food (D). A group of houses are settled in the middle of the flat land (E). Two main dwelling groups are linked by small houses. There are more houses on both sides to widen the scope of our valley (F, G). Beyond, two hills with terraced fields form a "V" (H). The foreground and background terraces are connected by a middle group of terraced fields on the right (I).

We may work a draft to guide us on our way.

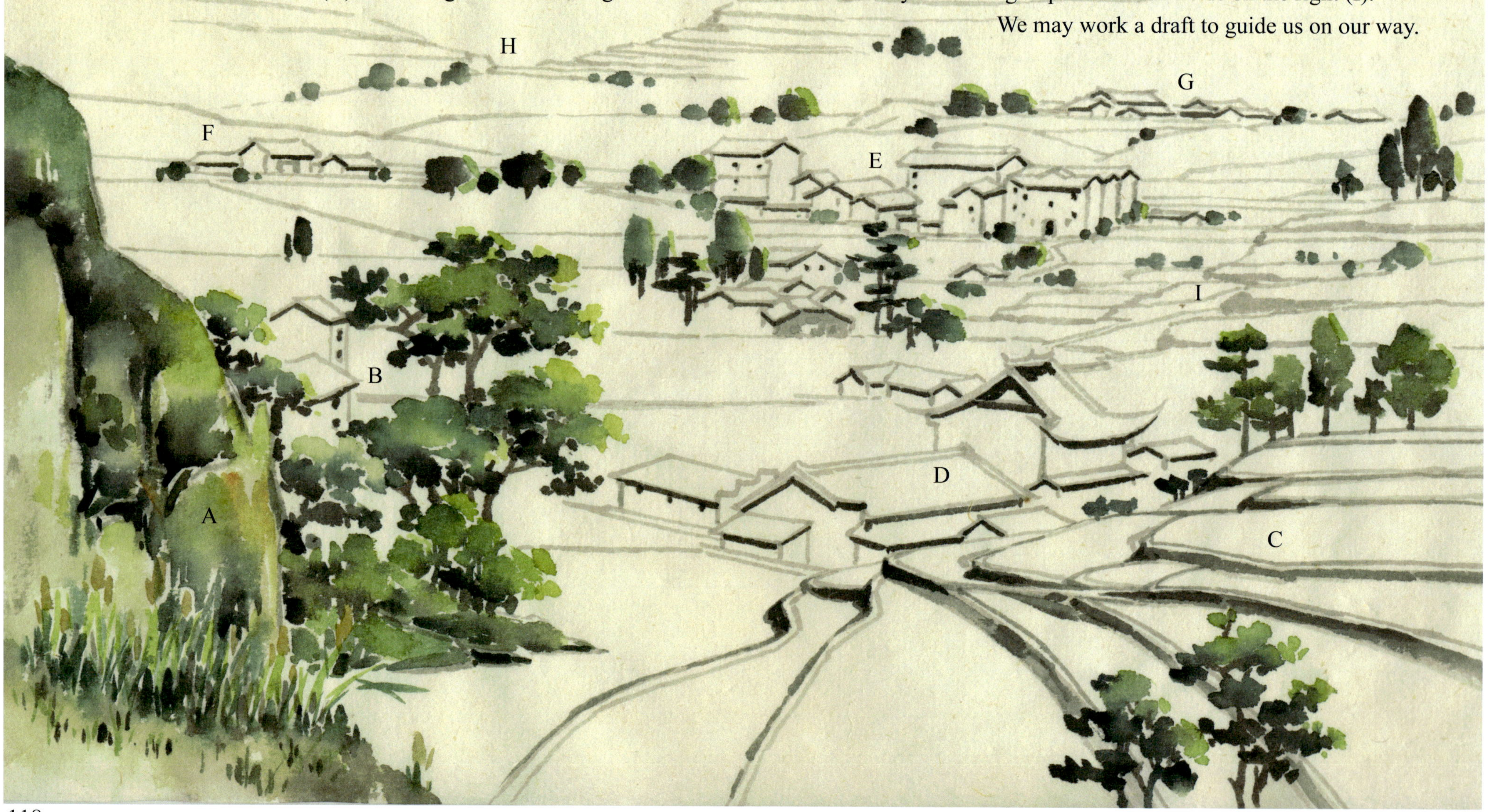

Step 1 Mountain

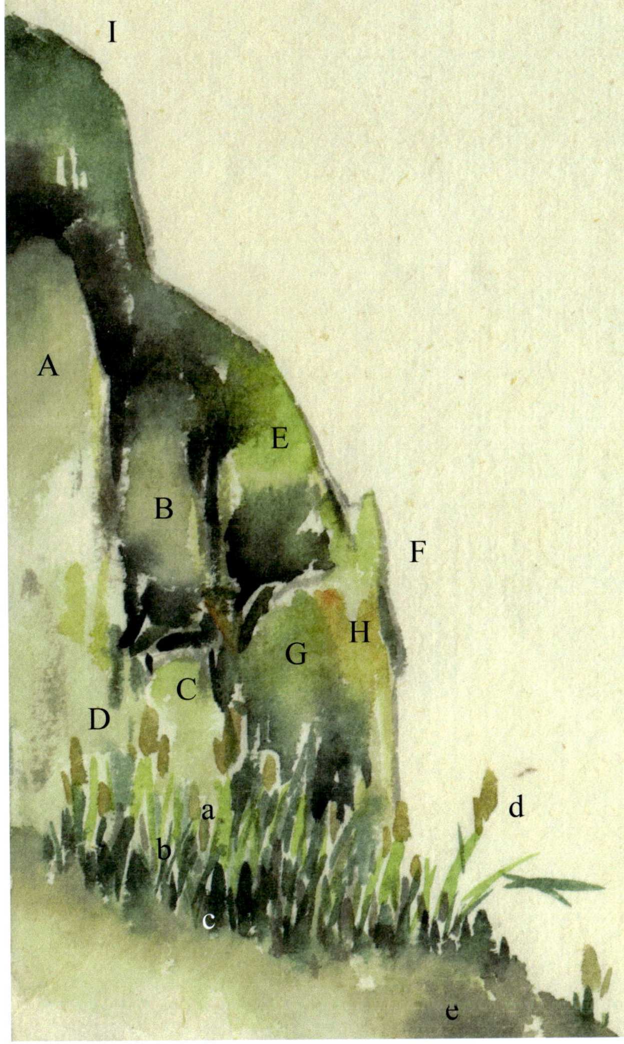

Grass: ℓ Flow or Small Mt. Horse, ❖ Light Green, work tall grass clusters (a). ❖ Dark Green, add darker ones below and on the sides (b). ℓ Flow, ❖ Shade, do shadow dots (c). ❖ Ochre, add dots on top (d). ❖ Beige, ↖ tilt and press from the roots of the grass downward to show the ground (e).

Mountain: ℓ Flow or Small Mt. Horse, ❖ Light Ink, dry brush. Do lines for the mountain. Show its divisions. ℓ Flow, ❖ Diluted White Green , ↖ tilt and press from the top downward to color the noses (A, B, C). Leave gaps for shadows. ❖ Diluted Shade, add light shadow lines between grass lines (D). ❖ Light Green (E, F, G). ❖ Ochre (H). ❖ Dark Green, color the rocks halfway down (I). ❖ Shade + Ink, ↙ tilt the tip and press upward to blend the shadows into the colors above. Well done.

Occasional spaces between strokes and shapes can add texture, dimension, and spontaneity to our painting. Treasure them.

Step 2 Tree Grove

ℓ Flow, ❖ Light Ink, dry brush. Do slope (1). ❖ Load Light Green + Dark Green, color the top of the slope from the tip inward. Leap over the painted elements. ❖ Diluted Shade, add along the lower part of the slope. ❖ Ink, extend shadows.

❖ Light Green + Dark Green, ↖ tilt tip and press halfway down to do the lower bushes. ❖ Light Shade with Ink, ↙ Tilt tip and press upward to blend the shadows into the colors above (2).

ℓ Flow, ❖ Light Ink, dry brush. Do the slope (3). ❖ Light Green + Light Shade, color the right side. ❖ Tip Shade + Ink, color the left side. Add shadows along the lower edge. ❖ Light Green + Dark Green, ↖ tilt the tip and press to work the tree dots (4). ❖ Medium Ink, add short trunks below.

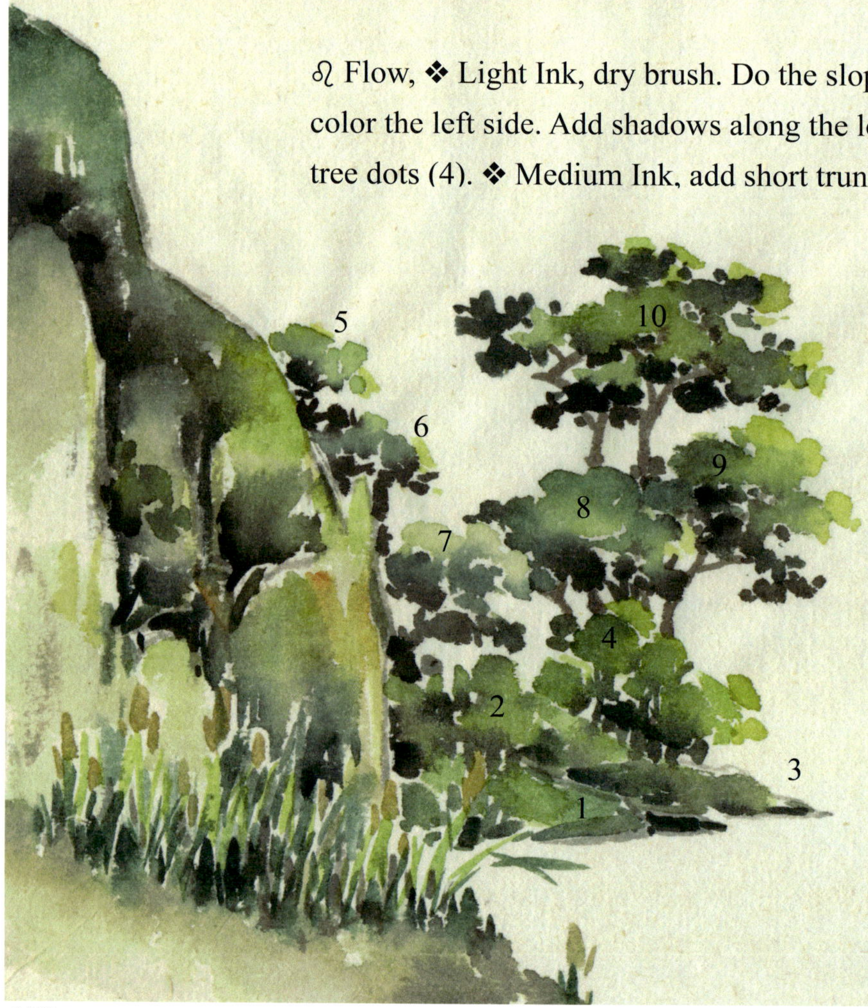

❖ Shade + Ink, add shadows below and behind. ❖ Mix Light Green with Yellow, add bright dots on top and to the left to show the light. Repeat this process to do all the foliage clusters.

Climb up the shoulder of the mountain, add more trees (5,6,7). Add foliage. Do the tall tree foliage from the lower clusters (8,9), then move to the top (10).

Show the dimension of the tree foliage using contrast. To give a cluster a rounded shape, use Light Green in the center area then use Dark Green, Shade, and Ink on the sides and below. Add bright dots with Light Green and Yellow along the upper right edges to reflect light.

❖ Medium Ink, insert branches and trunks through the foliage.

Step 3 Bottom-Half Line Work

Lower Right Tree Group: ℓ Flow, work a couple more trees using the same colors and technique as the previous ones (a).

Terraced Fields: ℓ Flow, ❖ Light Ink, dry body. Do the field lines. Double line the lower edges of the fields (1-14). ❖ Light Ink + Medium Ink + Ink, add shadows. Work more trees (b, c, check these little ones out).

Structures: ℓ Flow, ❖ Light Ink, dry body. Do lines to build structures from A to L . Building E is a temple. Wall H is a unique feature called "Horse Head Wall." ❖ Ink, add shadows and windows. Run a couple of horizontal lines to show flat land.

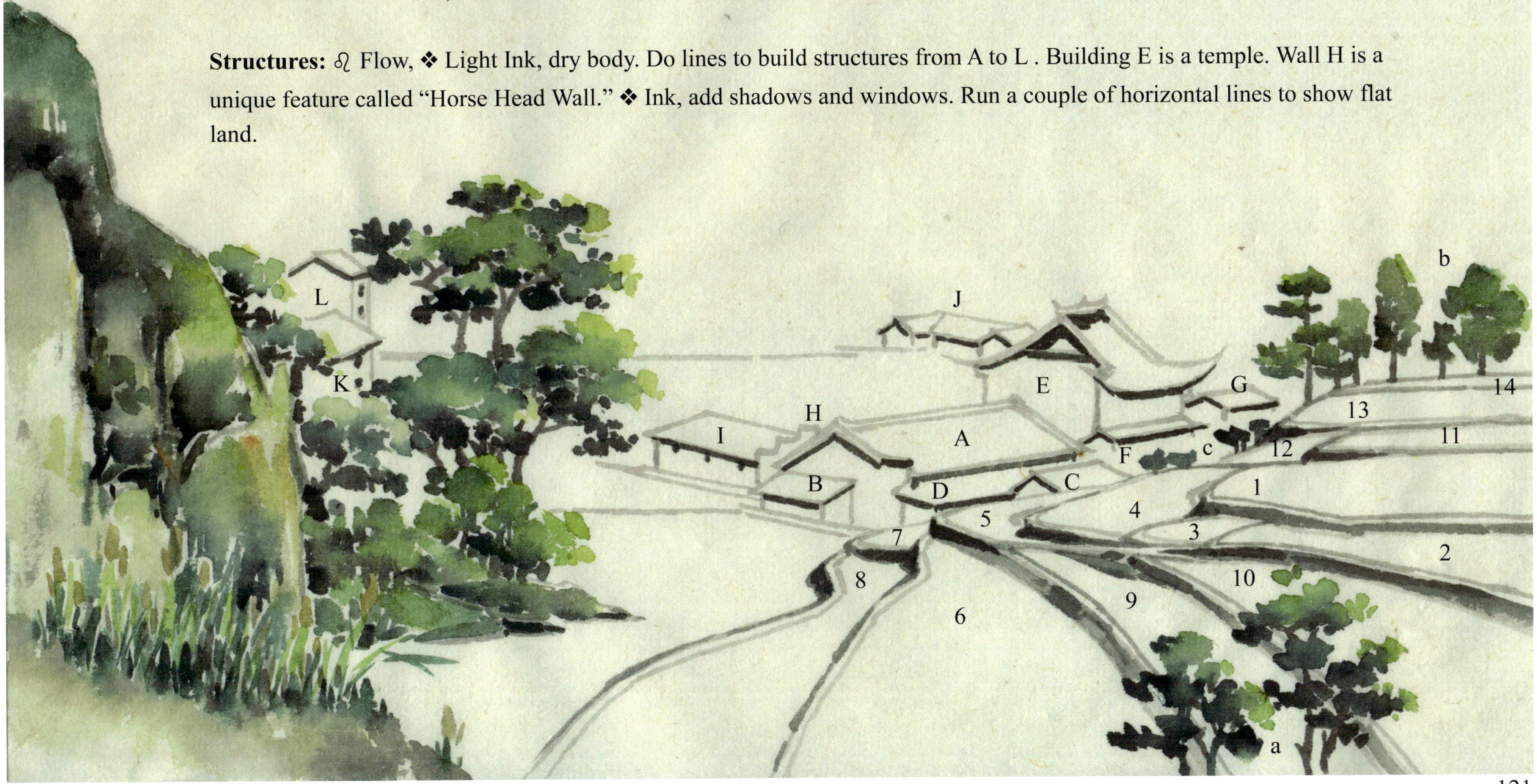

Step 4 Top-Half Line Work

Plant the middle tree group (a). Work a mid-level terrace field group (1-5). Add tree dots. Add more terraced fields and trees upward (6). Do the middle house group (A) with tree group on its left. Add horizontal lines on both sides (7, 8). Add a water closet (wc), important for tourists. I do not know where the local ladies go, but the farmers do it in the fields. Add Line 9 all the way across above the house group. Add a winding road (10) leading to house group (B). "Lead me to your door," as the Beatles would say. Add horizontal field lines, tree dots, and an outlying structure between the winding road and the mid-level terraced fields (11-13). Expand the valley with houses on the left (C). Link housing groups with trees and field lines. Add small hills (D, E) and houses on the right (F). Finish the line work with terraced hills in the distance (G, H). Add shadows and windows with Ink.

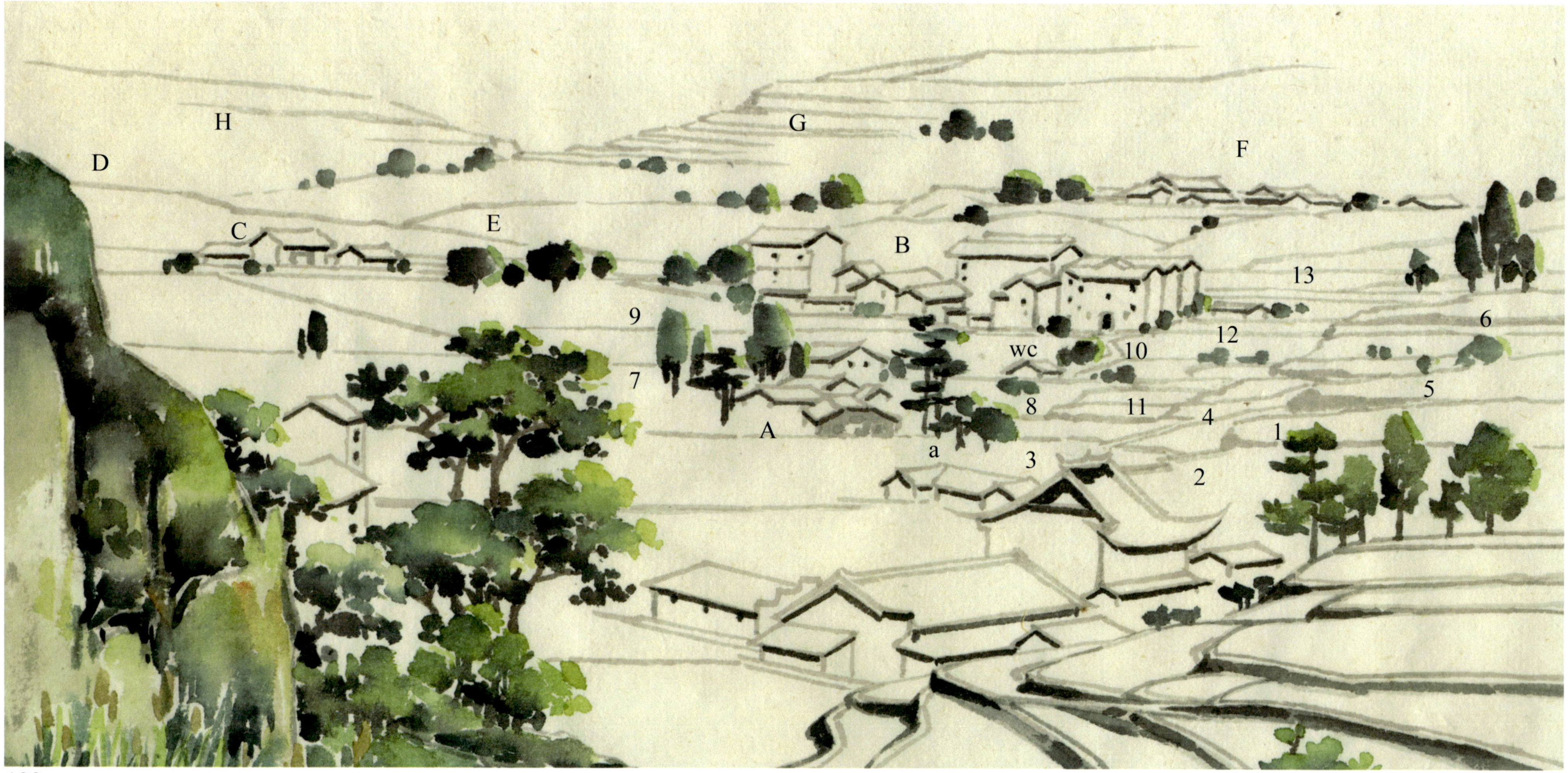

Step 5 Ink Work

♌ Flow, ❖ Light, Medium, and Dark Ink, apply to the houses, field lines, and terraces to show depth and dimension.

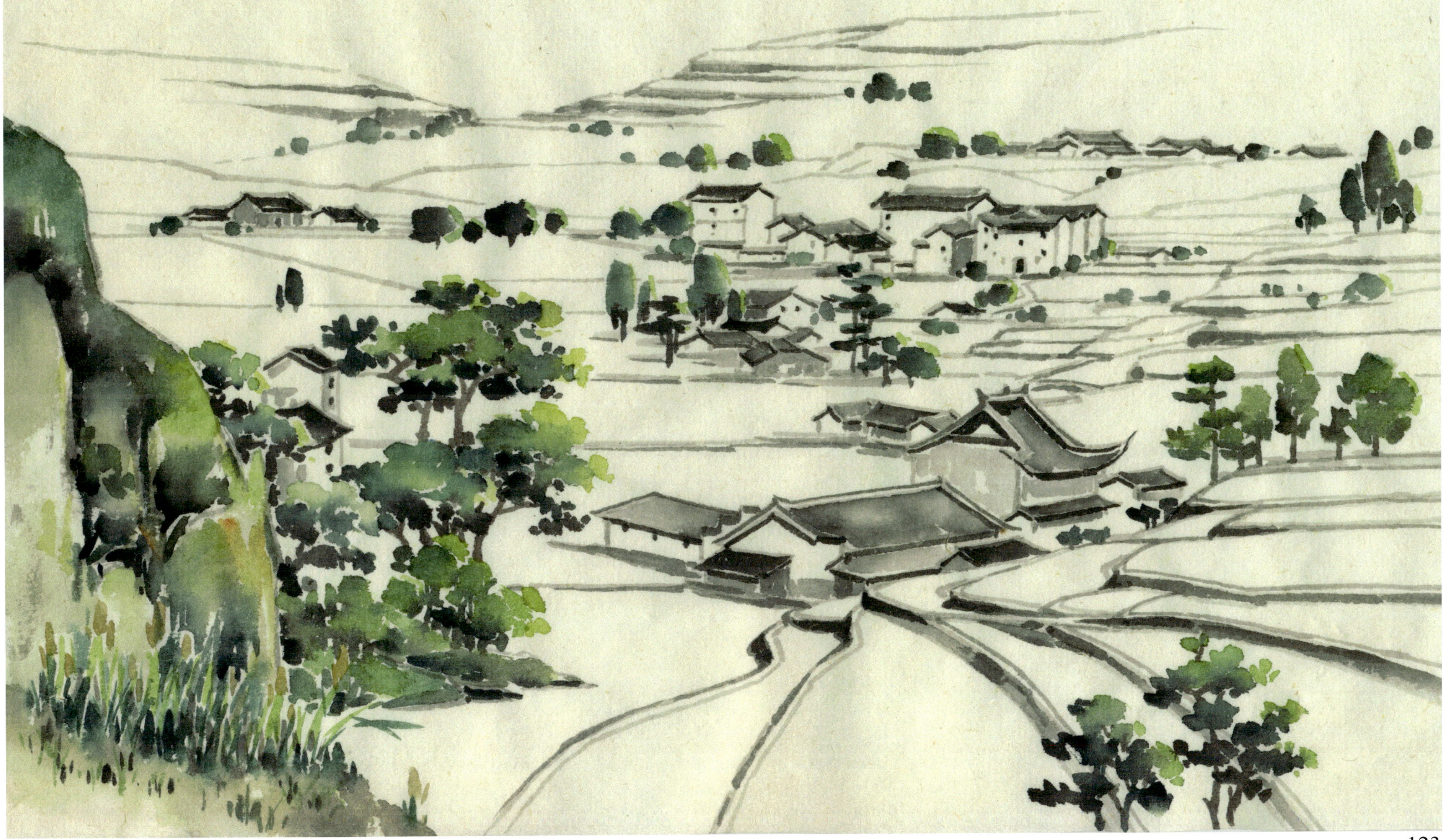

Step 6 Ink Work

ℓ Flow, ❖ Ochre (o), Beige (b), Red + Dark Red (r). Apply colors to the structures as indicated. Dilute the colors for houses in the distance.

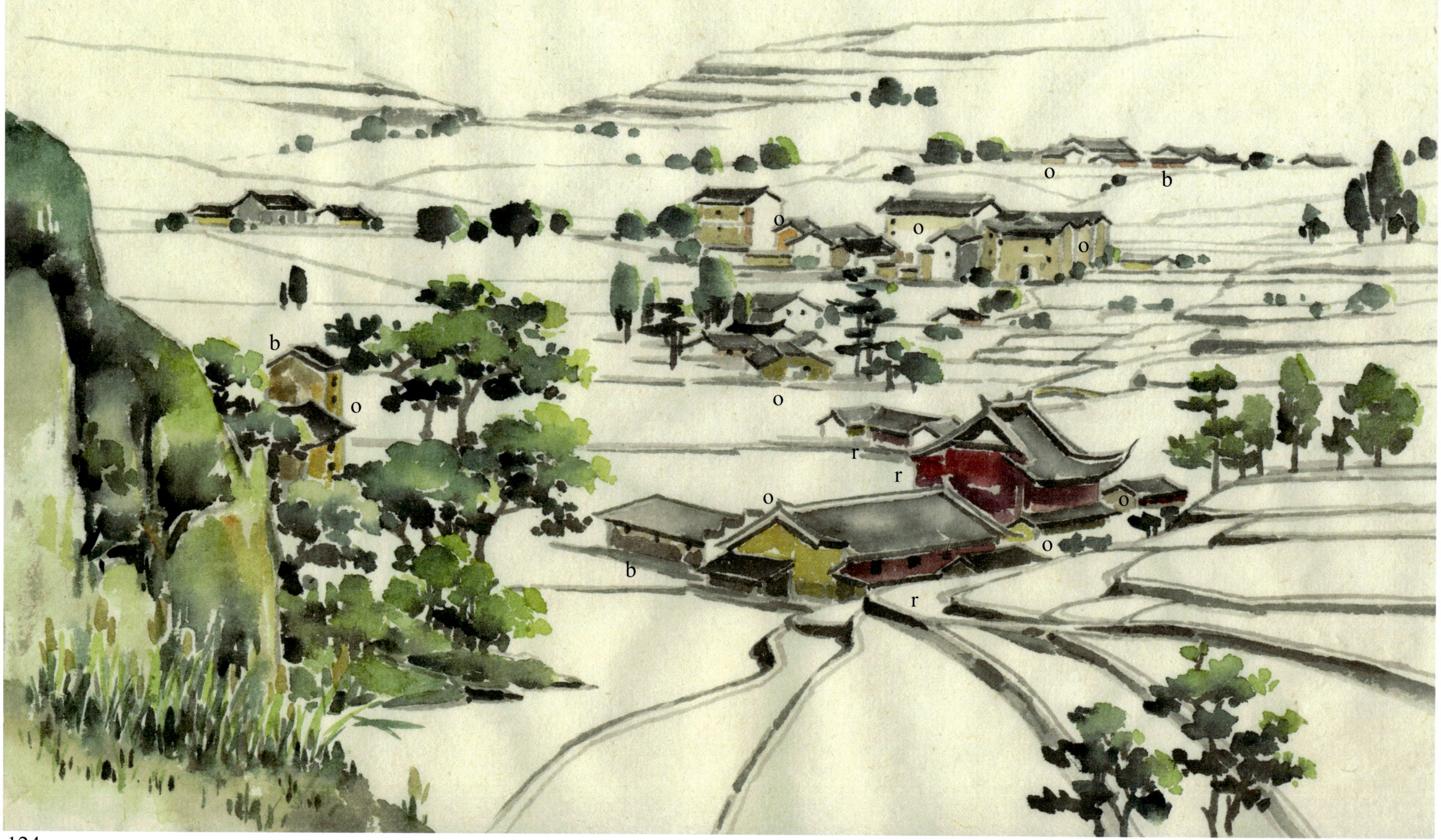

Step 7 Coloring Fields

♌ Flow, ❖ Ochre (O), color the paths between the fields, a couple of small hills and the ground by the houses. ❖ Light Green (LG) + Dark Green (DG), Color the darker fields (1-10). ❖ Light Green alone, or diluted White Green (WG) + Light Green, add color to the lighter fields. ❖ Light Manganese (M), use this on a few fields to show ponds. Children need to catch baby frogs sometimes. Leave hairline spaces occasionally. Begin strokes from the corners of the fields then use overlapping horizontal strokes.

The intensity of colors indicates where to start your stokes. ❖ Shade (S), add shadows.

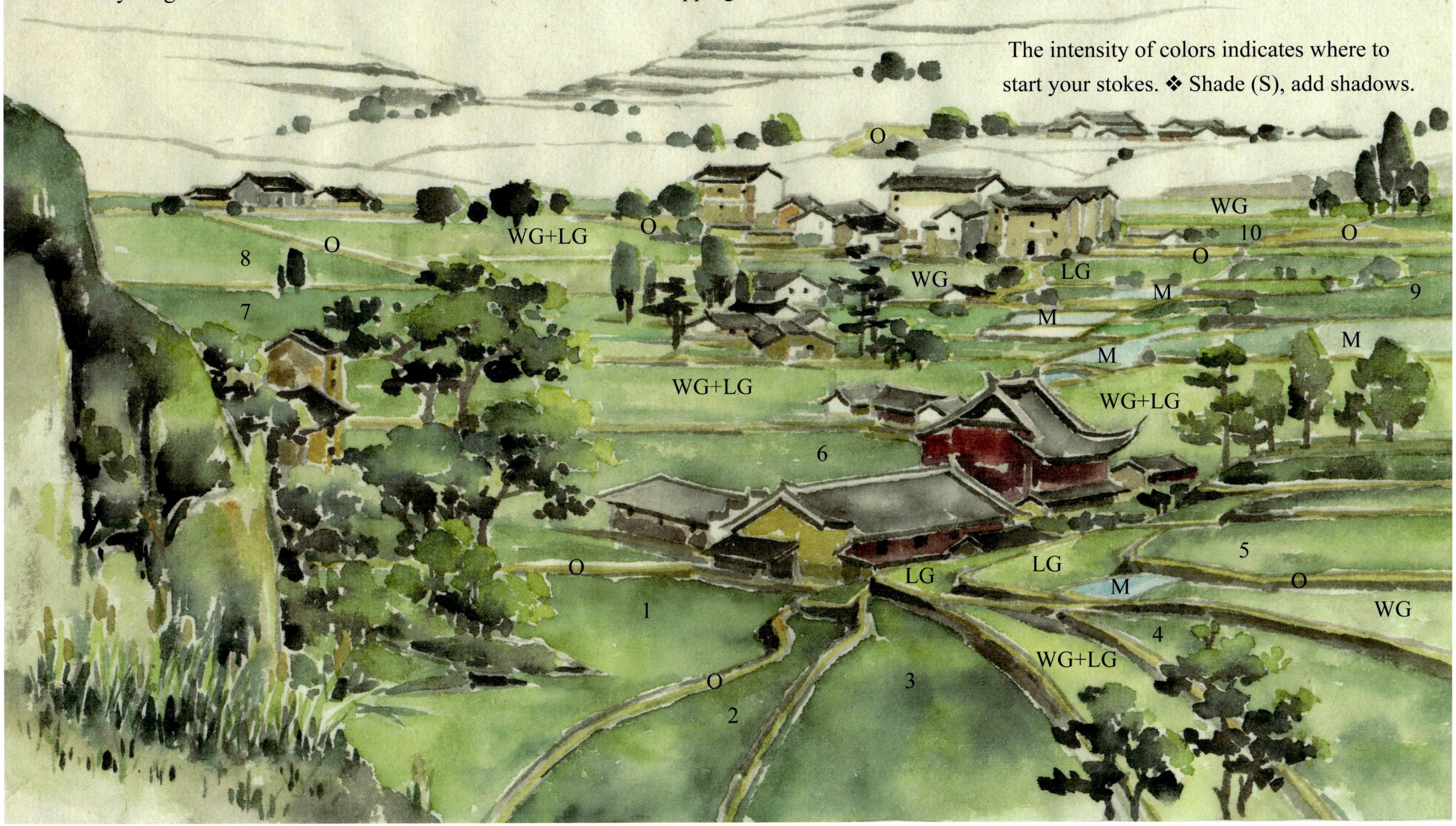

Step 8 Coloring Distant Hills and Sky

ᔕ Flow, ❖ Ochre (O), White Green (WG), Light Green (LG), Dark Green (DG), and/or Shade (S), color the distant hills as indicated. Fade the colors into mist areas. ❖ Manganese Blue (M), do the sky. ❖ Diluted Light Green (LG), accent areas of the sky.

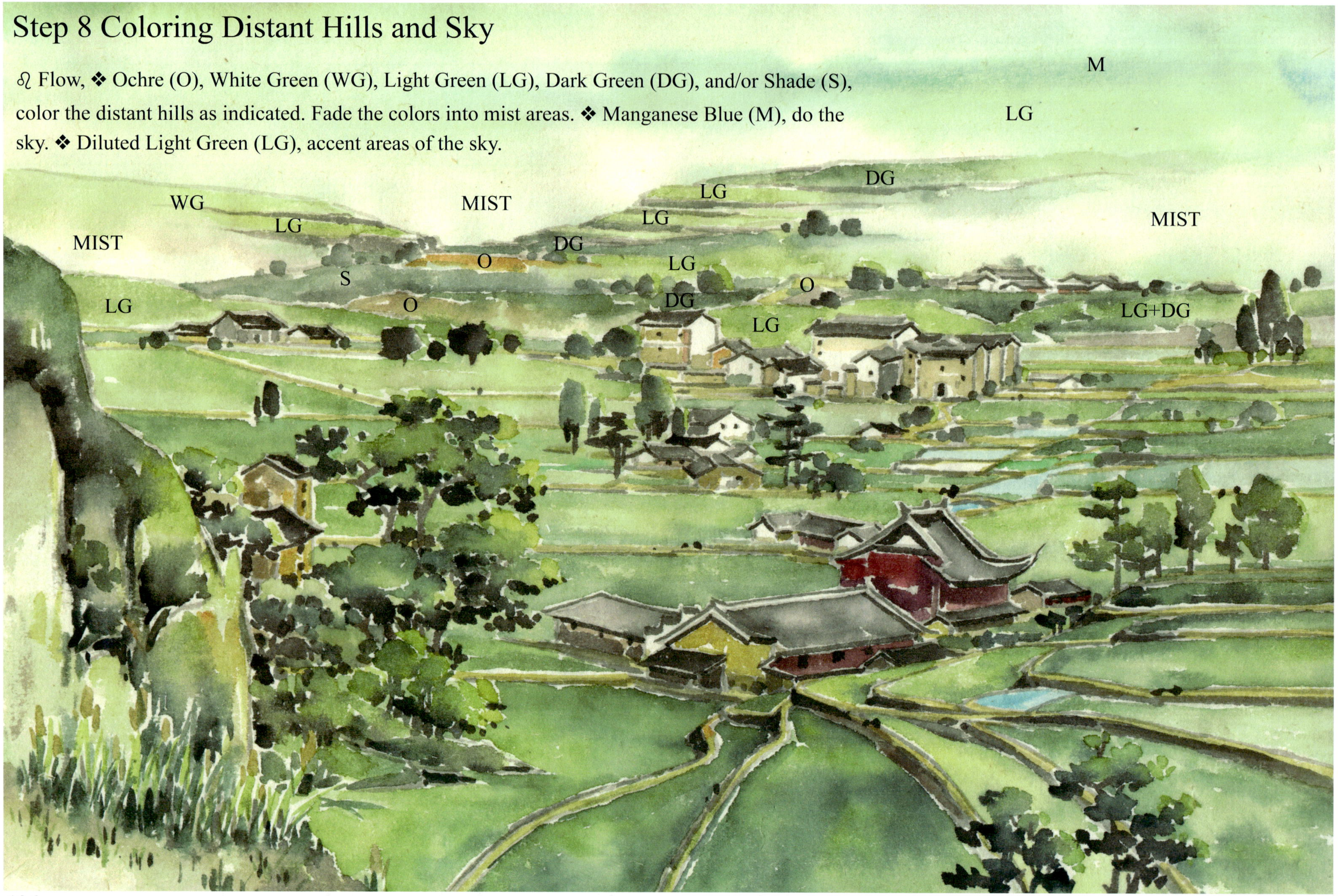

Lesson 14: Cherry Blossom Pagoda

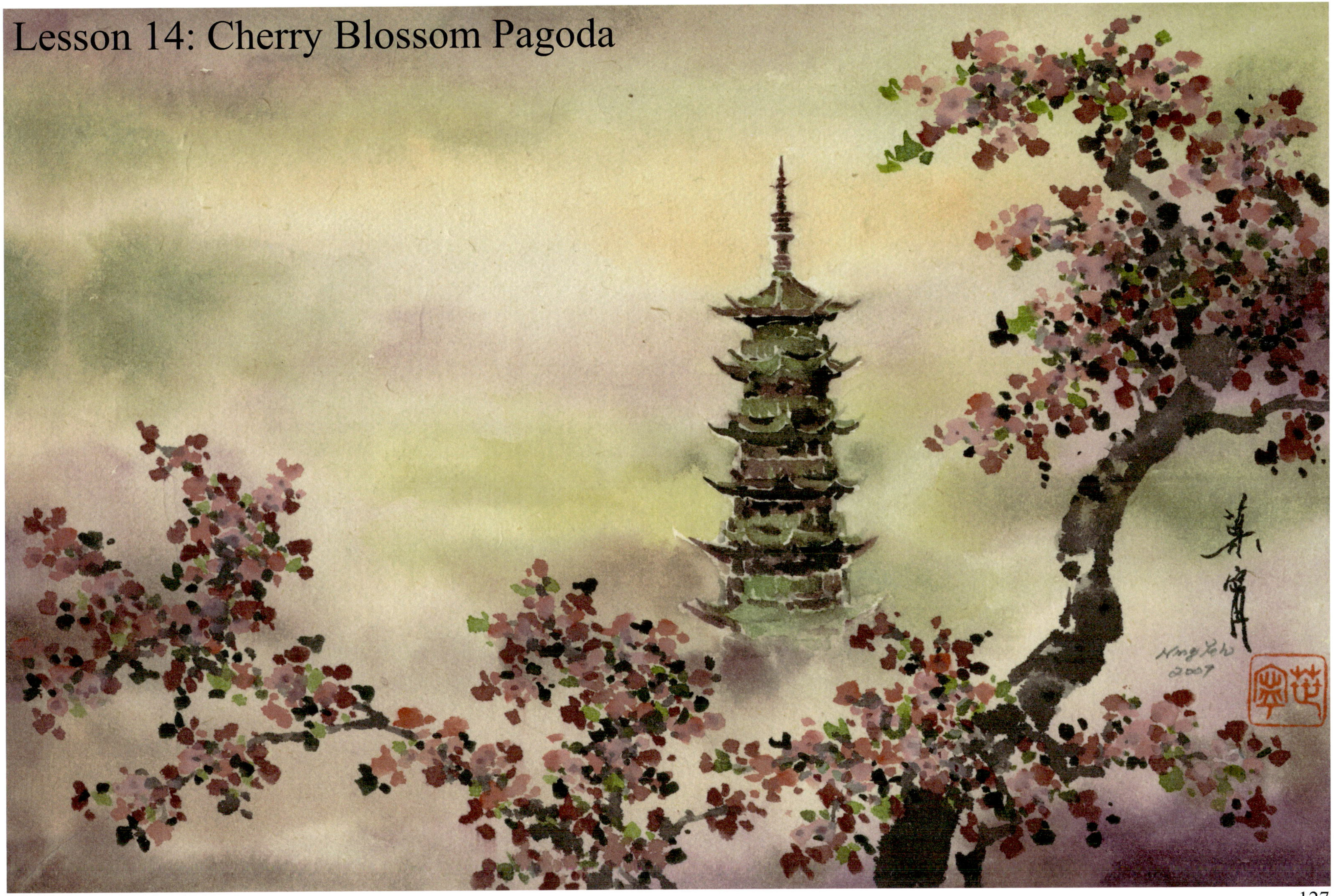

Lesson 14: Cherry Blossom Pagoda

Few structures are equal to the elegant, tall pagoda found everywhere in China.

Typically, the pagoda consists of many layers. Each floor has roof (shown in green), wall with windows, and railing (shown in red). I struggled for many years to teach this subject. The most difficult part of doing a pagoda is to achieve balance on both sides.

Fortunately, many pagodas in China are very old and badly need repair. Our pagoda definitely fits in the ancient category.

Now, let us find a workable solution.

If we look at the center sections alone, we see a series of roofs (green lines), walls (black lines), and railings (red lines), stacked like boxes in orderly layers. This is a piece of cake.

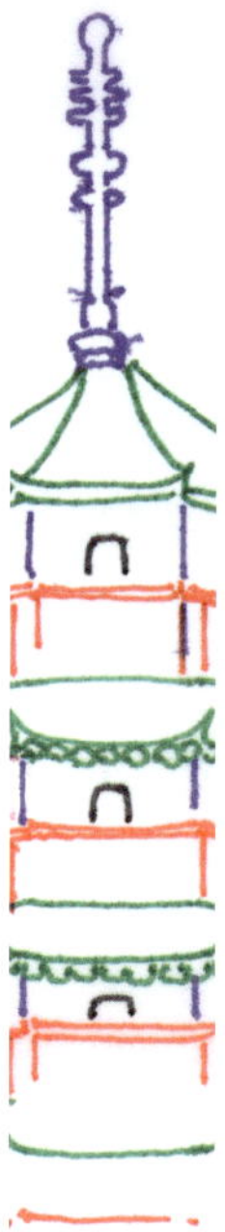

If we isolate the left side and just see one floor, we find a set of roof, wall, and railing tilting downward. We can do this.

Taking a second look at the entire left side, we find every floor the same. It is doable to stack the boxes in the middle. Stretch one roof, one railing out. Add a wall line in between and repeat several times.

I have overcome the hurdles and found a workable way to do pagodas with balance guaranteed.

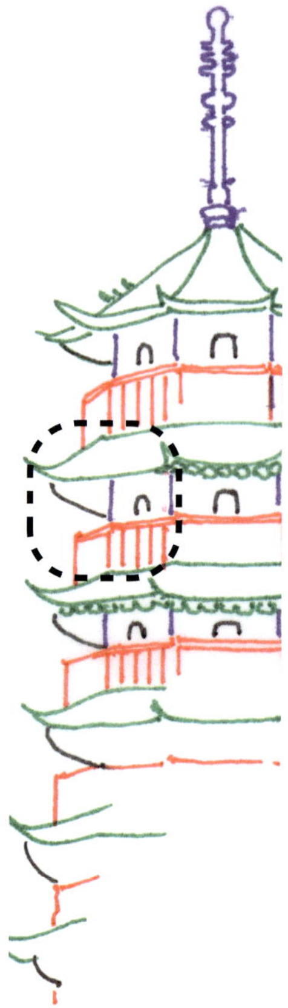

Fold a piece of paper vertically in half. Draft half of the pagoda on one side, then trace the image onto the other side. Unfold the paper to have a fool-proof and totally balanced pagoda.

The pagoda in this lesson is based on Shanghai's Longhua Pagoda which is more slender and graceful than this diagram.

I did not use the folding method for this lesson. Instead, I did the center panel slightly off center to offer a different angle.

Nevertheless, it is a good idea to prepare a draft of the pagoda with the folding method to make things easier. If so, make sure the centerline of the pagoda is along the fold.

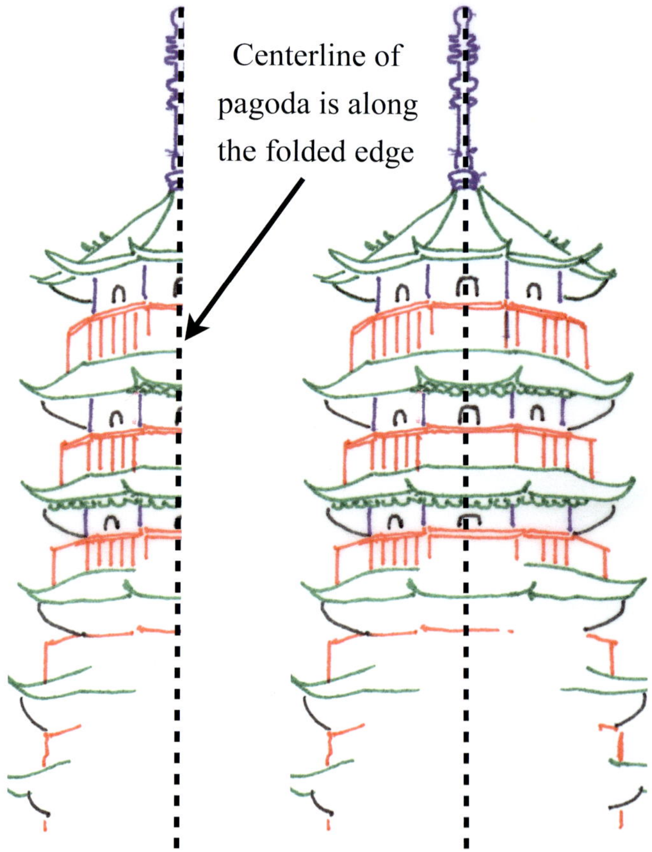

Step 1 Pagoda Line Work

Two options for drafting the pagoda are offered. Option A is done freehand, with its orientation slightly off-centered. Option B is done with the folding technique. Choose one option for preparing a draft. Place the draft under the painting paper and position it in line with A (slightly off-center to the right and equidistant from the top and the bottom). Use the draft as a guide for doing the line work.

ℓ Flow, ❖ Light Ink, do the pagoda from the top down. Work thick horizontal lines, slightly arched, in an overlapping series. Do the center spire (a). Make sure the centerline of the pagoda is vertical—not tilted—to guide the whole drawing.

Do an A-frame roof, with two sides balanced. Turn the ends up a little. Add a center line, Use two curves to connect the base (b).

Extend the sides outward and downward (c). Do two slightly arched lines to show the eave (d). Add wall lines below (e). Extend the railing out (f) a little wider than the walls so folks can have room to view the scenery.

Do the roof of the lower floor with two happy moons in the center. Extend the sides outward and downward (1). Add the eave (2). Do the wall (3). Show the railing (4). Repeat 1-4 to do the rest of the floors. The lines of the lower floors are less arched due to eye level. Fade the lower portion of the structure to prepare the pagoda to meet the mist below.

Simple, isn't it?

Option A

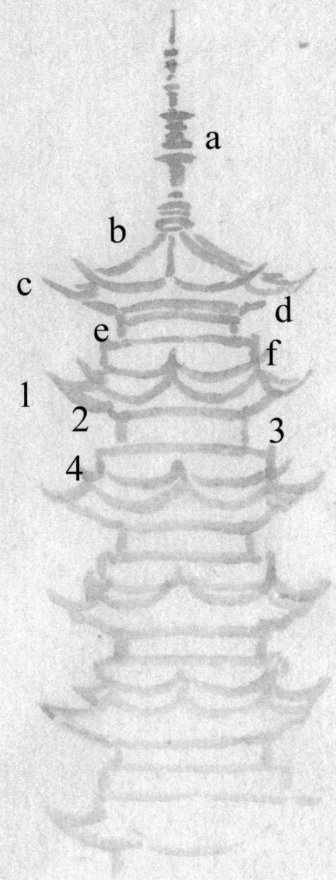

Option B

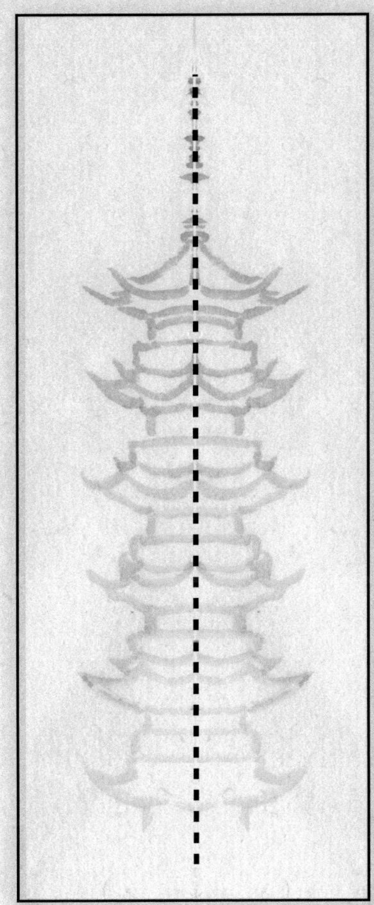

Step 2 Coloring the Pagoda

The pagoda is a vague image in the morning mist. We combine purple and green and apply them on different parts of the structure. Use different shades of Ink to add shadows.

♌ Flow, color the parts of the structure as suggested below but feel free to apply colors more randomly:

- ❖ Light Purple + Purple (1): spire, roof base, and extensions.
- ❖ Light Green + Light Purple (2): roof tops and left side railings
- ❖ Light Green + Dark Green (3): bottom layer
- ❖ Light Green + Dark Green + Shade (4): right side railings (in shadow).
- ❖ Medium and Dark Ink (5): eaves and wall areas in shadow.
- ❖ Diluted Light Green and Light Purple (6): fade the base of the structure.

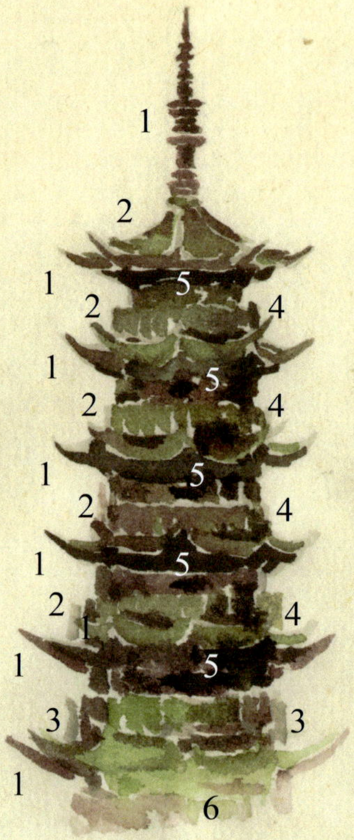

Step 3 Color Preparation for Wash (see diagram on p. 130)

Prepare the following colors for the background wash:

- ❖ White Yellow (WY): Mix Yellow with White, dilute into a light wash.
- ❖ Yellow Vermillion (YV): Mix Yellow with Vermillion, dilute to medium.
- ❖ Light Green Purple (LGP): Mix Light Green with Light Purple, watery but strong.
- ❖ Pink Purple (PP): Mix Pink with Light Purple.

Step 4 Background Wash

♌ Wash Brush, wait until the pagoda dries then wet the whole painting. ❖ Purple + Shade, load on one corner of the brush and blend. Hold the brush vertically, colored corner up. Stroke across the top (A). Reverse the brush, colored corner down. Work the lower edge (B), and the left side of the pagoda base (C), with occasional breaks. Shade area D above.

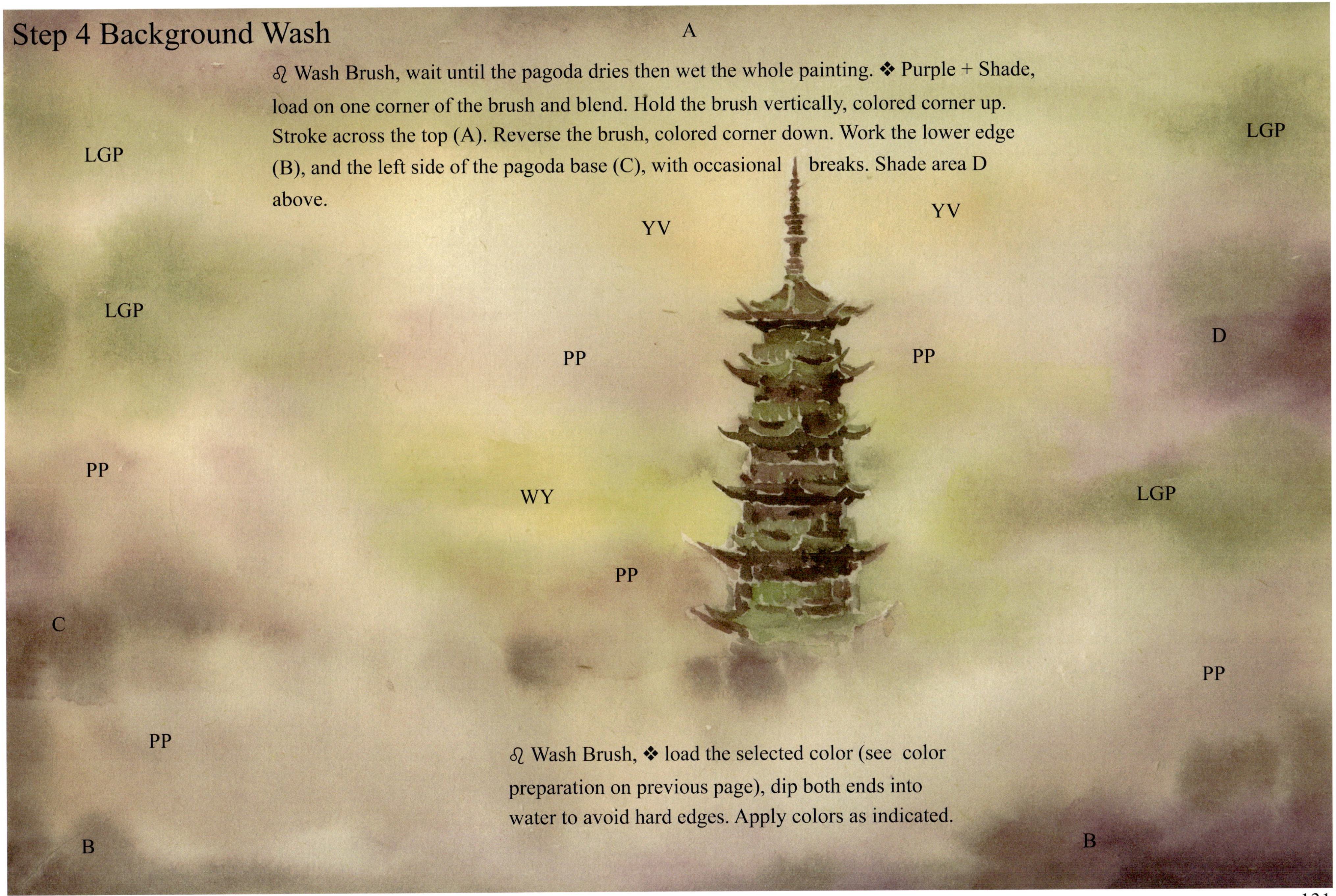

♌ Wash Brush, ❖ load the selected color (see color preparation on previous page), dip both ends into water to avoid hard edges. Apply colors as indicated.

Step 5 Tree Draft

ᘐ Flow, ❖ Medium Ink, prepare a draft of the branch pattern on a separate sheet.

Prepare the following colors for our blossom tree:

❖ Diluted White (milk-like)

❖ Pink: Mix White with Red (pasty)

❖ Red (pasty)

❖ Dark Red (pasty)

❖ Ink Red: Ink + Red

❖ Ink

❖ Light Green

❖ Dark Green

❖ Brown: Mix Vermillion with Ink, add some Dark Red and Dark Green.

I like to use the upper right branch group to illustrate the steps of doing the blossoms in detail (see the box with dashed outline).

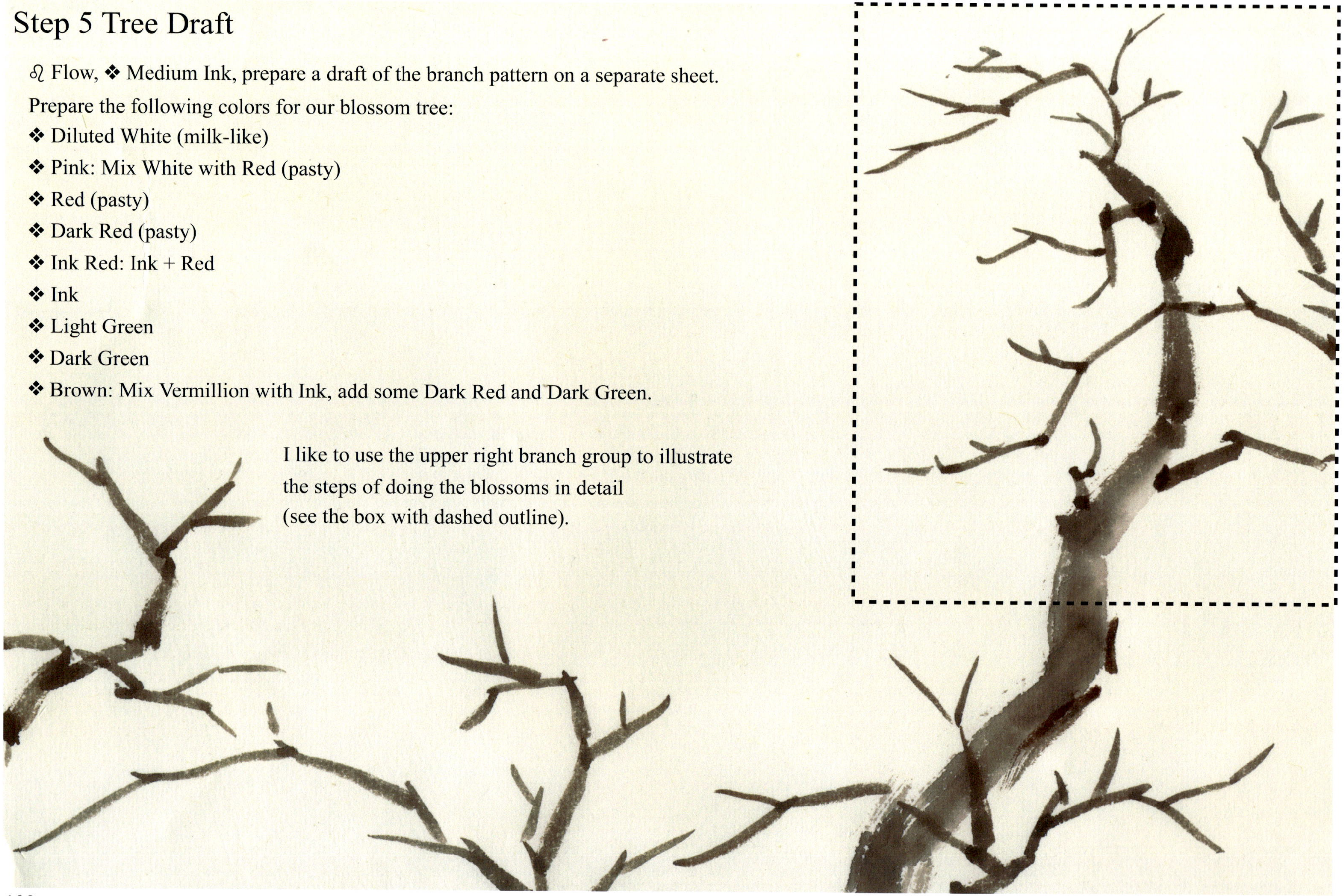

Step 6 Blossoms Demonstration

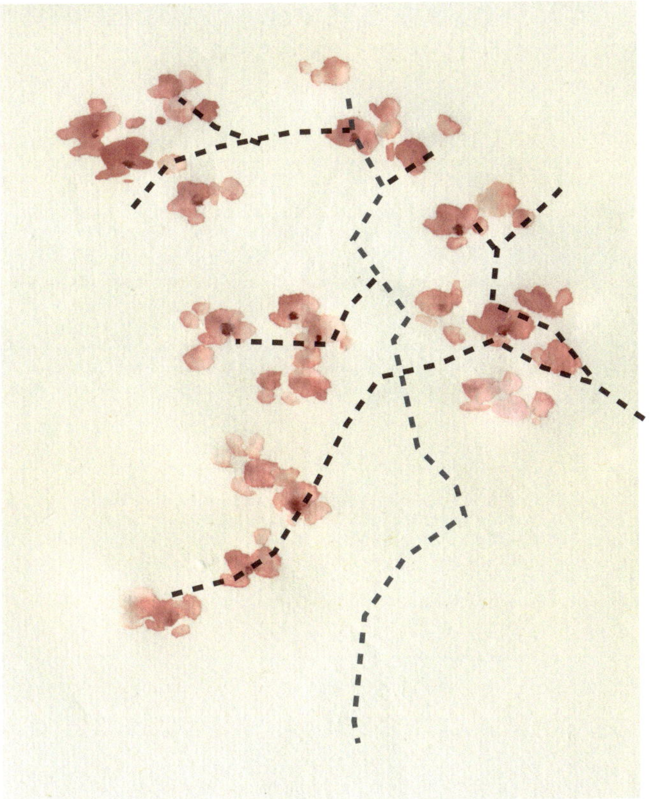

Place the draft branch pattern under the painting. The imaginary dashed lines above suggest this. Do not paint the dashed lines. Blossoms grow on twigs extending from these branches. They do not line up with the branches. Instead, they cluster and grow outward.

ℓ Flow, ❖ White + Pink, do dots in clusters. Each blossom can be one to five dots. ❖ Dark Red, add a center dot to full blossoms.

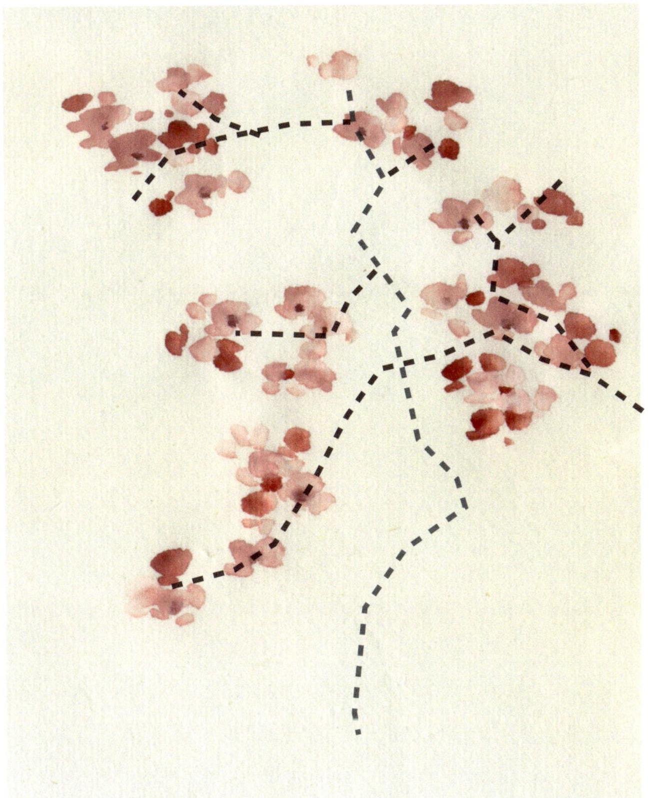

ℓ Flow, ❖ Pink + Red, do more blossoms to add variety.

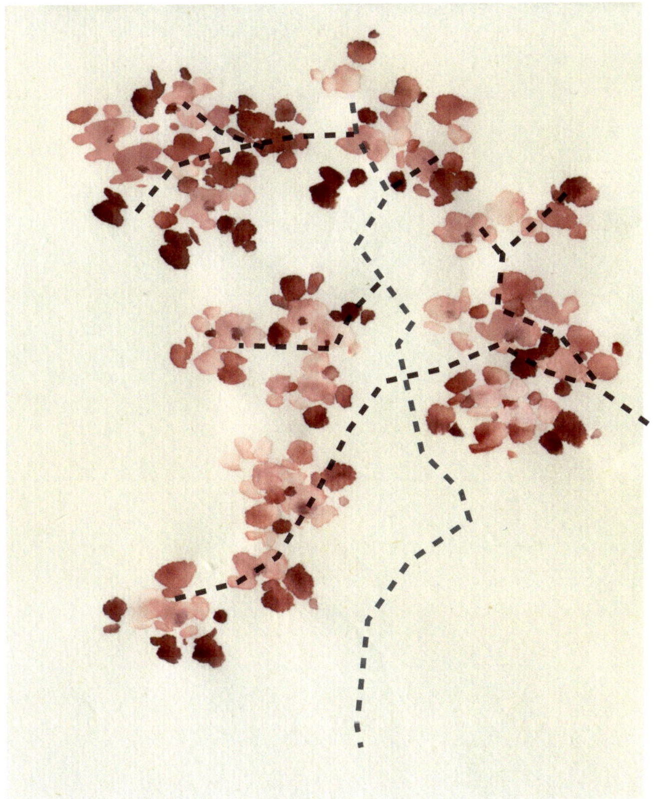

ℓ Flow, ❖ Red + Dark Red, show some shadow blossoms. Solidify and add dimension to the clusters.

Step 7 Leaves and Branches Demonstration

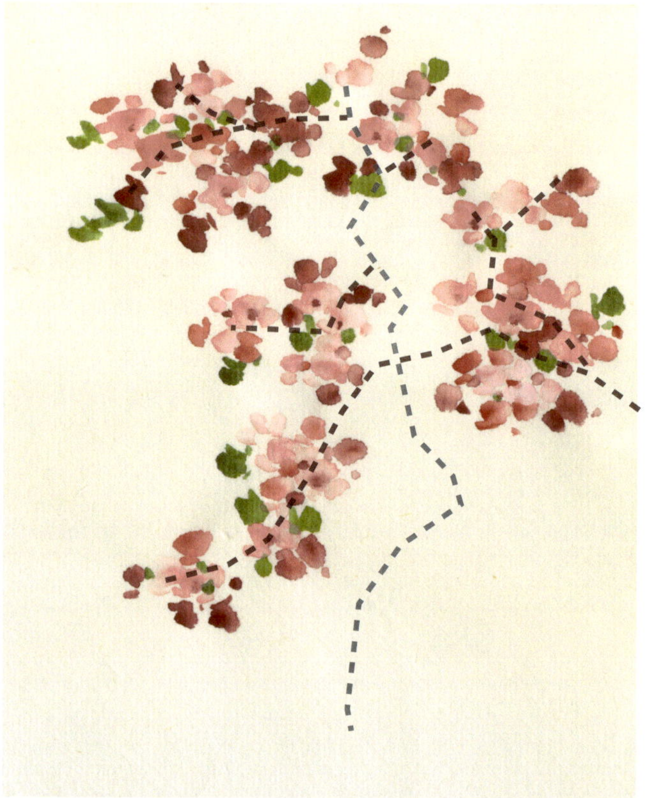

ℓ Flow, ❖ Light Green + Dark Green, do leaf dots. Leaves begin to appear after the full bloom. There should not be too many.

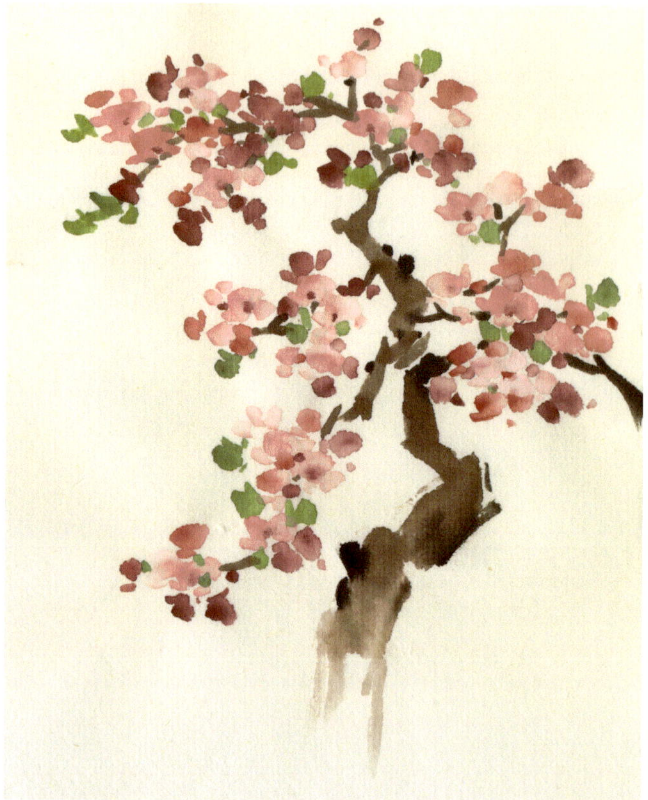

ℓ Flow, ❖ Brown, add small branches, threading through the clusters. Do the main branches wider and heavier. ❖ Brown + Ink, do darker branches. ❖ Ink, occasionally add outlines to the heavier branches. Do some happy dots to add interest.

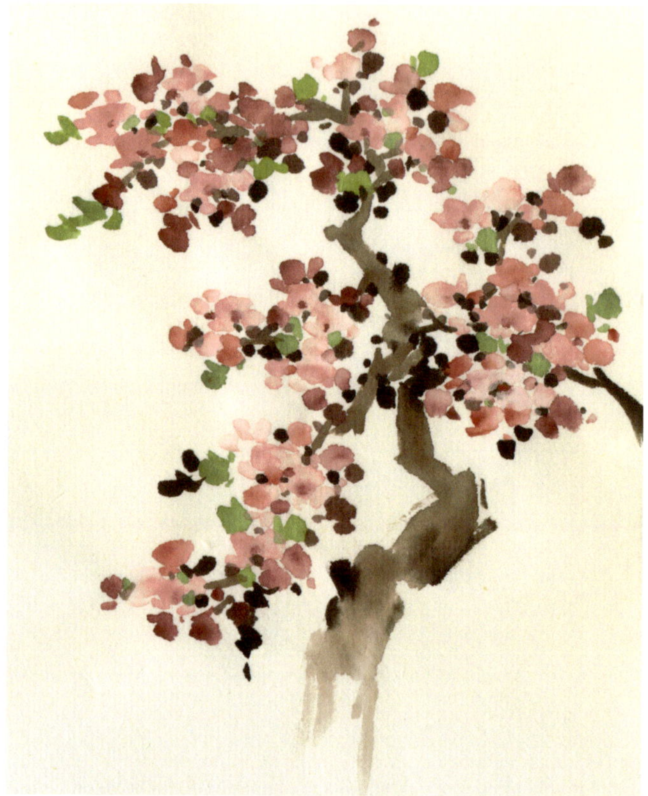

ℓ Flow, ❖ Dark Red + Ink Red, do more blossoms in the shadow areas. ❖ Ink, show leaf dots behind the branches.

Do dots one area at a time, to allow different colors to blend together.

Step 8 Blossoms, Leaves, and Branches

Bring the painting back and place the draft branch pattern underneath. Using the method demonstrated in Steps 7 and 8 we are now ready to add hundreds of these joyful dots to complete our masterpiece.

How nice it is to enjoy the heart-felt blossoming midway through our dream journey! Indeed, a grand finale to Landscape Lessons Book 1.

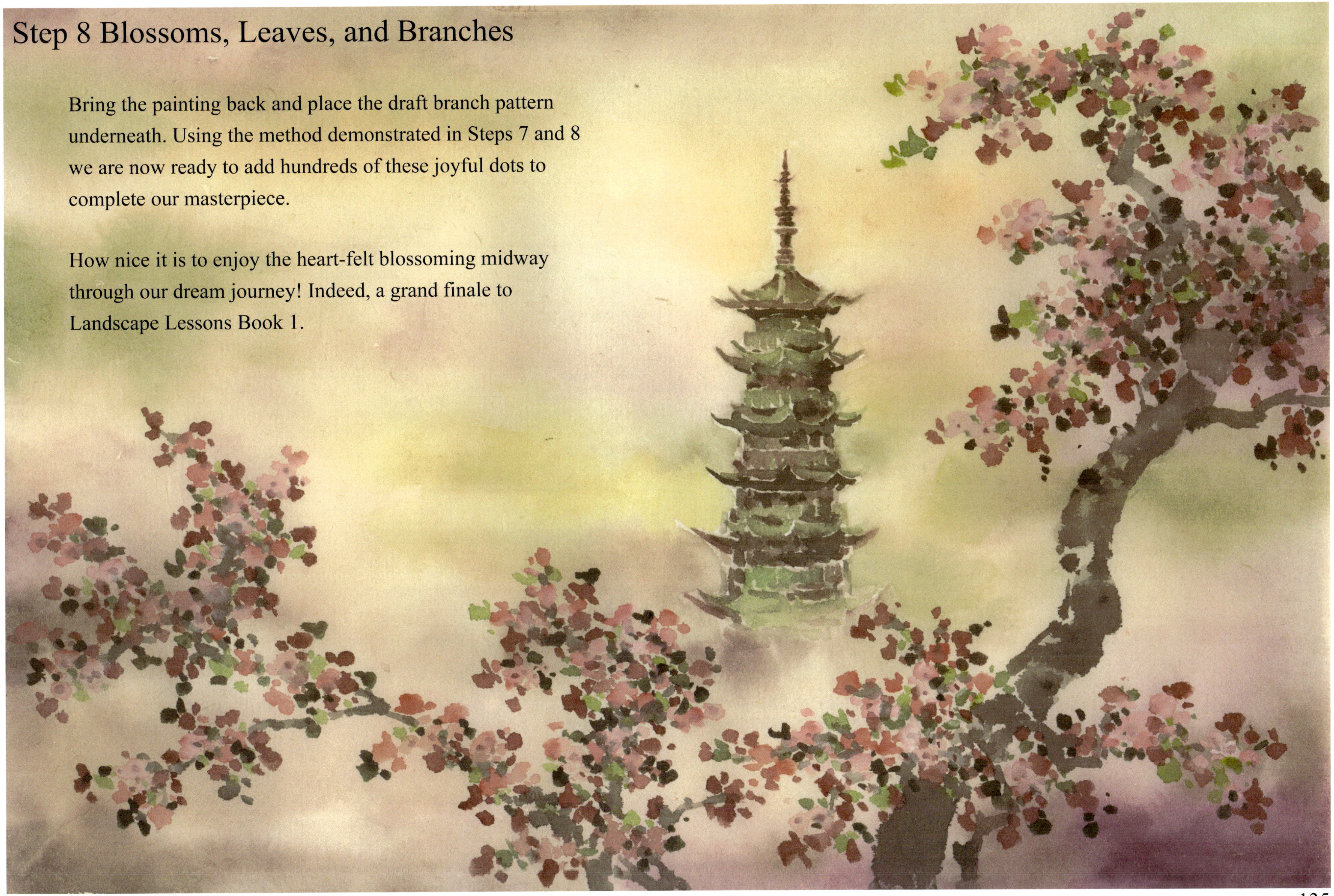

About the Artist

Ning Yeh was born in China into a family with an artistic tradition of many generations. Ning Yeh's art training began early after the family moved to Taiwan in 1949. As a top high school student, he became a draft choice of Taiwan's best university in humanities studies. In 1969, Ning Yeh accepted scholarships in America. He received his Ph.D. degree from Claremont Graduate University at The Claremont Colleges.

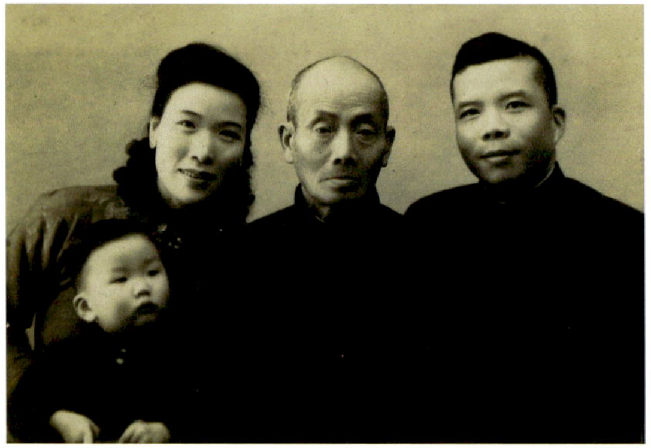

Above: Ning with parents and grandfather in China, 1948. Below: Top draft choice of Taiwan's best university in humanity studies, 1964

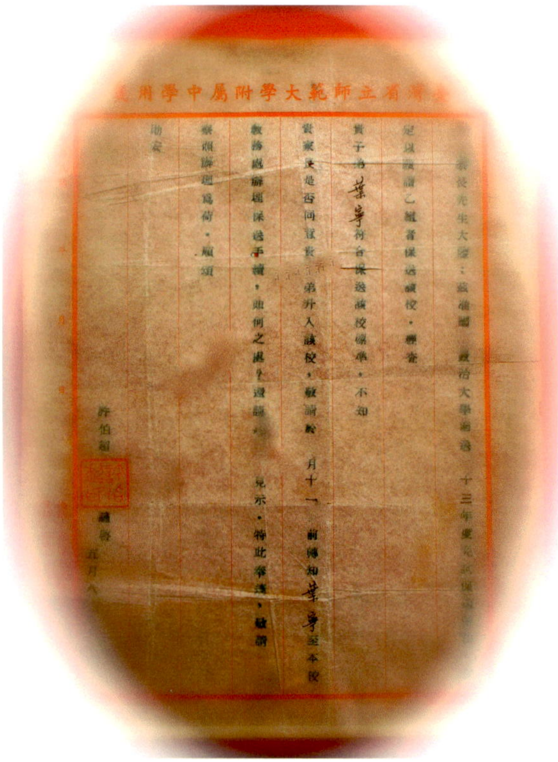

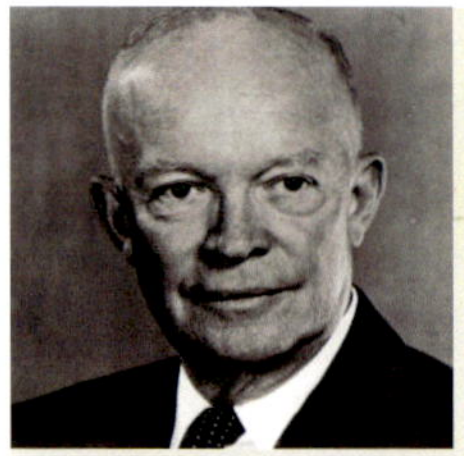

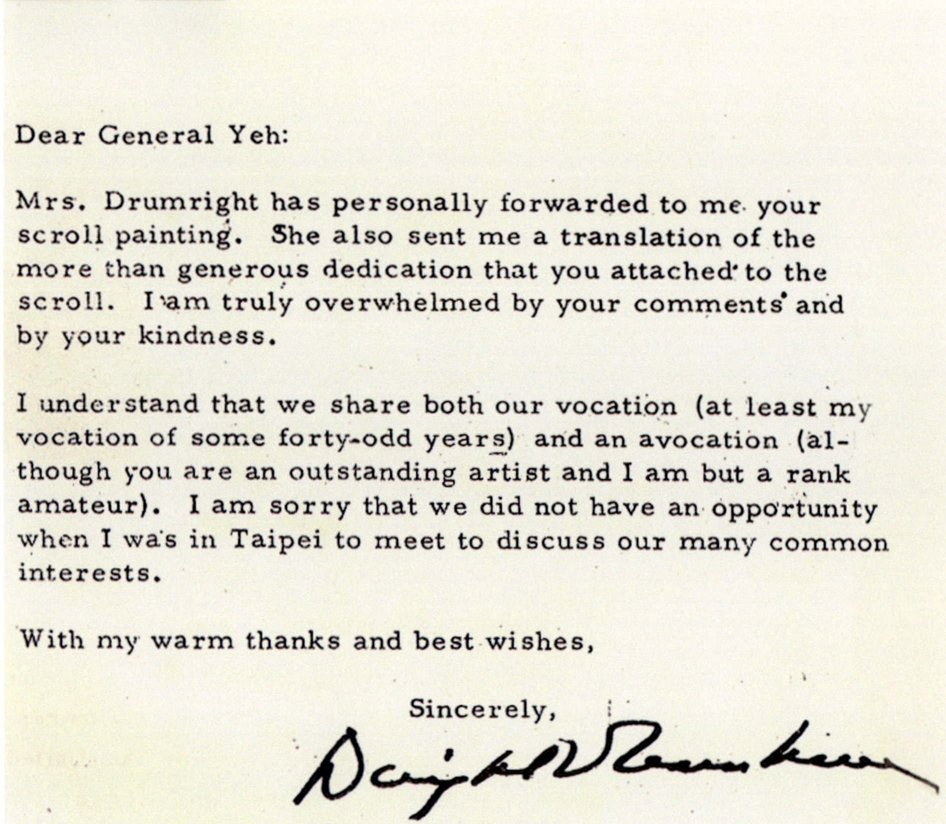

THE WHITE HOUSE

WASHINGTON

July 6, 1960

Dear General Yeh:

Mrs. Drumright has personally forwarded to me your scroll painting. She also sent me a translation of the more than generous dedication that you attached to the scroll. I am truly overwhelmed by your comments and by your kindness.

I understand that we share both our vocation (at least my vocation of some forty-odd years) and an avocation (although you are an outstanding artist and I am but a rank amateur). I am sorry that we did not have an opportunity when I was in Taipei to meet to discuss our many common interests.

With my warm thanks and best wishes,

Sincerely,

Dwight D. Eisenhower

Below: Painting in Taiwan with mother's supervision, 1964

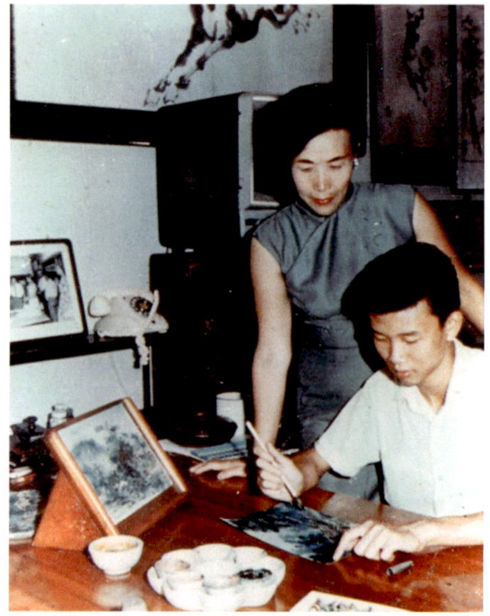

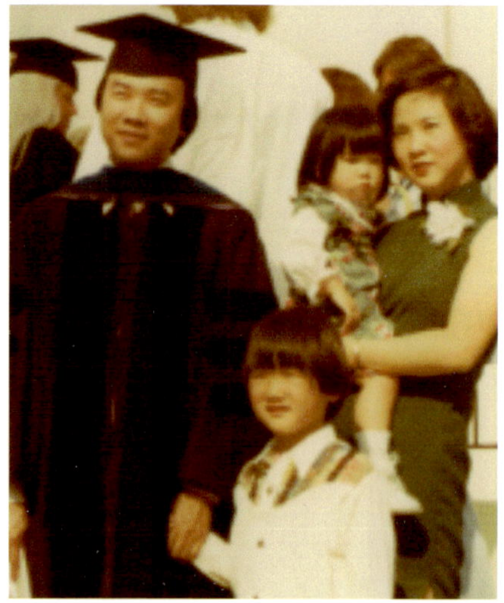

Above: A gracious letter from President Eisenhower to Ning's father, a renowned horse painter and an army general. Right: Ph.D. from Claremont with wife Lingchi, son Evan, and daughter Jashin, 1978.

Cine 1988

The Council on International Nontheatrical Events
congratulates
Ning Yeh
Artist
for the motion picture

Head Of The Horse

selected for its excellence to represent the
United States of America in international
motion picture events abroad and awards to it

ACADEMY
OF
TELEVISION ARTS & SCIENCES

40th ANNUAL
LOS ANGELES AREA EMMY AWARDS

Honors
NING YEH
ARTIST/ACADEMIC ADVISOR

for contributing to the winning of an Area Award

INSTRUCTIONAL SERIES
CHINESE BRUSH PAINTING
SERIES
KOCE

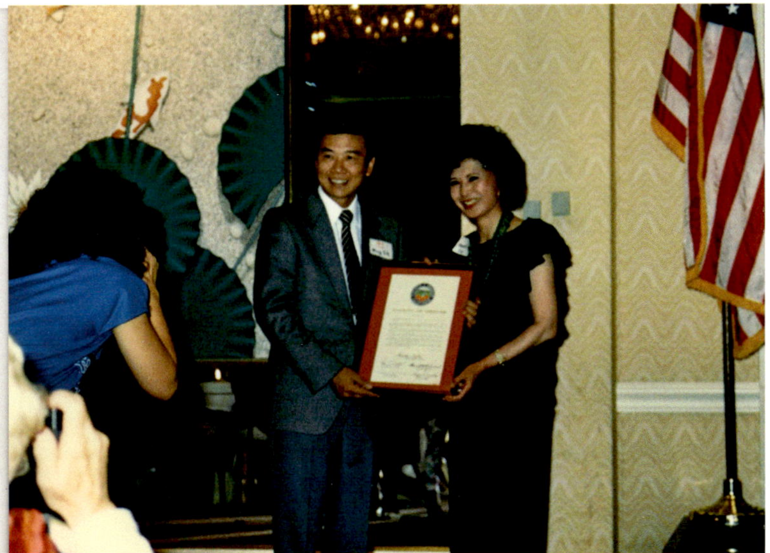

Ning Yeh's art has received many special awards and recognition: the Golden Eagle, the Emmy, the Great Seal of California, and a special Merit Award presented by Mrs. Dorothy Chandler, and Mayor Tom Bradley, among others.

March Fong Eu
Secretary of State

"THE GREAT SEAL OF THE GREAT STATE OF CALIFORNIA"

The Great Seal of the State of California was adopted at the Constitutional Convention of 1849. Thirty-one stars are displayed, one for each state which comprised the Union at the time. Beneath them appears the motto, Eureka! The peaks of the Sierra Nevada stand for the grandeur of Nature. Shipping on San Francisco Bay typifies commerce. A miner laboring with pick, rocker and pan represents industry. Agricultural wealth is seen in a sheaf of wheat and clusters of grapes. Keeping watch over this tableau is the armored figure of Minerva who, in classical mythology, was goddess of the arts and sciences, wise in peace and war. Like the political birth of California, she was born full grown from the brain of Jupiter, father of the gods and guardian of law and order. At her feet is a grizzly bear, independent and formidable, symbolizing the State of California. The Secretary of State is the keeper of the Great Seal.

By token of the Great Seal, the California Secretary of State extends to

NING YEH

sincere appreciation for the beauty of his art and its philosophy, commends his dedication to preserving this exquisite art form through his teaching and offers best wishes for every success with his new telecourse and in all future endeavors. This seal is offered as a token of lasting friendship.

Subscribed this 9th day of August, 1987

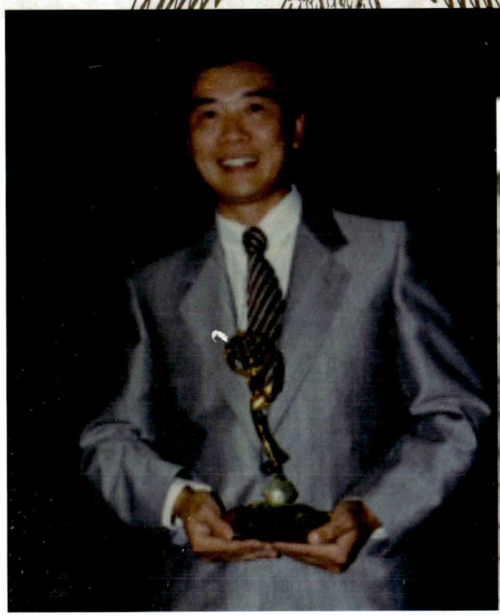

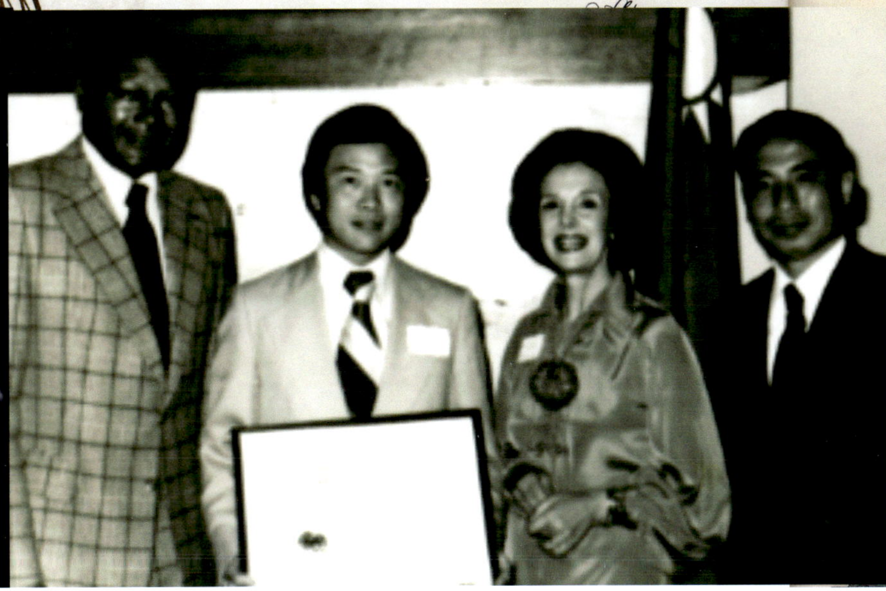

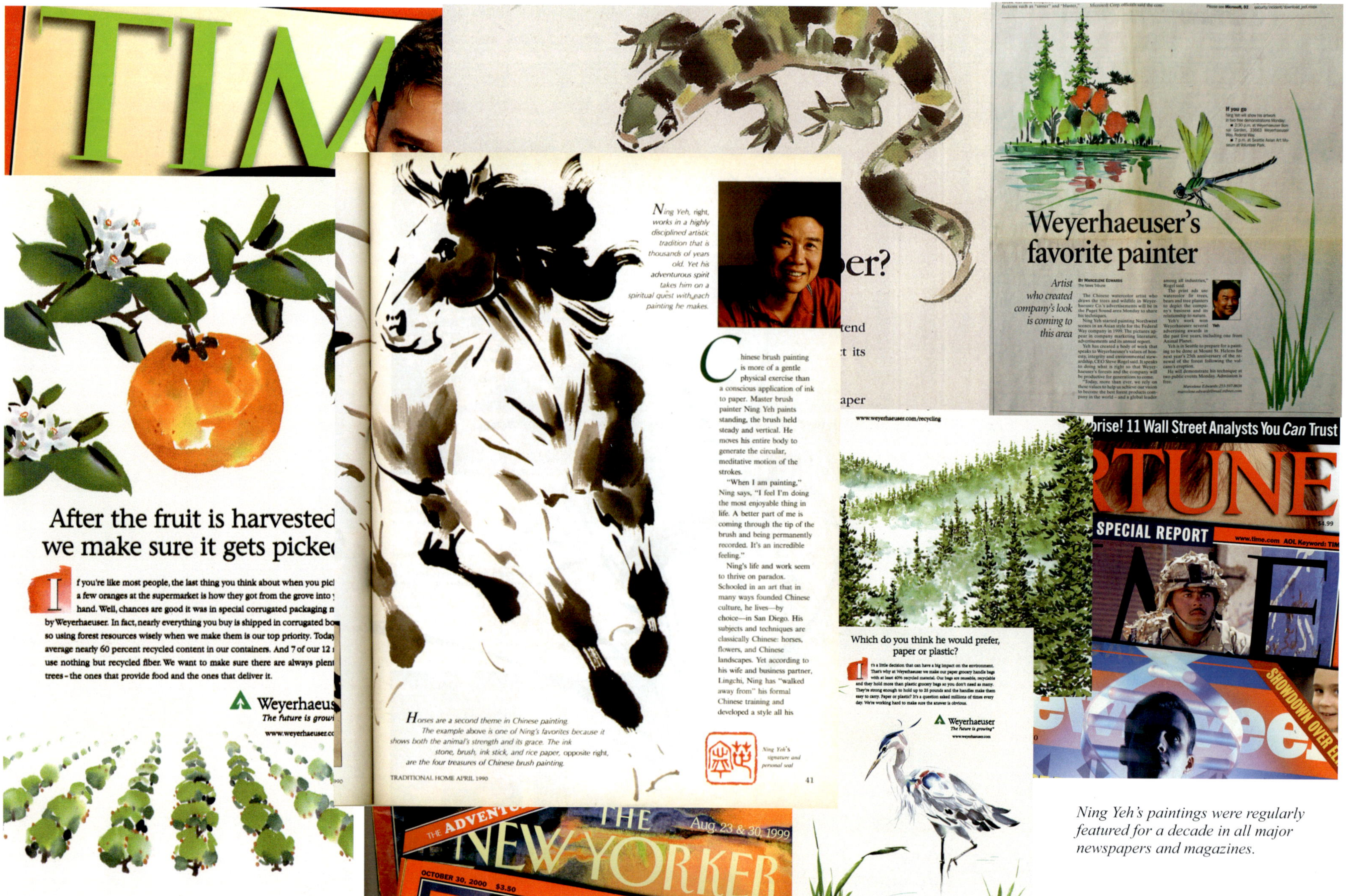

Ning Yeh's paintings were regularly featured for a decade in all major newspapers and magazines.

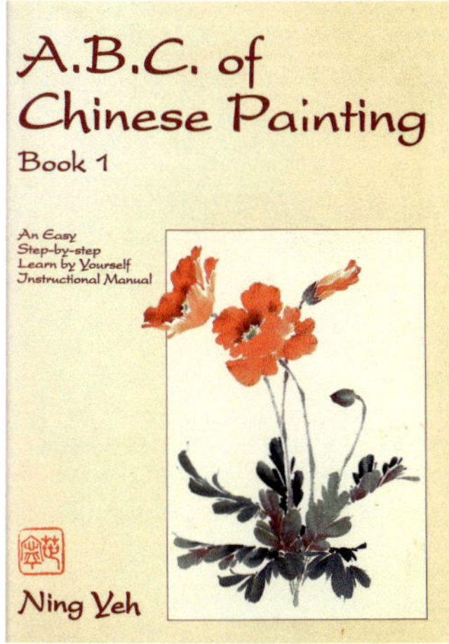

Dr. Yeh became a full-time art professor in 1972. He is a three-time recipient of the National Teaching Excellence Award. In 1987, his first television series, *Chinese Brush Painting with Ning Yeh*, won the Emmy Award for Best Instructional Series. In 1997, *Chinese Flower Painting with Ning Yeh (1 and 2)* began airing on PBS stations. In the 2000s, Dr. Yeh released his fourth television series *Chinese Animal Painting*. These TV series had 25 years of continuous airing in the United States.

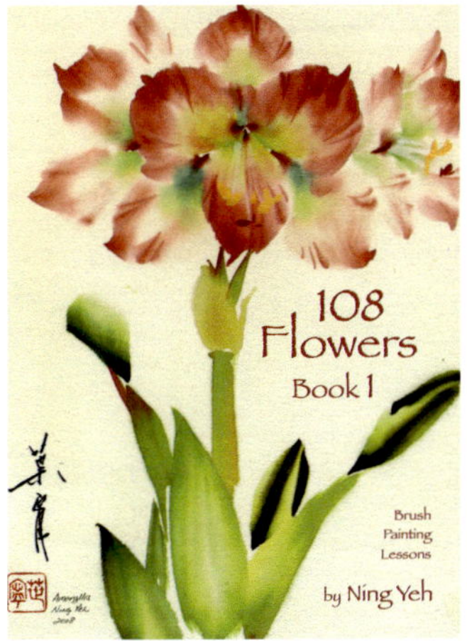

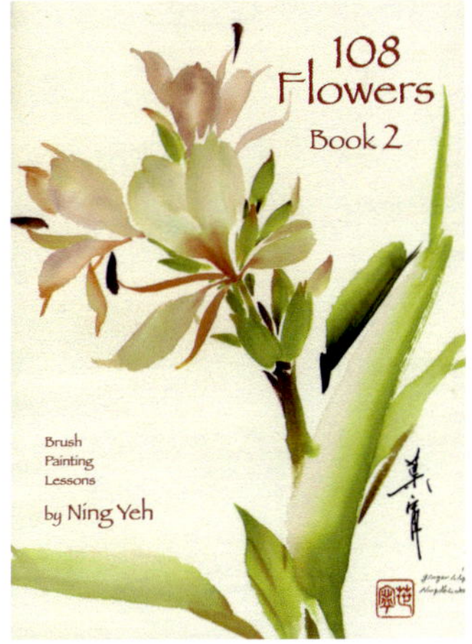

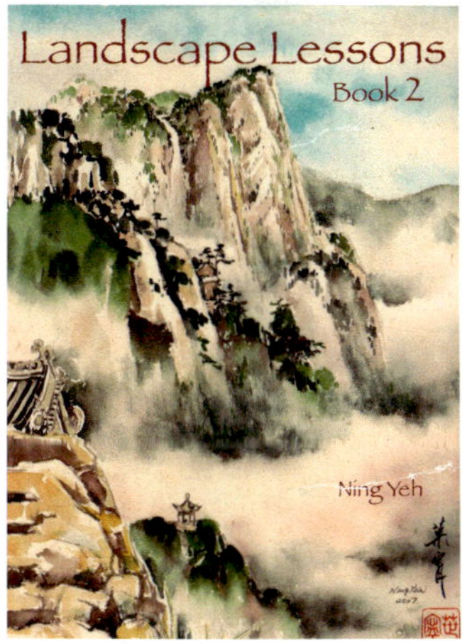

Dr. Yeh has published many books and art albums. His instructional books, *Chinese Brush Painting: An Instructional Guide* and *A.B.C. of Chinese Painting,* are best sellers with repeated editions. His four volume series, *108 Flowers,* accompanied by online step-by-step videos is his most endearing effort in sharing the magic of brush painting. *Landscape Lessons Books 1 & 2* document over 50 years of dream journeys to China and Taiwan, interpreting magnificent scenery in Dr. Yeh's classic and evocative painting style.

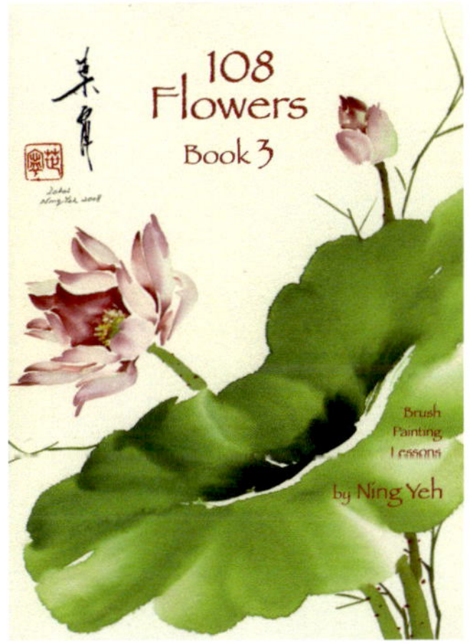

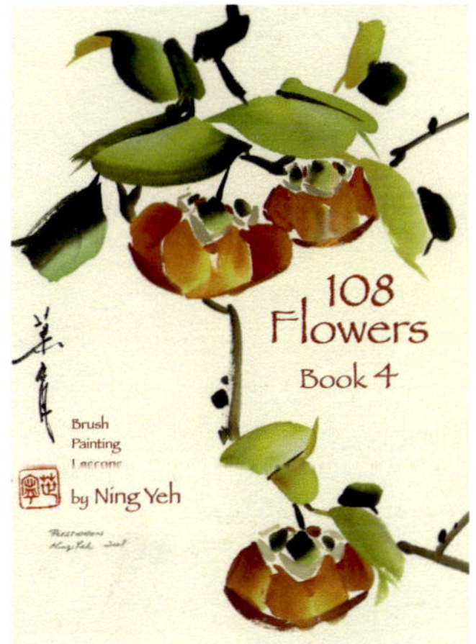

Dr. Yeh and his wife Lingchi live in Huntington Beach, California. His family owns Oriental Art Supply Company which provides the best painting materials for over 40 years.

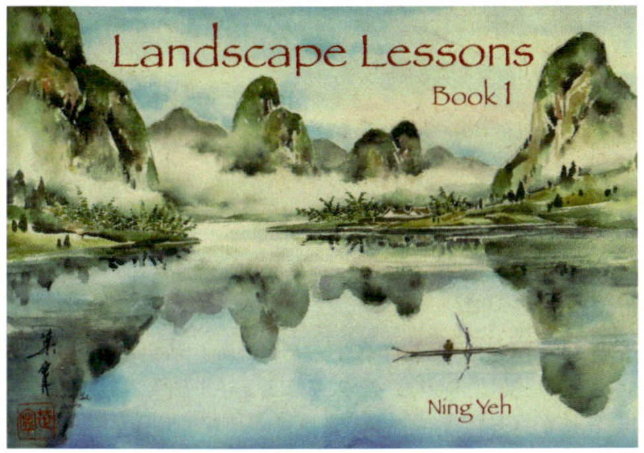

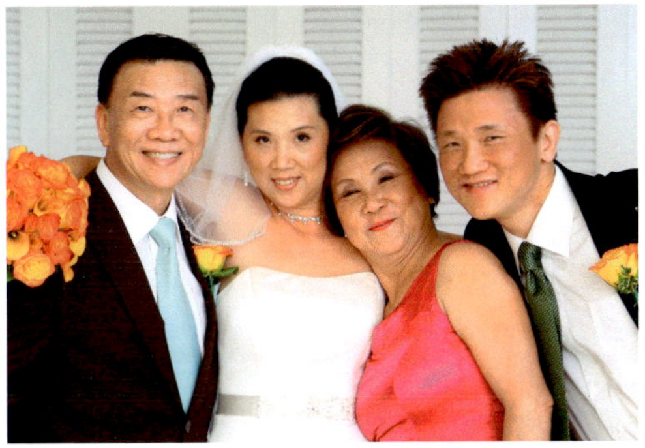

Ning, Lingchi, Evan, and Jashin 2012

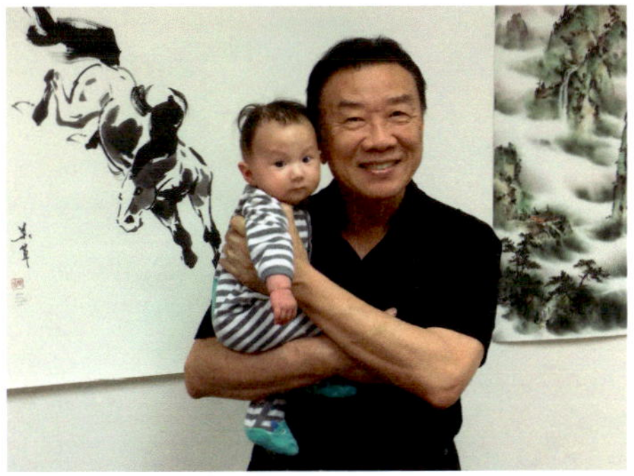

Ning and grandson Cody 2016

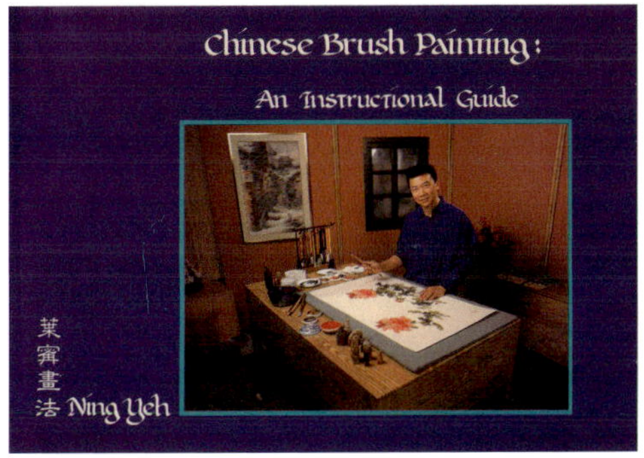

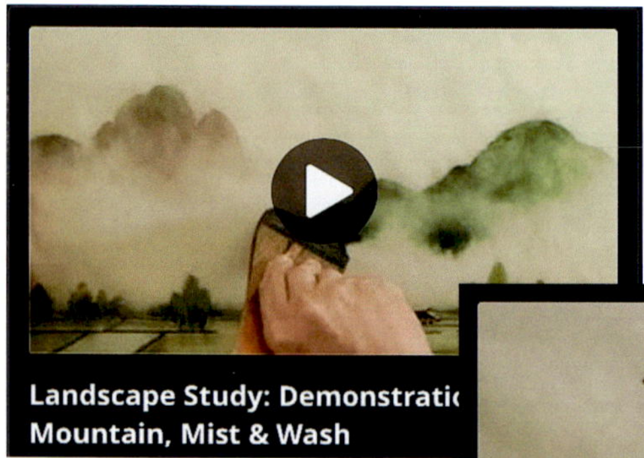

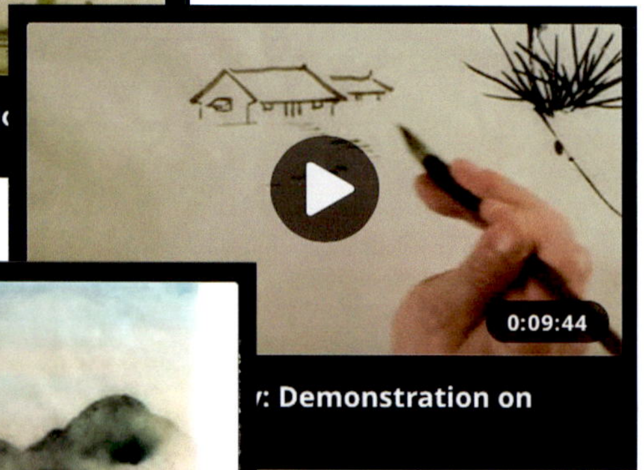

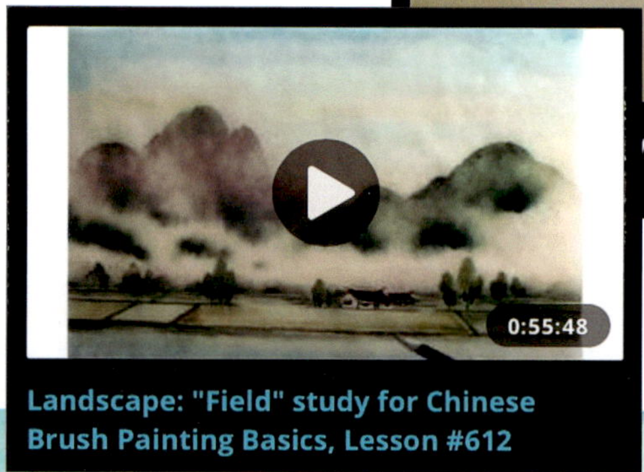

Learn with videos

Video demonstrations of Ning Yeh's landscape painting techniques are a perfect complement to this book series.

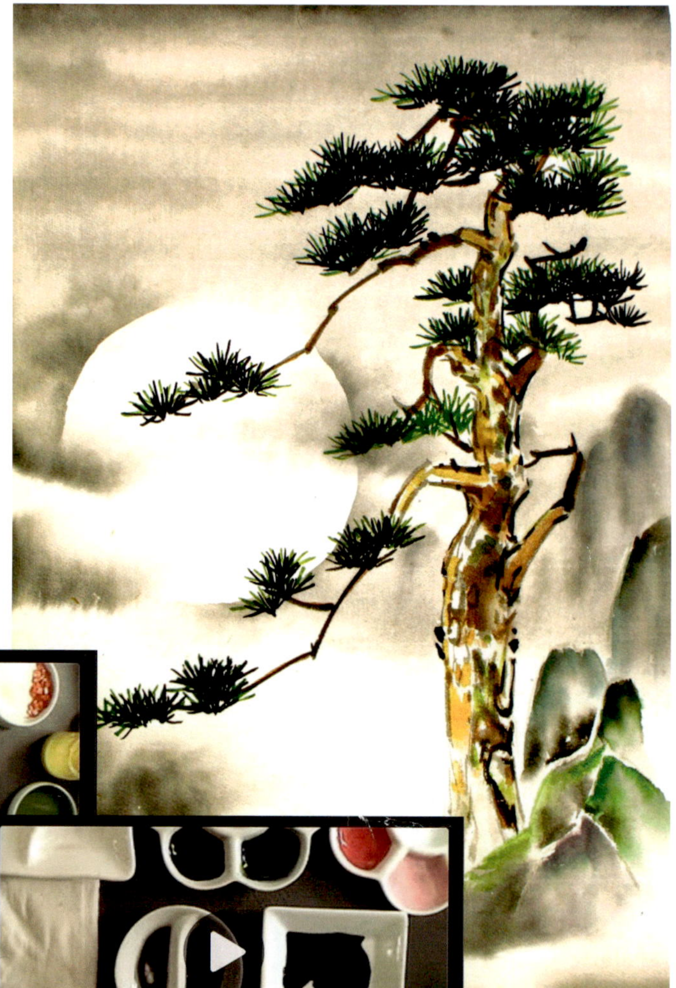

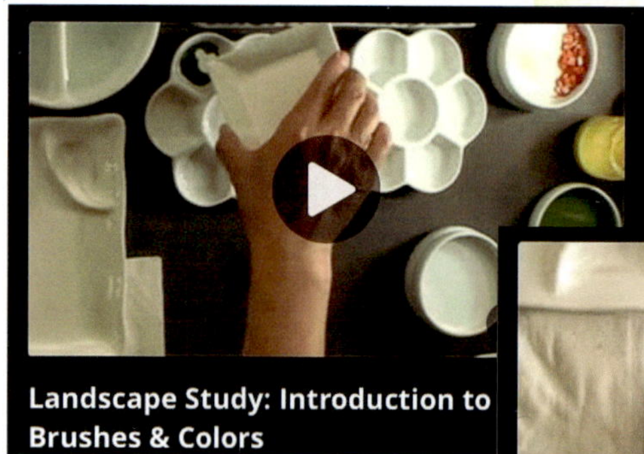

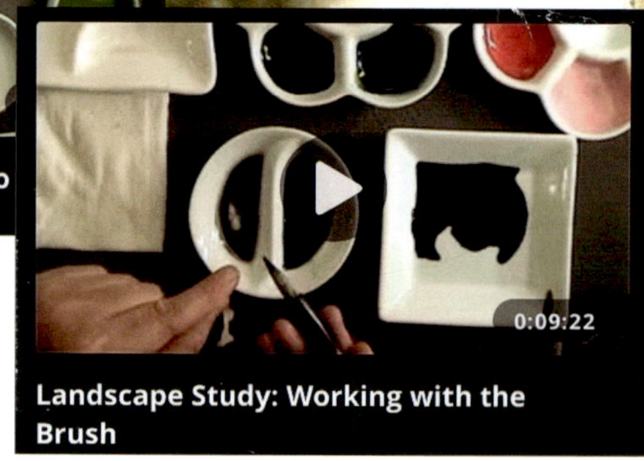

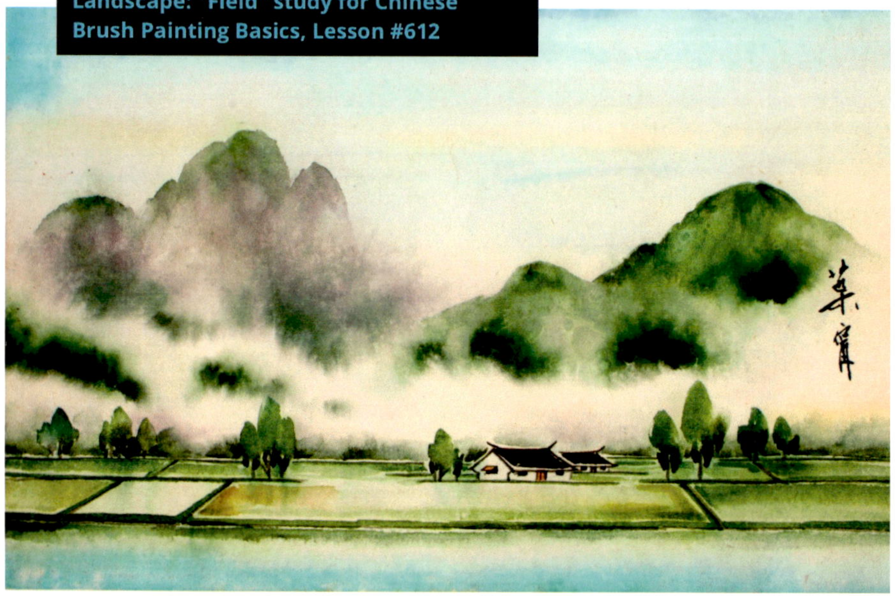

Available separately at

www.orientalartsupply.com